KV-339-171

Energy for Tomorrow's World

World Energy Council

CONSEIL MONDIAL DE L'ENERGIE

WEC COMMISSION

Energy for Tomorrow's World

– the Realities,

the Real Options

and the

Agenda for Achievement

KOGAN
PAGE

St. Martin's Press

First published in 1993 by Kogan Page Ltd.
Reprinted 1993 (twice)

Apart from any fair dealing for the purposes of research or private study, or
criticism or review, as permitted under the Copyright, Designs and Patents
Act, 1988, this publication may only be reproduced, stored or transmitted, in
any form or by any means, with the prior permission in writing of the
publishers, or in the case of reprographic reproduction in accordance with
the terms of licences issued by the Copyright Licensing Agency. Enquiries
concerning reproduction outside those terms should be sent to the publishers
at the undermentioned address:

Kogan Page Limited
120 Pentonville Road
London N1 9JN

British Library Cataloguing in Publication Data

A CIP record for this book is available from the British
Library

ISBN 0 7494 1117 1

Published in the United States of America 1993 by
Scholarly and Reference Division,
ST. MARTIN'S PRESS INC.,
175 Fifth Avenue,
New York, N.Y. 10010

ISBN 0–312–10659–9

Library of Congress Cataloging-in-Publication Data applied for.

Also published in French by Editions Technip, Paris

© World Energy Council 1993

Typesetting and Graphics by M G Schomberg, Oxford
Printed and bound in Great Britain by Clays Ltd, St Ives plc

WEC COMMISSION
ENERGY FOR TOMORROW'S WORLD
— *the Realities, the Real Options and the Agenda for Achievement* —

Chairman
Mr H J Ager-Hanssen
Senior Vice-President, Statoil Group, Norway

MEMBERS of the BOARD

Mr Abdlatif Y Al-Hamad
Director General/Chairman of the Board of Directors, Arab Fund for Economic & Social Development (AFESD)

Dr Ali A Attiga
Assistant UNDP Administrator & Director, Regional Bureau for Arab States & Europe, UNDP Headquarters, New York and formerly Secretary General OAPEC

Mr John W Baker
Chief Executive, National Power plc, UK

Mr Jean Bergougnoux
Directeur Général, Electricité de France

Mr Jacques Bouvet
Président Directeur Général, Charbonnages de France

Dr Klaus Brendow
Director, Energy Division, UNECE

Mr Lucien Bronicki
President and Technical Director, Ormat Turbines Ltd, Israel

Mr Tom Burke
Special Policy Adviser to the Secretary of State for the Environment, UK

Mr A Cardoso e Cunha
formerly Commissioner for Energy, Commission of the European Communities

Dr KunMo T Chung
Professor, Inst. for Energy Studies & Ambassador for Nuclear Energy Co-operation, Republic of Korea

Dr Anthony A Churchill
Senior Adviser, Vice Presidency for Finance and Private Sector Development, IBRD/World Bank

Mr Derek A Davis
Executive Director, WEC Commission

Mr W Kenneth Davis
Honorary Vice-Chairman WEC Executive Assembly and formerly US Deputy Secretary of Energy

Mr Juan Eibenschutz
Co-ordinador de Asesores del Secretario, Secretaria de Energia, Minas e Industria Paraestatal, Mexico

Mr Robert Evans
Chairman, British Gas plc, UK

Dr John S Foster
WEC Honorary President

Dr Z Sydney Gata
IES Zimbabwe Pvt Ltd and formerly Chief Executive ZESA Zimbabwe

Prof José Goldemberg
Instituto de Eletrotécnica e Energia, Universidade de São Paulo, Brazil, and formerly both Minister of Education and Secretary of State for the Environment

Prof Gordon T Goodman
Chairman, Stockholm Environment Institute

Mr Ted Hanisch
Director, CICERO (Center for International Climate and Energy Research), University of Oslo

Mr Enrique Iglesias
President, Inter-American Development Bank

Mr Toyoaki Ikuta
President, Japanese Institute of Energy Economics

Prof Dr Marek Jaczewski
Energy Institute, Warsaw

Mr John S Jennings
Managing Director, Royal Dutch/Shell Group

Mr Jia Yunzhen
Deputy Director, International Co-operation, Ministry of Energy, China

Dr V Krishnaswamy
Deputy Director, Energy & Industry Dept, Asian Development Bank

Mr Diby M Kroko
President Directeur Général, Energie Electrique de la Côte d'Ivoire

General R L Lawson
President, National Coal Association, USA

Dr Bong-Suh Lee
formerly Minister of Energy, Republic of Korea

Prof A A Makarov
Director, Institute of Energy Research, Academy of Science, Russian Federation

Mr Robert Malpas
Chairman, Cookson Group plc, UK, and formerly a Managing Director of the British Petroleum Group plc

Mr Alain Mongon
President, IFIEC

Mr Babacar Ndiaye
President, African Development Bank

Mr Carl-Erik Nyquist
President, Vattenfall, Swedish State Power Board

Dr Gerhard Ott
Chairman, WEC Executive Assembly

Dr R K Pachauri
Director, Tata Energy Research Institute, India

Prof David W Pearce
University College London, UK

Dr Heinrich v. Pierer
Vorsitzender des Vorstands, Siemens AG, Germany

Mr José Rosón
Chairman, Technical Programme Committee, 15th WEC Congress 1992

Mr Gabriel Sanchez-Sierra
Executive Secretary, OLADE

Prof Dr Ing. Ulrich Seiffert
Mitglied des Vorstandes, Volkswagen AG, Germany

Mr Yuri K Semyonov
formerly Minister of Electrification, USSR

Dr Chauncey Starr
President Emeritus, Electric Power Research Institute, USA

Mrs Helga Steeg
Executive Director, IEA/OECD

Dr Subroto
Secretary General, OPEC

Prof Jaroslav Suva
Czech Technical University, Czech Republic and formerly Minister of Energy, Czechoslovakia

Dr Sergio C Trindade
President, SET International Ltd, New York

Secretary
Mr I D Lindsay
WEC Secretary General

PROJECT MANAGEMENT UNIT

Executive Director
Mr Derek A Davis
sponsored by National Power, UK

Mr Martin Bekkeheien
sponsored by Statoil, Norway

Mr Esa Hakkarainen
sponsored by Vattenfall AB, Sweden

Mr Ian Israelsohn
sponsored by Eskom, South Africa

Mr Michael Jefferson
WEC Deputy Secretary General, UK

Mr Frank Jenkin
Consultant, UK

Mr Leslie Young
sponsored by the Finnish Energy Economy Association ETY, Finland

SPECIAL ADVISERS to the PROJECT MANAGEMENT UNIT

Dr J-R Frisch
Attaché à la Direction Générale, ELECTRICITE de FRANCE, France

Mr P-E Molander
International Secretary, SYDKRAFT, Sweden

Mr O Vapaavuori
President & CEO, Finnish Energy Economy Association ETY (WEC Member Committee of Finland), Finland

Mr M G Schomberg
Editor, WEC Survey of Energy Resources, UK

OFFICERS of the WORLD ENERGY COUNCIL

WEC President	Dr M Gómez de Pablos (Spain)
WEC EA Chairman	Dr Gerhard Ott (Germany)
WEC EA Vice-Chairmen	W Jack Bowen (USA) D M Kroko (Côte d'Ivoire) I Hori (Japan)
WEC Secretary General	I D Lindsay

MEMBER COMMITTEES of the WORLD ENERGY COUNCIL

Algeria	Iceland	Portugal
Argentina	India	Romania
Australia	Indonesia	Russian Federation
Austria	Iran (Islamic Rep. of)	Saudi Arabia
Azerbaijan*	Iraq	Senegal
Bahrain	Ireland	Singapore
Belgium	Israel	Slovak Republic*
Bolivia	Italy	Slovenia
Brazil	Jamaica	South Africa
Bulgaria	Japan	Spain
Burundi	Jordan	Sri Lanka
Byelorussia	Korea (DPR)	Swaziland
Canada	Korea (Rep. of)	Sweden
Chile	Kyrgyzstan	Switzerland
China	Latvia	Syria (Arab Rep. of)
Colombia	Lesotho	Taiwan, China
Costa Rica	Libya/SPLAJ	Tanzania (United Rep. of)
Côte d'Ivoire	Lithuania	
Croatia	Luxembourg	Thailand
Cuba	Malaysia	Trinidad & Tobago
Czech Republic*	Mexico	Tunisia (Rep. of)
Denmark	Monaco	Turkey
Ecuador	Morocco	Ukraine
Egypt (Arab Rep. of)	Namibia	United Kingdom
Ethiopia	Nepal	Uruguay
Finland	Netherlands	USA
France	New Zealand	Venezuela
Gabon	Nigeria	Yugoslavia
Germany	Norway	Zaire
Ghana	Pakistan	Zambia
Greece	Paraguay	Zimbabwe
Guatemala	Peru	
Hong Kong	Philippines	*awaiting
Hungary	Poland	confirmation

Contents

PART III – THE AGENDA FOR ACTION   223

PART IV – EPILOGUE   241

List of Figures

List of Tables

Conversion Factors and Energy Equivalents

1	calorie (cal)	=	4.196	J
1	joule (J)	=	0.239	cal
1	tonne of oil equivalent (net, low heat value)	=	42	GJ* = 1 toe
1	tonne of coal equivalent (standard, LHV)	=	29.3	GJ* = 1 tce
$1000\,m^3$ of natural gas (standard, LHV)		=	36	GJ
1	tonne of natural gas liquids	=	46	GJ
1000 kWh (primary energy)		=	9.36	GJ*

1	toe	=	10 034	Mcal
1	tce	=	7 000	Mcal
$1000\,m^3$ of natural gas		=	8 600	Mcal
1	tonne of natural gas liquids	=	11 000	Mcal
1000 kWh (primary energy)		=	2 236	Mcal[+]

1	tce	=	0.697	toe
$1000\,m^3$ of natural gas		=	0.857	toe
1	tonne natural gas liquids	=	1.096	toe
1000 kWh (primary energy)		=	0.223	toe
1	tonne of fuelwood	=	0.380	toe
1	tonne of uranium (current type reactors)	=	10 000	toe
1	tonne of uranium (breeders)	=	500 000	toe

1	barrel of oil	= approx	0.136	tonnes
1	cubic foot	=	0.0283	cubic metres

Notes

* WEC standard conversion factors (from Standards Circular No.1, 11/83)

[+] With 1 000 kWh (final consumption) = 860 Mcal as WEC conversion factor (assuming a conversion efficiency of 38.46%)

Because of rounding, some totals may not exactly equal the sum of their component parts, and some percentages may not agree exactly with those calculated from the rounded figures used in the tables.

Abbreviations

bbl	*Barrel (of oil), 159 litres.*
bcm	*Billion cubic metres ($10^9 m^3$).*
BOF	*Basic Oxygen Furnace.*
Btu	*British thermal unit. (1 Btu = 1 055.06 J).*
CCGT	*Coal-fired Combined Cycle Gas Turbines.*
CEE/CIS	*Central and Eastern Europe/Commonwealth of Independent States, Georgia and the Baltic States.*
CHP	*Combined Heat and Power (plant).*
CNG	*Compressed Natural Gas.*
DCs	*Developing Countries (ie all countries except OECD members and CEE/CIS).*
DH	*District Heating.*
DOE	*US Department of Energy.*
EAF	*Electric Arc Furnace.*
GATT	*General Agreement on Tariffs and Trade.*
GDP	*Gross Domestic Product.*
GJ	*Gigajoule.*
GREEN	*General Equilibrium Environmental Model.*
GtC	*Gigatonnes (elemented) carbon (10^9 tonnes C).*
Gtoe	*Gigatonnes oil equivalent (10^9 tonnes oil equivalent).*
GW	*Gigawatt (10^9 watts).*
IPCC	*International Panel on Climate Change.*
kgU	*kilograms of Uranium.*
kW	*kilowatt.*
LPG	*Liquified Petroleum Gas.*
MAGICC	*Model Assessment Greenhouse–Gas Induced Climate Change.*
Mtoe	*Million tonnes oil equivalent.*
MWh	*Megawatt hour.*
NICs	*Newly Industrialised Countries.*
OECD	*Organisation for Economic Cooperation and Development.*
OLADE	*Latin American Energy Organization.*
ppmv	*Parts per million by volume.*
R/P ratio	*Reserves to Production Ratio (years).*
RBMK	*Graphite moderated pressure tube type reactor designed and built in the former Soviet Union. (The Chernobyl accident concerned a reactor of this type.)*
RF	*Russian Federation.*
SAVE	*The European Community programme for encouraging energy efficiency, with as one of its goals to stabilise anthropogenic CO_2 emissions in the year 2000 at 1990 levels. A full description was provided in EC Directorate-General of Energy: "Energy in Europe", No 17, 1991.*
toe	*Tonnes oil equivalent.*
TWh	*Tera watt hours (10^{12} watt hours).*
UN	*United Nations.*
UNDP	*United Nations Development Programme.*
UNEP	*United Nations Environment Programme.*
UNIDO	*United Nations Industrial Development Organization.*
USEA	*United States Energy Association.*
WANO	*World Association of Nuclear Operatives.*
WEC	*World Energy Council.*

Glossary

Anthropogenic	*Man-made.*
Baseline Drag	*The basic aerodynamic resistance of vehicles.*
Biomass	*Organic, non-fossil material of biological origin constituting an exploitable energy source.*
Carbon Dioxide (CO_2)	*The gas formed in the ordinary combustion of carbon, given out in the breathing of animals, etc.*
Energy Intensity	*The proportion of energy used to Gross Domestic Product at constant prices, changes in which being taken as a measure of energy efficiency shifts.*
Enteric Fermentation	*The natural process of fermentation in the intestines of animals, such as of grasses in cattle, leading to the passing of methane and other gases.*
Fixed Capital Formation	*Investment in fixed capital and equipment.*
Flaring	*Burning (of surplus natural gas, etc).*
Fluidised Beds	*Beds of burning fuel together with non-combustible particles kept in suspension by upward flow of combustion air through the bed. Limestone or coal ash are widely used non-combustible materials.*
Gasifiers	*Tank for anaerobic fermentation of biomass residues from sugar cane, pulp and paper, etc, to produce biogas.*
Geothermal	*Natural heat extracted from the earth's crust using its vertical thermal gradient, most readily available where there is a discontinuity in the earth's crust (eg where there is separation or erosion of tectonic plates).*
Halocarbons	*A family of chlorofluorocarbons (CFCs) mostly of industrial origin – CH_3Cl is the main exception. Includes aerosol propellants (CFCs 11, 12, 114); refrigerants (CFCs 12, 114 and HCFC-22); foam-blowing agents (CFCs 11 and 12); solvents (CFC-113, CH_3CCl_3 and CCl_4); and fire retardants (halons 1211 and 1301). HCFC = hydrofluorocarbon.*
Methane (CH_4)	*A gas emitted from coal seams, natural wetlands, rice paddies, enteric fermentation (see above), biomass burning, anaerobic decay or organic wastes in landfill sites, gas drilling and venting, and the activities of termites.*
Photovoltaics	*The use of lenses or mirrors to concentrate direct solar radiation onto small areas of solar cells, or the use of flat-plate photovoltaic modules using large arrays of solar cells, to convert the sun's radiation into electricity.*
Sinks	*Places where CO_2 can be absorbed – the oceans, soil and detritus and land biota (trees and vegetation).*
Sorbent Injection	*The injection of sulphur 'absorbing' minerals such as limestone during the combustion process in order to limit sulphur emissions in the gaseous products of combustion.*
Suspended Particles	*Solid particles carried into the atmosphere with the gaseous products of combustion.*
Tropospheric Oxone (O_3)	*Oxygen in condensation form in lowest stratum of atmosphere.*
Venting	*Discharge (of natural gas, etc) into the atmosphere, thereby allowing excessive or unwanted products of gas to escape.*

FOREWORD

This report of the World Energy Council's (WEC) Commission "Energy for Tomorrow's World – the Realities, the Real Options and the Agenda for Achievement" has its origins in earlier WEC work on global energy supply and demand projections. When we decided, at the WEC's 14th Congress in Montreal, in 1989, to undertake this Commission we knew we were setting ourselves an immense task. Two and a half years have passed between the first and last meetings of our Commission Board, and in that time much has been achieved.

The Commission's aim is to identify a realistic framework for the solution of regional and global energy issues, whereby adequate sustainable energy at acceptable costs can be supplied to meet the needs of all people, using optimal production and end-use efficiency, whilst achieving socially acceptable care and protection of the environment.

The Commission's methodology employed the basic strength of the WEC, namely its membership in 100 countries. It required regional groups to be formed, multi-disciplinary wherever possible, to examine the future of energy and energy-related development in the nine regions (counting Central and Eastern Europe separately from the Commonwealth of Independent States) into which the world was divided. The main time horizon was to 2020, but as our work progressed it became clear that many issues and realistic resolution of issues related to a longer time-frame. Some topics relevant to our work, such as those examined by the Intergovernmental Panel on Climate Change, are being considered out to the year 2100. This is a very long period, and we have asked ourselves how much can usefully be said with any hope of accuracy on possibilities so far ahead. We have, nevertheless, in the Commission's Epilogue tried to sketch in outline some of those longer-term possibilities – both as challenges and as issues and opportunities which require attention now.

We no more have a crystal ball which permits us to foretell the future than anyone else. Although the whole Commission report is a qualitative study we have built into it four different Cases of global energy supply and demand possibilities out to the year 2020.

The regional reports stand alone, and have been summarised in Part II of the Commission's report presented here. They form, at the same time, one of the main foundation stones for the Commission's global report. To the many key issues, considerations and findings which emerged from the regional reports were added information and data drawn from central studies and advisers, and external experts, in order to compile the global report.

The result is a report which highlights:

- Above all else that the world's main energy issues will move from the industrialised world to the developing countries.

- In 1990 some 75% of the world's population (those in the developing countries) used only 33% of the world's energy consumption. By the year 2020 that 75% is likely to have risen to 85% and it will probably consume around 55% of the world's energy.

- The virtual impossibility of stabilising global anthropogenic CO_2 emissions at 1990 levels by the year 2020.

- The strong possibility that atmospheric CO_2 concentrations will rise for many decades to come.

- Precautionary measures are therefore required as a matter of simple prudence to start abatement of and adaptation to potential climate change. This particularly involves intensified scientific research to raise the level of understanding and a drive for greater efficiency and conservation in energy provision and use.

- Huge financial resources will be needed for investment in the period to 2020 – cumulatively perhaps US$30 trillion (10^{12}) at 1992 prices, which compares with global GDP in 1989 of US$20 trillion.

- The need for radical change within certain systems of markets, institutions, pricing and management if they are to attract sufficient finance with which to obtain sufficient energy.

This report is drawn to the attention of world-wide energy decision-makers in government, industry and elsewhere. Following the UNCED Earth Summit in Rio de Janeiro in June 1992 more and more governments will in the future be committed to addressing the "how" of sustainable growth in the most cost-effective way. We hope and believe the findings and recommendations of the Commission will therefore be timely and valuable to them. It was for them that this was written.

On behalf of the World Energy Council, we would like to thank all those who have so generously contributed their time, energy and other resources to provide this work.

Gerhard Ott	Henrik Ager-Hanssen	Ian Lindsay
Chairman	*Chairman*	*Secretary General*
WEC Executive	*WEC Commission*	*World Energy Council*
Assembly		

ACKNOWLEDGEMENTS

More than 500 people from all five continents of the world have given of their ideas, time and effort to produce the WEC Commission since its inception in 1990. Its estimated cost has totalled some US$5 million in man hours, travel, meetings and debate. In making our acknowledgements we would like firstly to record our thanks to the following who donated the vital finance without which the WEC Commission could not have been produced.

The Member Committees of Austria, Australia, Brazil, Canada, Denmark, Finland, France, Germany, Hong Kong, Iceland, Indonesia, Italy, Japan, Republic of Korea, Libya/SPLAJ, Malaysia, Netherlands, Norway, Portugal, Russian Federation, Sweden, Switzerland, Taiwan (China), United Kingdom and the United States of America.

In addition we received donations from six individuals and one single energy organisation: Lucien Bronicki, Walker Cisler, Kenneth Davis, Sven Hultin, John Kiely and Gerhard Ott together with OPEC.

The Commission report was supervised and inspired by its board of some 48 members, each of them eminent in his or her own field, and representing both a variety of disciplines and a variety of countries. The WEC is grateful to them for having given of their time, knowledge, inspiration and support.

The nine regional groups, which where possible were also multi-disciplined, compiled the vital basic local data and reports which form the foundation of the Commission report. Theirs was a colossal task and we are most appreciative to all of the Regional Co-ordinators and their teams who undertook it.

From its inception the Commission was developed and co-ordinated by the Project Management Unit located north of London under the direction of Derek Davis, the Commission's Executive Director. To them fell the responsibility of directing and marshalling the very considerable volume of opinions, information and statistics which were finally synthesised into the Commission report. They carried out their tasks with considerable efficiency, perseverence and tact. The small PMU staff were loaned and paid for by corporations within the Member Committees of Finland, France, Norway, South Africa , Sweden and the United Kingdom. The considerable thanks of the WEC go to them.

Finally it has fallen to Michael Jefferson, the WEC Deputy Secretary General, and to Michael Schomberg, the editor of the WEC Survey of Energy Resources, to write and format the complete document in preparation for the publishers. Theirs was a prodigious task completed under severe time pressures. Both are thanked warmly for their efforts.

In conclusion we would also like to record our appreciation of all those who so often are omitted from such acknowledgements – the secretarial and other staff whose input has enabled the Commission to keep to its planned schedule and timing.

INTRODUCTION

This is the report of the World Energy Council's Commission: "Energy for Tomorrow's World – the Realities, the Real Options and the Agenda for Achievement". It is aimed at energy policy-makers, politicians, the energy industry world-wide, and those members of the public who wish to engage in informed debate and action. The purpose is to achieve changes in energy policy which bring about realistic and desired goals in the most effective ways.

The World Energy Council (WEC) exists to promote the sustainable supply and use of energy for the greatest benefit of all.

The WEC was founded in 1924 and has Member Committees in some 100 countries and otherwise qualified geographic areas. In these Member Committees most major energy interests are represented – including the various industries, governments and energy-related sectors, professional institutions and specialist consultancies. Many global, international and regional organisations and agencies are associated with the WEC in its work – representing a range of interests and expertise which includes not only energy and economics but finance, technology, development and the environment. The WEC is a non-commercial body, and has long been an officially accredited Non-Governmental Organisation. It is also, and importantly for an understanding of this report, a multi-energy organisation: it does not represent the interests of any one form of energy or of traditional commercial fuels as distinct from others.

The WEC recognises the central role of the consumer and of consumer demand not so much for energy *per se* but for the services which energy can provide. Thus demand-side management is of critical importance.

The WEC has always been global in its viewpoint and latterly reinforced this by placing emphasis on regional analysis and understanding. Its membership represents the industrialised countries, the economies in transition, the centrally planned economies, the newly industrialising economies, the rapidly industrialising countries, and the many and varied countries forming the third world. The non-availability of energy, especially commercial energy, to meet basic needs has long been of prime concern.

At its 14th Congress in 1989, in Montreal, the WEC presented its Global Energy Perspectives 2000–2020. The supply and demand projections therein were widely regarded as objective, and the division of the world into five regions to examine more local realities was welcomed. But the need was felt for a closer look at the wide-ranging issues and a more detailed examination of the parameters relevant to future energy developments.

The WEC therefore took the initial steps in 1989 to create the Commission which has undertaken this work. Two facets are worth emphasis. First, the Commission's work has been guided by a board of 50 distinguished people drawn from many national origins, representing a variety of disciplines and experience.

Secondly, the Commission worked simultaneously on a bottom-up as well as a top-down basis. The former was achieved by creating eight regional groups, each with local co-ordinators – and multi-disciplinary representation where possible, and each of which produced regional reports. These regional reports were issued at the WEC's 15th Congress in Madrid in September 1992. They form the basis of Part II of the report, and provided important input to the other parts of this report. Details of regions and regional groups are given in Appendices A and B.

The aim of the Commission from its outset was to examine widespread concerns against assessment of current policies and what is realistically achievable in relation to stated goals.

> *The aim of the Commission is to identify a realistic framework for the solution of regional and global energy problems, whereby adequate, sustainable energy at acceptable costs can be supplied to meet the needs of all people whilst achieving socially acceptable care and protection of the environment. It is to identify the realities, the real options and the agenda for achievement.*

Although those who have been involved in producing this report are mainly energy practitioners, there has been important input from others – not least those with specialised experience in environmental politics and economics. Key inputs have been made by those who combine long-standing experience and concerns in the energy, economics and environmental fields. There has been a real attempt at every stage to deal in a balanced way with the interlocking issues of energy, social development, environment, finance, technology and institutional realities.

The situation demands a strategic approach to energy problems rather than emphasis on numerical aspects. This is quite apart from the fact that, given the uncertainties surrounding the future, figures relating thereto are inclined to carry with them a spurious precision. Nevertheless, numbers have been provided as an indication of future possibilities wherever appropriate. They can provide a useful framework for highlighting issues and policy requirements provided they are not taken too literally. By their nature they should not be permutated too far: in this report four Cases of possible future energy demand and supply have been considered, against only one population projection and two economic growth assumptions. Many other Cases could have been considered, with rapidly diminishing returns – especially those with longer time-horizons.

The year 2020 was selected as the main time-horizon for this Commission, but, recognising that some major energy issues are likely to come to a head after this date, possibilities out to the year 2100 were also considered.

This report it is an attempt to view the issues in the interests of mankind as a whole. Delegates (of which there were over 3000) and representatives of the Press at the WEC's 15th Congress in Madrid, Spain in September 1992 recognised and supported this goal when a draft summary version of this report was debated there. Substantial points made during those debates have been incorporated in the present report. They highlighted the need for action now to tackle present and future problems – some of which may not emerge in their full starkness for another 30 to 60 years. Lead times in the development of energy are normally long, and this needs to be recognised and governments mobilised to assist in the necessary processes of change.

Two points in particular were raised in Madrid. First, the concern that in those developing countries where population is already large and growing rapidly, the intensity of energy use (that is, the ratio of energy use to gross domestic product) may well rise over the next two to four decades before falling in line with the historic experience of industrialised countries. Even if, as is generally the case, the trajectory of energy demand in presently developing countries is lower than was the case for industrialised countries at a similar stage of development, this implies significantly higher global energy demand prospects than would otherwise be the case. For this final report a sub-case (B_1) to Case (B) has been developed to examine the implications of this point more fully.

Secondly, growth of world population (which, as is generally recognised, will take place overwhelmingly in presently categorised developing countries) will combine with intensifying apprehension over reducing reserves to production ratios for oil and natural gas in the second-quarter of the next century.

The likelihood is that global energy demand will rise in the coming decades, primarily due to population growth in the presently categorised developing countries. The fossil fuel in greatest abundance to meet that expansion of demand is coal. Continued and expanded nuclear power generation could make a contribution. New renewable forms of energy will also make a growing contribution, but major governmental support (and subsidy to demonstration plant stage) will be required if that contribution is to be significant and rapid. None of these forms of energy are without accompanying problems and concerns – not least environmental concerns. If a wider and more flexible energy resource base is to be achieved, and energy efficiency and conservation promoted, then end-user price rises will be required to encourage and to help fund developments.

This report follows the UN World Commission's Report on Environment and Development, "Our Common Future" (1987) and the UN Conference on Environment and Development (Rio de Janeiro, June 1992). There can be no doubt that the confluence of growing world population, rising global energy demand, and environmental constraints present an enormous challenge to the world and its inhabitants over the next few decades. However, this report examines much more profoundly, on both a regional and a global basis, what practical strategic options are open and required for global energy and its related sectors.

The many complexities of adequate, efficient and secure energy supply and demand; care for the environment; capital and technical resource requirements; and the needs of the developing countries and economies in transition are among the parameters analysed. Some very challenging assumptions have been made, not least about the world's capacity and willingness to improve efficiency in energy provision and use, and reduce the energy intensity of economic development. These challenges are directed particularly at energy policy-makers, politicians and energy consumers. The Commission's aim has been to identify a realistic framework for tackling regional and global energy and energy-related issues. The goal has been the supply of adequate and sustainable energy at acceptable costs to meet the needs of all people, using optimal production and end-use efficiency, while achieving socially acceptable care and protection of the environment.

The Commission ends this report by identifying major concerns, conclusions and recommendations which would form the basis of an agenda for action. Action has to begin now.

EXECUTIVE SUMMARY

The work reported on in this book results from a unique project which has sought to reconcile major views on the important energy issues confronting our times with realistic prospects for the economic, technical, environmental, social and institutional development of the various regions of the world. The work is the result of an interactive bottom-up and top-down study to identify the key issues for continued energy development and to test global views on these issues by regional analysis and viewpoints.

The study concentrates, from a global aspect, on those key issues which will shape energy provision and its use in the future such as population growth, economic and social development, access to sufficient energy for the developing world, local and regional environmental impact, possible global climate change, efficiency of energy supply and use, financial and institutional issues, technological innovation and dissemination, and single energy issues.

In the bottom-up approach, nine regional groups analysed their own regional energy issues and requirements. These were tested with the facts, uncertainties and probabilities of the global energy scene prior to listing their own priorities for energy development, expectations and options.

The synthesised global and regional results were discussed in detail at the 15th WEC Congress in Madrid in September 1992. Resulting constructive comment was then built into the final study.

The results of the Commission study are summarised hereafter under three headings:

- Global perspectives.

- Regional perspectives.

- Conclusions and recommendations.

GLOBAL PERSPECTIVES

Energy issues should be viewed in their total, global, social and institutional, as well as economic and environmental, perspective. In particular, what people demand is not energy as such but the services which energy can provide – heating, cooling, cooking, lighting, mobility and motive power. Attention should therefore in future focus on how these services can be provided most effectively and efficiently – which may eventually mean in ways very different to those with which we are now familiar.

Given this starting point, it is not surprising that this study is a qualitative document. However, to support its top-down analysis, the Commission developed four energy Cases, each representing different assumptions in terms of economic development, energy efficiencies, technology transfer and the financing of development around the world. These Cases were developed to illustrate future possibilities. They are not predictions. In all four Cases, covering a wide range of possibilities (none of which represents a "business as usual" situation) major improvements in energy efficiency compared to historic performance are required – though to differing degrees within the various economic groupings of countries. The main horizon year adopted is 2020. The key characteristics of the four Cases are given in Table 1.

The Reference Case (B) represents an updated version of that developed by the WEC at its 14th Congress in Montreal in 1989. The other three are variants to illustrate sensitivities to changes in the basic assumptions.

The Ecologically Driven Case (C) is included to illustrate the size of the challenge and the far-reaching and immediate actions which are required if annual carbon dioxide emissions are to be broadly stabilised by 2020 at their 1990 levels.

In all four Cases the critically important projection of population growth is assumed to be the same and is taken from the current UN projection (Base Case). This implies an explosive increase in world population from 5.3 billion in 1990 to 8.1 billion in 2020 (and further to 10 billion in 2050 and 12 billion in 2100). More than 90% of this "explosion" will take place in the developing world.

As can be seen from Figure 1, it is only in the OECD and CEE/CIS that there is potential for containing future energy demand. Population "explosion" and economic development in many of the presently categorised developing countries make it inevitable that they will, for many decades, consume considerably increased amounts of energy. Even the Ecologically Driven Case C (which assumes a dramatic improvement in developing countries' energy efficiency far beyond historic experience, and despite static per capita energy consumption in some areas resulting

Case	A	B₁	B	C
Name	High Growth	Modified Reference	Reference	Ecologically Driven
Economic Growth % p.a.	High	Moderate	Moderate	Moderate
OECD	2.4	2.4	2.4	2.4
CEE/CIS	2.4	2.4	2.4	2.4
DCs	5.6	4.6	4.6	4.6
World	3.8	3.3	3.3	3.3
Energy Intensity Reduction % p.a.	High	Moderate	High	Very high
OECD	−1.8	−1.9	−1.9	−2.8
CEE/CIS	−1.7	−1.2	−2.1	−2.7
DCs	−1.3	−0.8	−1.7	−2.1
World	−1.6	−1.3	−1.9	−2.4
Technology Transfer	High	Moderate	High	Very high
Institutional Improvements (World)	High	Moderate	High	Very high
Possible Total Demand (Gtoe)	Very high 17.2	High 16.0	Moderate 13.4	Low 11.3

Table 1   Description of the four WEC Energy Cases

from continuing poverty) projects major increases of energy consumption within these countries.

Conversely, cost-effective energy efficiency measures cannot be implemented indefinitely. It is therefore likely that the rate of reduction in energy intensities (the amount of energy consumed to yield a unit of GDP at constant prices – or more positively the increasing amount of GDP which can be generated from a given amount of energy) will slow after 2020 in both the OECD and CEE/CIS. On the other hand, improved energy efficiency in the developing countries will reflect their more efficient use of manpower, capital and natural resources. Much of this may therefore happen after 2020.

As it is, the improvement in energy efficiency assumed in the Ecologically Driven Case C – in particular for the CEE/CIS and developing countries – is such that it will require a massive programme of technology transfer, financing and commercial implementation of energy-efficient technology if it is to be achieved before 2020. Even with major governmental assistance this may not be possible. History suggests that it is turnover of capital stock in favour of more efficient processes in general which reduces energy intensity, along with changes in the general struc-

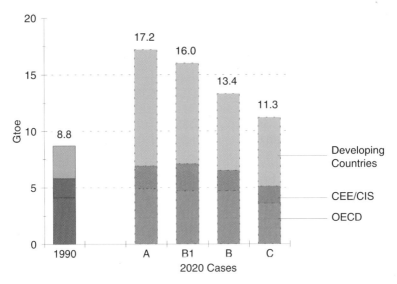

Figure 1   Primary Energy Demand by Economic Group

ture of economic activity. The world has little experience of what can be achieved by policies and decisions directly focused on improving energy efficiency and energy conservation.

Figure 2 compares possible global energy supply mixes for the four Cases in the year 2020 with the corresponding mix for 1990. It will be seen that fossil fuels continue to dominate the energy mix over the next three decades and are likely to do so well beyond this period. The only exception is shown in the Ecologically Driven Case C which is based on extreme assumptions thought unlikely to be achievable before the horizon year of 2020.

Many of the energy mix elements in the four Cases line up against their theoretical maxima on today's knowledge and capabilities. Two, however, demand special consideration.

The contribution from nuclear power to increasing electricity production is assumed to grow in all cases. This cannot be taken for granted. It will first require resolution of several issues of public concern, such as: technical safety in operation, management skills, effective international inspection, and safe long-term disposal of radioactive wastes. If these concerns can be resolved, nuclear power could have a large potential for satisfying a substantial part of the increasing demand for electricity, and would do so without significant emissions of greenhouse gases. In the longer term *if nuclear energy does not develop* it is likely to be replaced by coal.

New renewable energy sources will play an increasing role in the energy mix in absolute terms. However, with the exception of the

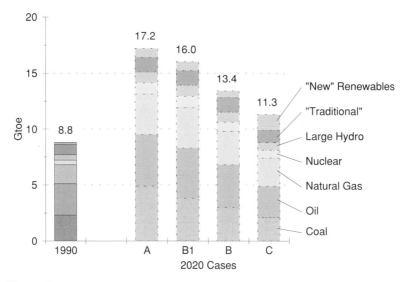

Figure 2   Primary Energy Supply Mix

Ecologically Driven Case C they will make a modest contribution up to 2020 in relative terms. Cost effective research, development and installation involving financing which only governments can supply will be needed if these sources of energy are to be implemented on the large scale shown in the Ecologically Driven Case C. Even then upfront capital costs (which apart from biomass represent most life-cycle costs) and local environmental concerns could slow their large-scale commercial development.

Many references to the relationship between fossil fuel burning and environmental protection relate to the overall context of carbon sources and sinks. It is thought by the Intergovernmental Panel on Climate Change that 1990 source emissions totalled 200 GtC while sinks worldwide absorbed 194 GtC. Fossil fuel burning probably accounted for 5.9 GtC of emissions in 1990 – some 3% of global CO_2 emissions from all sources. The crucial question requiring scientific proof is whether this 3% anthropogenic contribution, and an increase in it, will disturb the balance to create global climate change.

From Table 2 it can be seen that the Ecologically Driven Case C is the only one which will have global CO_2 emissions from fuel combustion in 2020 close to their 1990 level. As has been pointed out, stabilisation of annual CO_2 emissions was the theoretical requirement for this Case. All the other Cases show large increases in annual CO_2 emissions. However, none of the Cases allows a stabilisation of greenhouse gas concentrations in the atmosphere within the next few decades – the objective of the Climate Convention signed by 161 countries and the European

Cases	1990	2020			
		A	B₁	B	C
Emissions (GtC)	5.9	11.5	10.2	8.4	6.3
Concentrations (ppmv)	355	434	426	416	404

Notes:
1   Emissions are from commercial fossil fuels only.
2   Concentrations provided by the Climatic Research Unit, University of East Anglia, using the MAGICC climate model.
GtC = gigatonnes of elemental carbon.
ppmv = parts per million by volume.

Table 2   Carbon Dioxide Emissions from Commercial Fossil Fuel Combustion and Estimated Atmospheric CO_2 Concentrations

Community and ratified by 17 countries (as of March 1993). If the hypotheses which link anthropogenic emissions to global climate change are eventually proved to be correct, significant rises in global mean sea level and temperature over the next century may be anticipated. In this event, the process of adaptation to such conditions will be more success-ful the earlier it is started, in order to reduce the scale on which it would otherwise occur.

Major change of energy supply structures and of energy utilisation systems cannot be achieved rapidly. They must be built up over time, but equally they require to be built up to follow international strategic planning to ensure sustainability – sustainability of economic develop-ment and sustainability of environmental protection. The two are indivisible but can and should be interdependent.

Against this background the Commission with respect to possible global climate change advocates, as a matter of necessary prudence, action based upon the following approach:

- Recognising the uncertainties, the need for intensified research to improve scientific understanding in this field.

- The need to raise energy efficiency whenever it can be justified on the basis of cost/benefit analysis and to increase energy conservation.

- The application of rational adaptation measures now, because if the hypotheses about global climate change are scientifically proven then the world is probably already past the point where it can be avoided.

- If rational abatement and adaptation strategies are to be adopted with the necessary speed and effectiveness then government involvement is required to provide stimulus and leadership. Such government action should allow for the optimal use of market instruments and industry-initiated responses to the potential problem; for example, tradable emission permits; and road user pricing.

Measures must be effective, their implementation cost effective, and they need to have the joint support of governments, energy operatives, and the consumers who will have to pay the costs – in order to reap the benefits of such measures.

REGIONAL PERSPECTIVES

From the regional analyses it was found, not unexpectedly, that the first priority for the majority of the world's population is access to sufficient affordable energy. Some 70% of the world's population lives at a per capita energy consumption level one-quarter of that of Western Europe, and one-sixth of that of the United States. In many cases this inhibits even minimal economic growth (eg in certain African countries), and restricts services basic to human needs. In other developing countries (eg China) sufficient energy is available to support planned growth but not without potentially serious environmental implications.

The second priority highlighted by the regions is the need to surmount the urgent and severe local environmental problems faced by many countries such as deforestation, soil erosion, unplanned and uncontrolled urbanisation, unchecked industrial pollution, water scarcity and contamination, and loss of natural habitats for wildlife. All these are local problems demanding management and investment. The challenge to the developing countries is emerging as the need to achieve the right balance between investment for growth, investment for efficiency and investment for the local environment. Sometimes these are mutually supportive but in other cases they are in competition with each other.

The third priority is an important contributor to the solution of local and global environmental problems. It is the need to raise the efficiency with which energy is provided and used around the world. The regions confirmed that there is a large potential for meeting economic and social aims using less energy. Such improvement can only be achieved, however, with considerable investment in old as well as new plant, buildings, processes, appliances and in fuel substitution. This requires government encouragement, support and regulation as well as market forces which should play a dominant role. Above all, it requires the right conditions in order to harness international investment and equity capital and know-how, to create joint ventures, to mobilise local capital and provide investors with a satisfactory rate of return.

Among other key issues highlighted are the need for:

- Massive investment to expand existing energy systems and technologies. This could total US$30 trillion[1] by 2020. By comparison world GDP in 1989 was some US$20 trillion. Much more capital than hitherto will have to be mobilised locally and a much larger proportion than historically will need to achieve a satisfactory commercial return. Competition for investible funds will increase greatly.

- Through such investment the transfer or local development of modern energy technology suited to local needs, such as mini-hydro and small-scale solar schemes.

- The provision of education, training and technological support for the development of energy systems and local technological independence. Without the development of local infrastructure and expertise to sustain them, well-meaning projects frequently result in failure.

- Substantial institutional change to facilitate the progressive introduction of market systems, foreign equity participation and the mobilisation of local capital markets. The World Bank has noted a recent explosion in private sector financial flows to developing countries, both of portfolio capital and foreign direct investment. Equity capital inflows to Latin America, for example, rose nearly 14-fold between 1989 and 1992 (to US$5.6 billion).

By contrast to the discussions in many industrialised countries, the reactions from most regions are that the perceived problem of global climate change is not a high priority, particularly among the developing countries.

CONCLUSIONS AND RECOMMENDATIONS

From the global and regional perceptions there emerges a clear distinction between the energy priorities of the developing, transitional and industrialised economies.

- For the developing countries, despite the disparate nature of such a grouping, the key issues are economic growth,

---

[1] Trillion=10^{12}

access to adequate commercial energy supplies and the finances needed to achieve these.

- For the CEE/CIS countries in transition, the key issues are the modernisation and expansion of their existing supply infrastructures, the promotion of the rational use of energy, the transition to market-orientated policies and enterprises, and the introduction of stable legal and fiscal regimes which foster investment and satisfactory returns thereon.

- For the industrialised countries, the dominating issues are securing greater energy efficiency and continuous improvement to the technologies deployed in their own countries and elsewhere.

The challenge for the world's institutions is to rise above these different priorities and to secure broad progress on all fronts rather than allow sectoral or political difference to inhibit necessary progress.

The consequences of the huge forecasted increase of global population will be the accelerated consumption of the reserves of fossil fuels, with coal depleting less rapidly than oil and natural gas. The result will be increased reliance on coal and ultimately a shift (probably well into the 21st century) to other fossil resources (such as tar sands, shale oil, synthetic gas, etc) which can only be developed at higher cost, with the application of improved technologies, but with the risk of increased environmental impact.

The higher cost of fossil fuels and environmental considerations will place increased emphasis on energy efficiency, and should stimulate the development and implementation of the various other energy sources.

Ensuring the Functioning of Energy Markets

Ensuring that global and regional energy demand can be met in the most cost-effective way will require energy markets to function effectively, and this will depend on:

- Achieving a high degree of market liberalisation, albeit within government regulatory frameworks.

- Identifying and implementing appropriate improvements to institutional problems, both national and international. It is particularly in the CEE/CIS and developing countries that such improvements are required in order to mobilise capital, create efficiency and separate the State from day-to-day energy operations. These countries need to ensure the protection of private and intellectual property, and to recognise the right to use the resulting profits, in order to foster the effective functioning of energy markets.

- Reordering support and assistance from the industrialised countries to ensure the optimisation of the use of such aid to cover not only the transfer of technology but the training of operatives and the setting up of local equipment and other manufacture.

Long-Term Oriented Research and Development

The most important requirement for securing an adequate global energy supply up to 2020 will be the efficient and responsible use of fossil fuels and of nuclear energy. Other fossil fuels (oil shales and tar sands) and new renewable energy sources will make a growing contribution.

Research and development of these latter energy sources should principally be left to market forces and industry responses. For economic reasons, however, there is likely to be difficulty in ensuring research and development are based upon a long-term global vision.

- Although the long-term price of oil and therefore of other fuels will increase, prices in the shorter term may vary and blur this perspective. Research and development should nevertheless be based on the longer-term price outlook.

- The technology for efficient energy application must be developed and implemented for world-wide application.

- The development of new renewable energy technologies will need investment in research, development and installation which is not yet generally perceived to be justified by economic returns. Government support would appear necessary.

- There is a need to improve the safety, capacity and efficiency of long-distance energy transport facilities.

- One of the greatest challenges is how best to meet the demand for mobility, given the current level and prospective expansion of road use and transport infrastructures, and the possibility of greatly increased air traffic.

These are all areas where governments should set longer-term frameworks.

Improving Environmental Quality

The technology for abating local and regional pollution of energy provision and use has advanced to a point where the industrialised countries can gradually reduce energy-related pollution to acceptable levels. For them, the new and even more challenging concern is now potential global climate change resulting from CO_2 emissions and other greenhouse gases.

The developing countries and the economies in transition see, however, the urgent and severe local environmental problems with which they are faced as being of a much higher priority to them.

To ensure that resources are used in an efficient and balanced manner as seen from both a global and regional point of view, it is important in seeking international agreement on greenhouse gas emissions that:

- Economic growth is seen and achieved as an essential part of any policy of sustainable development, necessary not only to meet peoples' needs and aspirations but also to generate the investment capital needed to use energy more efficiently and to protect the environment.

- The claims of local priorities, based on local judgement, and upon available resources, are recognised. This may require considerable assistance to flow from the industrialised countries to the CEE/CIS and developing countries if local energy efficiency levels and other methods of reducing local emissions are to be implemented.

- Precautionary measures to reduce the emissions of greenhouse gases should be adopted since scientific evidence does not so far justify any other policy.

Abatement policies should be based on the principle of expenditure optimisation across the globe such that private and public funds are spent, not on a national basis to secure national targets irrespective of global impact, but in a manner which secures maximum global improvement. This is a principle which can usefully be applied not only to potential global environmental concerns, but to local and regional pollution also.

Finding a Path to Sustainable Energy Development

The top-down and bottom-up analysis of this study demonstrates clearly that the perception of what is important in the further development of the world energy system varies widely from region to region. In finding a path to sustainable global and regional energy development it will be of the utmost importance to address these widely different concerns in a realistic and balanced manner to reduce – as far as possible – the associated stresses between countries and regions. Without sufficient attention to this dimension of the world energy problem, there will not be sustainable development consistent with the expected population explosion in the developing world. Although there is no single universal formula, there are a number of important measures which when taken together indicate a path to world-wide sustainable development.

- To ensure that the available resources are used in the most cost-effective and productive manner.

- To ensure that markets function as effectively as possible to attract the capital necessary to provide the energy services needed.

- To ensure that governmental measures are directed principally at providing the framework within which markets function effectively and avoiding market distortions which prevent the development of the necessary longer-term solutions to problems – in particular with respect to research and development and the world-wide dissemination of useful results.

- To ensure that energy conservation and efficiency, wherever justified on cost/benefit grounds, are maximised to reflect both economic and environmental goals.

- To place energy issues in their broadest social and institutional context globally, recognising that people seek the services which energy can provide – not energy as such. Policies, processes and equipment related to energy provision and use should focus on how the provision of energy services can be more effectively and efficiently provided in future.

This Commission report forms the basis of the WEC's integrated views on energy development to 2020, and beyond. However, the Commission's work process will not end with this report. Ongoing WEC study programmes will be devoted to the updating and amplification of major elements.

This report will therefore act as the foundation for debating energy policy and increasing understanding of energy-related issues in the future.

The 1993–1995 work programme and its policy implications will be presented at the 16th WEC Congress, to be held in Tokyo in October, 1995.

WORLD ENERGY TO 2020

CHAPTER

1

THE PATTERN OF ENERGY USE

What people seek from energy use is the services energy provides – such as heating, cooling, cooking, lighting and motive power. Energy is not a mere commodity or set of commodities unrelated to other human requirements or concerns. The provision and use of energy has powerful social and environmental impacts. No report on energy can ignore how people use energy, whether they use it efficiently, and – above all – whether they have the means to use it.

Until the 18th century, almost all energy use was supplied locally, from such traditional energy sources as human and animal power, wood, dung, crop residues, charcoal, peat and the utilisation of wind and water power. With the decline in infant mortality, the rise in average life expectancy, and improvements in sanitation and health care came rising population closely linked with the industrialisation process. Admittedly this provided the goods and services required in part to sustain the population growth and eventually provided the technology to mitigate many of the problems it had caused. But even in those countries which industrialised earliest the health hazards from the burning of traditional fuels in the home, the filth and inefficiencies occasioned by the use of horse-drawn traffic, and the low conversion efficiency and high pollution of earlier technologies were widespread. Many of the problems remain to this day, and intensify, in developing countries.

The growth of population, the desire for comfort, material acquisition, mobility and communication, and access to the materials, processes and technology to meet such desires by an increasing number of people has brought with it, among other things, rising energy demand and the incentives to meet that demand. Inevitably, suppliers tended to seek out the more readily available and cheaper sources. Consumers have a general preference for lower prices and ready availability than otherwise. This does not itself encourage efficiency in commercial energy use nor minimise adverse environmental impacts. Nevertheless, steady techno-logical progress has raised efficiency in both provision and use as well as mitigated environmental effects.

Over the past 30 years, the world's energy requirements have risen considerably. In 1960 the world used 3.3 Gtoe of energy. In 1990 the world used 8.8 Gtoe – an increase of 166% or an average increase of 3.3% pa.

Not all energy is supplied on a commercial basis. Some traditional fuels, such as fuelwood, are largely accessed non-commercially. Fuelwood, the major source of energy for heating and cooking in many developing countries, is becoming more difficult to obtain for growing numbers of people.

But there are wide divergences in energy use. By far the largest energy consumers are the industrialised countries – the OECD, Central and Eastern Europe, and the CIS. (Throughout this report CIS refers to the Common-

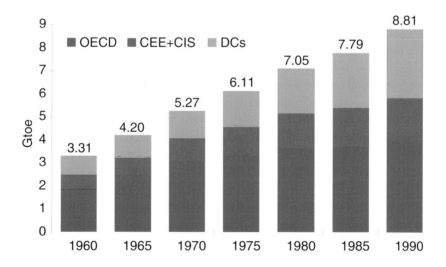

Figure 1.1 Primary Energy Demand by Economic Group

wealth of Independent States, plus the three Baltic States and Georgia, that formerly comprised the USSR.) Energy use per capita is even more varied. In 1990 primary energy consumption per capita in North America was 7.82 toe (tonnes of oil equivalent). By contrast the figure for Western Europe was 3.22 toe, for the CIS 5.01 toe and for Central and Eastern Europe 2.91 toe. This last figure was nearly three times the level prevailing in Latin America, the Middle East and North Africa, and the Pacific Region (despite the upward distortion provided by consumption in such countries as Japan, Taiwan China, the Republic of Korea, etc). In Sub-Saharan Africa primary energy consumption per capita was barely one-sixth the level in Central and Eastern Europe (at 0.53 toe), it was even less in South Asia (0.39 toe). In North America primary energy consumption per capita in 1990 was about 15 times the level in Sub-Saharan Africa and over 20 times the level in South Asia. With a world average primary energy per capita in 1990 of only 1.66 toe it may seem surprising that this was little more than 20% of the per capita consumption in North America, and little more than a third of the level in the CIS. The details are given in Figures 1.1 and 1.2.

CURRENT REALITIES AND POLICIES

There are not only imbalances in the use of energy around the world. Energy resources – particularly fossil fuel resources – are unevenly distributed. The costs of extracting or collecting, transporting and converting the various forms of energy vary widely. Some forms of energy

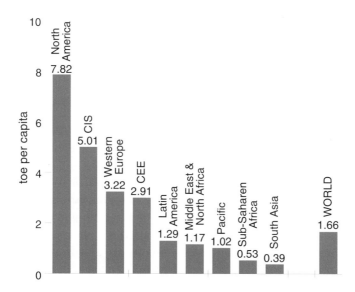

Figure 1.2 Energy Demand per Capita in 1990 by Geographic Region

are currently readily available using existing technology – particularly the fossil fuels. Others will require many decades to bring on stream in substantial quantities, using technologies in their infancy or still to be developed – this is particularly the case for some forms of new renewable energy and for advanced forms of nuclear power generation (the fast-breeder reactors and fusion).

Growing environmental concerns have naturally propelled action to tackle local and regional emissions from energy provision and use. There is increasing pressure to take steps to counter anthropogenic greenhouse gas emissions, which may cause global climate change. But there are many trade-offs between efficiency and environmental gains. In general technologies and processes which clean up or reduce harmful emissions also reduce energy efficiency.

There are many fields where current policies do not promote efficiency in energy provision and use, nor encourage conservation. Energy prices are widely subsidised, inducing excessive consumption and waste. Price subsidies hinder the introduction of cleaner processing of existing fuels and the development of alternative, cleaner forms of energy. But the removal of price subsidies requires a willingness and financial ability to achieve this end. In many countries major institutional changes and shifts in attitudes of policy-makers and end-consumers would be required. In poverty-stricken or potentially unstable societies sharp price rises are not practicable. Without price rises waste and profligacy will continue, the funds for investment in improved and new forms of energy and energy-using equipment will be reduced, and publicly pronounced policy goals will remain out of reach.

This incompatibility between goals and current policies reaches a pinnacle when related to potential global climate change. Despite many public pronouncements by world leaders, and the setting down of goals for the reduction of carbon dioxide emissions (thereby ignoring most other greenhouse gas emissions – though halocarbons have been tackled separately), there are few policies in place and actions taken which will bring the desired result about within the timetable set down. This is simply within the limited context of bringing carbon dioxide emissions back to 1990 levels within a decade or so, and keeping them at that level. It does not begin to embrace realistic policies for reducing current annual anthropogenic carbon dioxide emissions by the 60% or so claimed to be necessary to avoid further global warming. There are virtually no policies in existence to tackle methane emissions directly (though constraints on venting and flaring do exist in some countries), and policies to curb nitrogen and nitrous oxide emissions directly are also wanting.

Most of the growth in future global energy demand will come from the present developing countries. Few developing countries have the financial means to acquire modern, efficient and clean technology. Little such technology will simply be handed over at no cost by richer countries. Whereas the sums of money required for such investment in new technology are not large in relation to annual global fixed capital formation, they need to be harnessed. This can only come about through attracting private finance, joint ventures and equity participation, and developing local capital markets. Present realities are far removed from the attainment of these objectives in many countries.

Even current technology, when available, is widely used to less than best effect. Poor management, lack of education and training, and inappropriateness to local circumstances are the usual causes of ineffectiveness.

Institutional rigidities and an unwillingness of policy-makers and politicians to will the means to attain their stated ends are among the causes of incompatibility between words and actions. It serves no useful purpose to pretend otherwise.

THE ROLE OF POPULATION GROWTH

The reality is that in the present world some 50% of the 1990 population of 5.3 billion do not have access to commercial energy, and the services it brings. This is principally because the great majority of the 2.5 billion-plus people in the developing world have no energy other than muscle power, perhaps a few domestic animals, and traditional fuels increasingly difficult to obtain in the desired quantity. In 30 years' time there are likely to be nearly 3 billion more people in the world, over 90% of them in countries which are already economically poor. Thus most of these additional people will be unable to have the services and goods regarded as basic now in developed countries unless the energy is available to provide them.

Yet the growth in energy demand has for some time past been fastest in the developing countries. In the past decade, it has risen in developing countries by 49%; in the developed countries by only 14%. Although most energy is still consumed by the developed industrialised countries, the proportion accounted for by the developing countries can be expected to continue to increase. Indeed, even if the expected additional numbers of people achieve only the current per capita consumption of energy (in the form of fuelwood and/or fossil fuels) as that currently prevailing in developing countries, then by 2020 the present developing countries will account for the major part of the world's greenhouse gas emissions from fuel burning. Indeed they will probably do so before 2010.

This should be seen primarily as the inevitable confirmation of past trends. The two main forces driving energy demand in developing countries have been population growth and economic development. Over the past 30 years the developing countries accounted for 87% of the world's population growth, increasing their share of world population

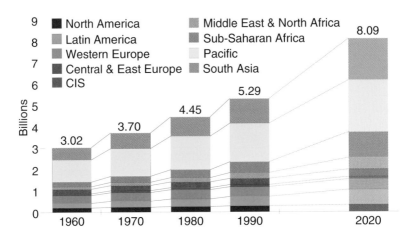

Figure 1.3 World Population by Geographic Region

from 68% to 76% in 1990. Figures 1.3 and 1.4 provide world population growth and growth rates 1960–2020 based on UN population projections.

Population forecasting has long been a hazardous business, and the past two centuries are littered with erroneous forecasts. But most of the errors have been due to underestimating population growth and even forecasting declines due to falling net reproduction rates. Although population growth is expected to continue in the developing countries,

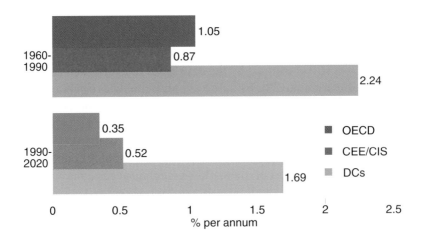

Figure 1.4 World Population Growth Rates by Economic Group

> ***By 2020 nearly 85% of world population will be in the developing countries.***
>
> UN Population Projections and Prospects.

the pace is expected to slow. Indeed it is already showing some decline: from over 2% per annum in the 1960s down to 1.75% in the 1980s. Virtually everywhere in the world fertility rates are falling. In Thailand fertility rates have fallen from over 6 children per woman to 2.5; in Bangladesh from 7 to 4.5; in Brazil from 6 to 3.2. However, life expectancy is also increasing rapidly in most countries – as shown in Table 1.1. Further, because the world's population has already passed the 5.4 billion mark the actual growth of population will be the largest ever in a single 30-year period, despite declining fertility rates. Thus between 1960 and 1990 world population rose nearly 2.3 billion (breaking all previous records); between 1990 and 2020 the UN anticipates 2.8 billion more people; and in the 30 years following 2020 the UN anticipates a further 2.0 billion people. Standard estimates for future world population are given in Table 1.2.

In this report the median figure, the "Base Case" of the World Bank, has been used throughout. It is believed by some demographers that world population growth is likely to approach stability during the second half of the 21st century within the range 10–15 billion people (Figure 1.5).

Such a population expansion will provide great challenges, but also great opportunities for human imagination, adaptation and innovation. Even if wealth per head grows only slowly, the rise in human numbers

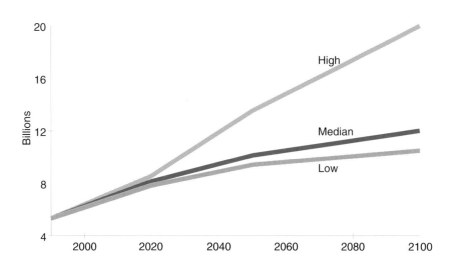

Figure 1.5 World Population Estimates to 2100 *(Source: UN and World Bank)*

Country	Fertility Rate (births per woman)		Overall Life Expectancy (at birth – years)		Population (millions)		
	early 1960s	1990[1]	early 1960s	1990[1]	early 1960s	1990 (actual)	2025 (est)
Algeria	7.44	5.08	50.20	65.40	12	25	52
Brazil	5.65	3.20	57.10	66.20	84	150	246
China	6.36	2.48	54.90	70.20	715	1139	1513
Egypt	6.76	4.04	48.80	60.20	29	52	90
Mexico	6.72	3.30	59.60	69.70	45	89	150
Ethiopia	5.80	7.50	42.80	48.00	25	49	127
India	6.23	3.94	45.20	59.00	487	853	1442
Indonesia	5.51	3.06	44.10	61.80	105	184	286
Iran	7.09	6.22	52.20	62.90	25	55	114
Kenya	8.00	6.52	47.50	58.90	10	24	79
Morocco	7.11	4.50	49.40	61.80	13	25	46
Myanmar	5.82	3.82	47.70	61.40	24	42	73
Nigeria	6.89	5.98	41.70	51.50	58	109	281
Pakistan	7.00	5.84	45.80	55.80	53	123	267
Peru	6.68	3.80	50.60	62.70	11	22	37
Philippines	6.80	3.54	55.50	64.40	32	62	112
Saudi Arabia	7.26	7.02	48.30	64.50	5	14	45
South Africa	6.15	4.26	51.10	62.00	20	35	65
Sudan	6.67	6.28	40.20	50.40	12	25	60
Tanzania	6.56	6.56	42.90	47.50	12	27	85
Thailand	6.25	2.50	55.60	65.90	31	56	81
Turkey	5.66	3.70	53.80	66.60	31	56	88
Uganda	7.04	7.30	47.20	46.90	8	19	53
Vietnam	5.98	3.84	49.00	66.60	38	67	117
Zaire	5.96	6.24	43.40	52.00	17	36	99
Zambia	6.64	6.74	44.30	49.70	4	8	26
Zimbabwe	8.00	4.92	48.00	60.80	4	10	23
TOTAL					1910	3356	5657
As % of Total World Population					63	63	67

Note : [1] strictly "Most recent estimate"

Source: "Social Indicators of Development, 1991-92"; World Bank, 1992 and "World Resources, 1992-93"; World Resources Institute/UNEP/UNDP, 1992

Table 1.1   Basic Demographic Data for Selected Countries

Range	1990	2020	2050	2100
"High"	5.3	8.5	13.5	20
"Median"	5.3	8.1	10.1	12
"Low"	5.3	7.8	9.4	10.5
Sources: UN "World Population Prospects: Estimates and Projections as Assessed in 1990", 1991 and World Bank: "World Development Report, 1992: Development and the Environment" 1992. Fig. 1.1, p.26				

Table 1.2   World Population – Actual and Estimates (Billions)

will add immensely to the world's demand for energy. By the end of the next century the presently developing countries will account for 90% of the world's population (Figure 1.6). This report does not assume in any of the four Cases examined that the present developing countries will catch up with the rest of the world (OECD, Central and Eastern Europe, and the CIS) in terms of GDP per capita or energy consumption per capita over the next few decades. In some parts of Sub-Saharan Africa for example, it may prove difficult to increase per capita use of energy at all due to economic, social and institutional barriers.

ECONOMIC GROWTH AND ENERGY INTENSITY

The other major factors influencing energy demand, additional to population growth, are economic growth and the efficiency with which energy is used. Figure 1.7 provides information on economic growth since 1960.

Economic growth is of vital importance for human development, but care needs to be taken in defining what growth is and what purposes it

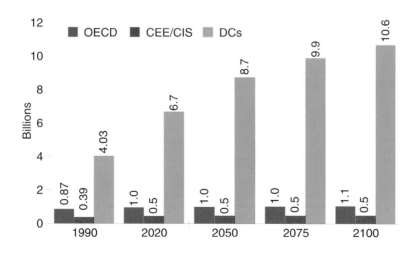

Figure 1.6   World Population – Actual and Estimates to 2100 by Economic Group

serves. Three steps would greatly assist in making the measurements of economic growth more meaningful and acceptable: the inclusion of all costs in pricing, so that social and environmental externalities were incorporated; the full allocation of such costs to the private sector when it is the private sector which incurs them or should properly incur them, rather than – as at present – leaving "governments" (ie the general taxpayer) to pick up the bill; and the incorporation of future actual or potential liabilities into current accounting. The speed with which such steps can realistically be taken will depend on local circumstances.

Since the beginning of the industrial revolution the efficiency of energy production, conversion, transport and end-use has risen markedly. The efficiency of lighting has improved by some three orders of magnitude over the past 100 years, the efficiency of natural gas power plants has risen greatly, and so on. One result is that the ratio of energy consumption to GDP expressed in constant prices (the measure of energy intensity) has been falling in the leading industrial nations for decades. In the United States and the United Kingdom energy intensity has been declining by about 1% per annum for the past 100 years. In France and Germany a similar picture emerges from the 1920s. In Japan a broadly similar story develops after 1950. Thus the idea that there was a constant relationship between energy demand growth and GDP growth at constant prices (which was sharply broken by the impact of the 1973 oil crisis) is seen to be incorrect. Figure 1.8 demonstrates the more likely picture, although the earlier data points are somewhat uncertain.

The downward trend of energy intensity over time provides other important insights. First, there is no simple 1:1 relationship between

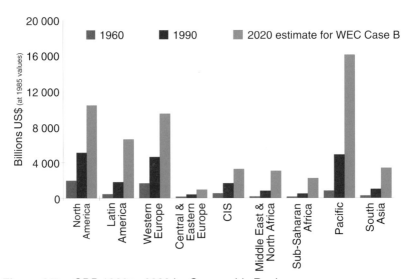

Figure 1.7 GDP 1960 to 2020 by Geographic Region

future economic growth and energy demand projections. Second, it makes clear that different countries can be on different trajectories of energy demand and that countries which industrialised later tend to be on a lower trajectory. Those countries which industrialised later seem to benefit from the knowledge, skills and technologies which have been gained earlier elsewhere. This is sometimes claimed to be part of a "leap-frogging" process which could be enhanced to promote the well-being of energy consumers in developing countries. However, the influence of warmer climate in many developing countries is another factor at work. Third, it provides hopes that presently developing countries will not only have *lower* energy intensity trajectories (which is generally the case) but will also arrive earlier at the point of downward inflection. This is the assumption built into three of the four Cases examined in this report. However, there is debate on this point – with some specialists believing that economic and social development needs will require many developing countries to experience rising energy intensity over the next few decades before decline is achieved. Part of the problem here is that as people and countries switch from traditional non-commercial fuels to commercial fuels and electricity there is more of an apparent than a real expansion of energy use. Nevertheless, as more efficient technology and processes are applied to energy provision and use in the developing countries, so energy efficiency gains will permit resources to be used for other purposes. These other purposes may include energy consumption.

There is also a more general and obvious point which can get overlooked. Energy intensity generally falls because productivity gains have

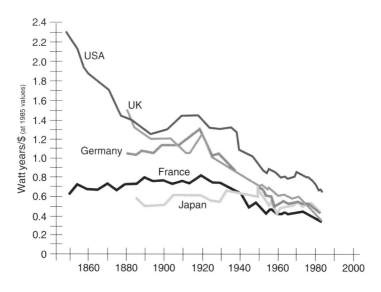

Figure 1.8   Primary Energy (including Wood) per Constant GDP
(Source: Grübler, IIASA, 1989. Data: Nakicenovic, 1986 and Martin, 1988)

raised the value added per unit of energy used, and because of structural shifts in the economy. These changes may have little or nothing directly to do with deliberate efforts to raise energy efficiency. Similarly, techno-logical innovations may well have as a by-product the reduction of energy usage, without this having been a deliberate objective. In the future, this situation may change due to shifts in energy policy and prices. In the past there has been little experience of the impact of measures to raise energy efficiency.

It is fortunate that innovations and, above all, turnover of capital stock across the broad economic spectrum result in declining energy intensity. But as an International Energy Report ("Energy Efficiency and the Environment", 1991, p.48) warned: "The progress of energy efficiency within the demand trends examined needs to be evaluated with care because it is intertwined with so many other factors affecting demand. An energy efficiency improvement is defined as any action by a producer or consumer of energy that reduces the use of energy without affecting the level of service provided."

THE STRUCTURE OF DEMAND

Commercial fossil fuels supplied over three-quarters of the world's total energy requirements in 1990. "Traditional" and mainly "non-commer-cial" energy (such as fuelwood and dung) provided 11%, nuclear 5%, hydropower 6% and "new" renewables 2% (Figure 1.9). Even though non-fossil energy sources are expected to increase their share, as dis-cussed below, fossil fuel supplies will continue to meet the bulk of the world's energy requirement for a long time to come.

Table 1.3 shows the breakdown of commercial energy use in industri-alised countries and for eight developing countries. The first three lines show energy use for households and services, transport and industry other

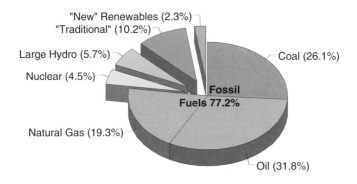

Figure 1.9   Fuel Mix in 1990

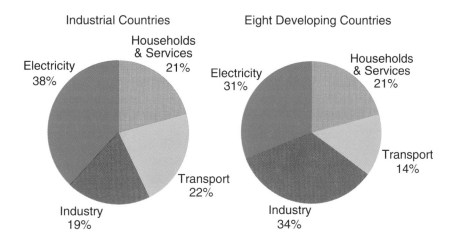

Figure 1.10   Consumption of Commercial Energy in 1988 for Industrial
Countries and Eight Developing Countries

than through the electricity route. The fourth line shows total energy consumption via electricity (Figure 1.10).

Transport and electricity are the two fastest growing sectors in terms of energy demand.

Transport activities account for about 30% of the energy used by final consumers, and about 20% of the gross energy produced. Of this, movement of people takes about 70% and movement of freight about 30%. Within this sector road transport accounts for the largest proportion: over 80% in industrialised countries, with air transport next at 13%. The transport sector is mainly dependent upon oil, and the road transport sector's use of oil in the OECD countries rose from 30% of total final oil consumption in 1970 to 47% in 1987. The transportation market has been virtually the only growth sector for the oil industry over the past 20 years.

	Industrial Countries	Eight [a] Developing Countries
Households & Services	21	21
Transport	22	14
Industry	19	34
Electricity	38	31
[a] Brazil, China, India, Indonesia, Malaysia, Pakistan, Philippines and Thailand. These countries account for more than 50 % of total energy and 35 % of oil consumed in developing countries (detailed data not available for all developing countries) Source:OECD, 1990; Imran & Barnes, World Bank 1990		

Table 1.3   Consumption of Commercial Energy in 1988 (% of Total)

As the OECD in 1987 used 80% of the world's passenger cars and 67% of its goods vehicles, these figures capture much of the total picture.

The rapid increase in road transport in recent years is a major contributor to the rise in oil demand. Further, motor vehicles are believed to be responsible for 14% of all CO_2 derived from fossil fuel combustion. Road transport is a cause of congestion and expanding infrastructures and is posing severe challenges both in richer countries and the urban centres of poorer ones. While recent research has raised doubts over whether car ownership and use around the world will rise to the levels earlier predicted, some OECD countries have approached 600 cars per 1000 population while most non-OECD countries average less than 20 per 1000 population. This suggests an enormous potential for road transport expansion and energy demand increases by the transport sector.

Nevertheless, the rate of increase in road transport energy demand has slowed in the most developed countries since the late 1960s (Figure 1.11). This has reflected both improved vehicle efficiency and a slowing down in the level of acquisition of cars by households (though by contrast the number of households with two or more cars has risen steadily for much of the past two decades). These developments have encouraged hopes that saturation levels may operate at lower levels than sometimes projected, but it would be unrealistic to anticipate that the road transportation sector will cease to be a major force in global energy demand growth over the next few decades.

Road transport will continue to depend mainly on oil over the next three decades. The huge investment in current transport systems – not only vehicles but infrastructures and supply facilities – and the value of these systems to society means that they are likely to persist for a long time to come. The use of oil for transport has been found very convenient and easy, while ease of mobility is valued highly by users. Determined efforts will be made in the coming decades to switch to alternative fuels (methanol, ethanol, synthetic oils, LPG, hydrogen), more efficient vehicles and new transport systems. Efforts will also be made to price vehicle use and congestion higher. Significant changes, however, are likely to come about only slowly. Much will depend on whether threats from scarcely constrained vehicle usage are perceived as real by whole communities and legislators. These threats may come from the build-up of tropospheric ozone, other harmful emissions with local effects, or the possibility of global climate change.

The various forms of transport-related pollution work, in some respects, counter to each other. Thus the build up of tropospheric ozone – for which nitrogen oxide emissions from road vehicles bear heavy responsibility – has a warming impact on mean air temperatures close to ground level. Emissions of nitrogen oxides from aircraft flying in the stratosphere – hitherto limited to some military, supersonic and mostly trans-Atlantic subsonic flights – reduces stratospheric ozone, and thus tends to offset global warming in doing so. However, reduction of the ozone layer in the stratosphere has other, harmful, consequences for humans and many other species. Thus the rapid increase in air travel and air traffic movements, especially those involving substantial flights through the stratosphere, which has taken place in recent decades may also have had adverse environmental impacts. Given the likelihood that both road vehicle use and aircraft use will increase in the coming decades determined efforts to mitigate their environmental impacts are an urgent necessity.

Technology has an important role to play in addressing these problems. Improvements in vehicle design and alternative fuels can have a major impact in improving efficiency and reducing emissions. Much of the forward momentum achieved in the decade to 1985 has slowed in response to downward oil price

	Millions of cars	Persons per car
USA	145	1.7
Canada	13	1.9
Italy	28	2.0
France	24	2.4
UK	23	2.4
Spain	13	3.1
Japan	37	3.3
Czecho-slovakia	3	4.8
Greece	2	5.5
Poland	6	6.2
Malaysia	2	8.4
Taiwan, China	2	11.5
Korea, Rep. of	2	15.5
ex-USSR	17	17.0
India	2	121.4
China	2	680

Table 1.4   Cars in 1991

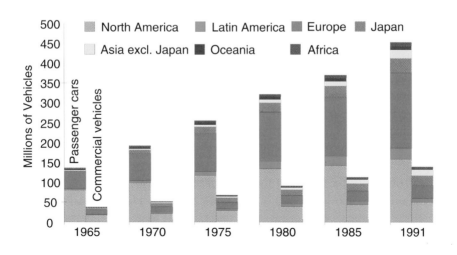

Figure 1.11   Growth in Passenger Cars and Commercial Vehicles
1965–1991 *(Source: Society of Motor Manufacturers and Traders, UK)*

movements and apparent consumer preferences. There is a clear need for renewed efforts when major motor vehicle manufacturers are able to produce road vehicles with fuel consumption barely a quarter of the existing fleet average, and special prototype machines have travelled 300 times as far as the average automobile on a single gallon of fuel.

The focus, however, needs to go beyond vehicle efficiency and technology. In the longer term it can only be tackled through an imaginative approach to urban planning and integrated public transportation planning. This needs to be aimed at stemming the otherwise seemingly inevitable domination of the motor car in the developed countries and the potential for the same phenomenon in the developing countries. In the United States, mass transport accounts for only 6% of all passenger travel; in Germany the figure is over 15%, and in Japan 47%. This partly reflects geography and human settlement patterns. Nevertheless, merely expanding infrastructure without an attendant comprehensive strategy which takes account of consequential transportation movements will perpetuate the seemingly insoluble problems faced by many developed countries today. Much more effective policy responses are required to lessen the dominance of the motor car, while satisfying so far as it is possible the desire for mobility and other social aspects which those who have or aspire to vehicle ownership associate with the motor car. Similar imaginative efforts will be needed to improve means of communication, and encourage their adoption, in order to undermine the upward pressures on air travel and freight.

Economic resources are also more efficiently used if those who make decisions about them are fully informed about the cost of their decisions. Users should be fully charged for their road usage as well as for the full costs of vehicle manufacture and parking. These full costs include environmental damage both arising from vehicle ownership and use and from associated infrastructural investments. An important part of the process of successful policy implementation will be to ensure that road pricing is seen as a use charge rather than a tax, and to ensure that revenues generated from this source are largely ploughed back into collective modes of transport, road maintenance and improvement, traffic calming schemes, and environmental enhancement. International efforts will be needed to introduce full cost pricing to air travel and air freight.

Electricity has virtually doubled its share of energy consumption since 1960 on a world-wide basis and has increased sharply in all three groups of countries: the developed (OECD) economies, in Central and Eastern Europe and the Commonwealth of Independent States, and in the developing countries. In 1990, 58% of global electricity was produced in OECD countries (USA claimed 26%) and only 23% was in the developing countries. The rate of penetration of electricity use in the OECD has slowed since the early 1980s, with electricity as a percentage of total energy use flattening. In the CEE/CIS area a similar flattening can be discerned from the mid-1970s (Figure 1.12). This flattening has caused electricity consumption per unit of economic activity on a global basis also to flatten out (Figure 1.13). However, electricity demand continues to rise rapidly in the developing countries, and the extension of electricity availability will provide an important means of improving the quality of life for many in the developing countries.

Electricity generation not only absorbed larger volumes of coal and oil world-wide between 1960 and 1990 but also increases in natural gas, nuclear, large hydro and new forms of renewable energy. Pacific Region members of the OECD increased their consumption of natural gas between 1970 and 1990 by nearly 14% annually, particularly Japan which pursued a policy of diversification away from oil after 1973 and where the electricity industry now accounts for over 70% of primary gas demand. In the longer term the increased use of renewable energy sources is likely to be deployed via the electricity route. The continued penetration of electricity in the developed world must depend to some extent on environmental attitudes, not least in the transportation sector.

Nonetheless the major growth area is likely to be in the developing countries, because electricity, generated by gas, oil or coal, or, increasingly, from renewable energy sources, and distributed either via an interconnected network or by local distribution systems, must be seen as a major currency whereby commercial energy can be brought to millions presently relying on depleting supplies of non-commercial fuels. Estimates based on a variety of sources suggest electricity growth rates in the developing countries beyond 2000 at two to three times those in the

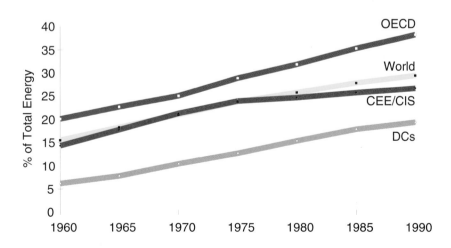

Figure 1.12 Electricity Consumption as a Percentage of Total Energy Consumption

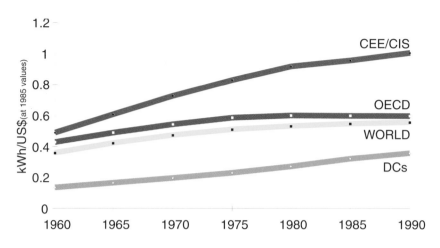

Figure 1.13   Electricity Consumption per unit of GDP

developed world.[1] Electricity has direct benefits of versatility in end-use, including its being the only means of providing many household, industrial, commercial, agricultural and medical facilities; cleanliness in end-use; and, in a world increasingly conscious of the health hazards associated with hitherto unchallenged human activities, its benign nature as an energy source provided well established safety standards are observed (Figure 1.14). There are also the secondary benefits of communication, education and other spin-offs from the use of electricity as opposed to other energy sources.

But electricity is by and large capital intensive in generation, transmission and distribution; and its expansion to the benefit of growing populations in the developing world must depend on the provision of very substantial funding by means discussed elsewhere in this report.

Key Themes

The effect of trends in developed countries of shifts from manufacturing into services is clearly demonstrated by the lower proportion of commercial energy consumption by industry. A similar process will eventually take place in the developing countries and economies in transition. At first sight, Table 1.3 appears to show that the share of commercial energy consumption going into households and services may not appear to rise significantly for developing countries. However, through the increased

---

[1] Khatib and Munasinghe: Electricity, the Environment and Sustainable World Develpment: World Energy Council, 15th Congress, Madrid, September 1992.

access to electricity this will in fact occur, if not at the rates often anticipated.

There are a number of common themes running through this chapter which need to be made absolutely clear. Demand pressures act upon the pattern of supplies with the cheaper more readily available resources exploited first. There is an understandable reluctance to exploit more expensive and more remote resources. But energy resources are not evenly distributed and are, in the case of fossil fuels, finite – though reserves of coal are enormous and relatively widespread. The implications of supply constraints have already been felt in respect of oil, although oil importing nations have enjoyed a period of remission on prices since 1985. In Chapter 3 there is discussion of how a growing import dependency of a larger number of countries will have serious implications for oil and natural gas availability and prices in the future. These relate to lengthening supply lines and a trend outside the Middle East to exploit reserves (often in smaller pockets) in more remote areas which are frequently exposed to geopolitical uncertainties.

On the demand side consumers have been attracted by low prices and convenience. Electricity consumption in the home, and oil consumption in transportation, have been among the obvious beneficiaries.

In the case of both supply and demand people's likes and dislikes are likely to prove a major barrier to rapid change. Full-cost pricing, effective competition and technological innovation will strongly influence people's preferences.

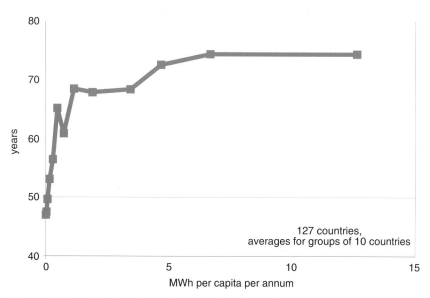

Figure 1.14 Life-time Expectancy *vs* Electricity Use

PRICING

Energy prices frequently do not cover even production costs, still less the wider social and environmental impacts called externalities.

It has been estimated, in OECD and other studies, that commercial energy prices in general are subsidised at an average rate of between 30% and 50% in the economies in transition and most developing countries. Energy is generally less subsidised in the more dynamic developing economies.

For some years the World Bank has been drawing attention to the fact that electricity is sold in developing countries at on average only 40% of the cost of its production. As a recent World Bank study has pointed out: "Such subsidies waste capital and energy resources on a very large scale. Subsidising the price of electricity is both economically and environmentally inefficient. Low prices give rise to excessive demands and, by undermining the revenue base, reduce the ability of utilities to provide and maintain supplies. Developing countries use about 20% more electricity than they would if consumers paid the true marginal cost of supply. Underpricing electricity also discourages investment in new, cleaner technologies and more energy efficient processes." ("Energy Efficiency and Conservation in the Developing World", World Bank, January, 1993, p.14.)

Subsidised energy prices are one of the principal barriers to raising energy efficiency in developing countries, where it is only 50% to 65% of what would be considered best practice in the developed world. Studies indicate that with the present state of technology a saving of 20 to 25% of energy consumed would be achieved economically in many developing countries with existing capital stock. If investments were made in new, more energy-efficient capital equipment, a saving of the order of 30 to 60% would be possible.

This report therefore also concludes that such policies encourage inefficiency in both provision and use, waste and extravagance in consumption, and exacerbate adverse environmental impacts. Why are policies and practices contrary to announced goals and apparent rationality? There are various reasons:

- Lack of knowledge of the accounting required to reflect the relevant costs – production, capital, environmental and other externalities.

- The desire to subsidise energy prices for social reasons or to gain political support among those subsidised. This is particularly prevalent in the developing countries, in many of the economies now in transition, and in rural areas elsewhere.

- Attempts to gain advantage in international trade and inward investment.

- The outcome of the interplay of market forces including competitive pressures, so that some products can benefit from the prevailing price of alternatives or can be sold cheaply because other, related products can be sold at a premium. Thus natural gas prices can follow oil prices up (and down), while gasoline and other products from the lighter end of the oil barrel can fetch a premium permitting fuel oil and bitumen from the black end of the barrel to be sold cheaply.

- A traditional practice had grown up of responding to increases in actual or prospective energy demand by expanding supply or supply capacity. Only in very recent years have least-cost planning and demand management approaches been promoted, which look at the energy supply-demand system as a whole and consider whether by using supply capacity more efficiently or by encouraging greater efficiency in use expensive expansion of supply capacity can be avoided.

There has long been a widespread view that low energy prices, like low prices more generally, are somehow "a good thing". They may not be. This report does not go to the other extreme and argue that high prices are necessarily beneficial. But prices which cover production costs and externalities are likely to encourage efficiency, mitigate harmful environmental effects, and create an awareness favourable to conservation. Such an approach produces marginal costing of new energy production which is an important planning tool for evaluating existing supplies. There are many examples where the opposite approach, seeking to drive prices down below full costs, then rapidly leads to non-availability.

The conventional market and price mechanisms have not traditionally allowed for externalities. In particular, they have not allowed for the wide array of local, regional and potential global environmental impacts which energy provision and use can have. Thus the market has not, and will not, provide the answers to environmental concerns and the costing of environmental impacts unaided. In this respect there is a fundamental contradiction between market pricing and full-cost pricing. By definition markets have not operated in "the global commons" or with "public goods". In consequence prices cannot yet be reliably attached to many of the assets involved, and neither costs nor benefits can be accurately determined. This is an area where valuations and costings are in their infancy, where basic inter-relationships and their impact are uncertain, and where many environmental assets cannot readily be valued. This is therefore a proper and important area for further research, valuation, debate and experimentation.

A number of policy measures, particularly economic instruments, which would be required to tackle local, regional and potential global environmental concerns require the ability to assess costs in relation to benefits of action. Similar measures to capture other externalities also require the assessment of costs and benefits with some semblance of accuracy. Even where costs and benefits cannot yet be ascertained with any degree of accuracy, this remains an ultimate goal.

The role which pricing can play is complex. What can be put into practice varies with local circumstances. For instance, it would be unrealistic to expect early introduction of full-cost pricing in the economies in transition or most developing countries, or even in some cases before 2020. Thus there can be no single solution. Nevertheless, this report recommends that the world seeks to move towards full-cost pricing which encompasses all production costs and related externalities in the provision and use of energy.

COMPETITION

Effective competition and the availability of choice also have a powerful role to play. The spur to innovation and improvement which competition brings in its wake is part of the valuable information exchange inherent in competition. Effective competition has underpinned the relative success of those market economies which in recent decades have achieved greater efficiency and prosperity. The comparison and contrast is frequently made with the depressed performance of the former USSR and other countries where centralised State planning and overt control have been imposed. Effective competition needs to take place not merely between firms but between related sectors, in order that substitution can take place and alternatives be sought out. Important competition has been taking place in recent years between coal, oil and natural gas. In the future, "new" renewable forms of energy will play a larger and more effective role on the competitive scene. Cleaner processes and more efficient energy using equipment are also an important result of effective competition.

If the world is to drive towards greater energy efficiency, larger energy resources and a wider variety of forms, and reduced environmental impacts, then governments must ensure both full-cost energy pricing and effective competition.

However, governments will also need to ensure that pricing and competition take place on a level playing field – where the rules are fair and known to all. For instance, they will need to ensure that all forms of energy are priced to reflect their full costs – including their full environ-mental costs. Competition alone is more likely to reduce costs and prices, thus additional measures are unavoidable. They will need to ensure that unacceptable barriers are not raised to new entrants, newer energy forms, or cleaner supplies and processes. One means at their disposal is the effective implementation of anti-monopoly, mergers and restrictive practice policies.

Governments have an important role to play in maintaining competition by instituting appropriate policies to curb monopolies, mergers intended to reduce competition and restrictive practices. The record of governments in history is in this respect to be found more in the breach than the observance, because all too often governments themselves have created and supported monopolies and restrictive practices.

THE ROLE OF TECHNOLOGY

Whereas sound institutions and policies are important in enabling both improvements in overall efficiency of energy provision and use, and environmental protection and clean-up, it is technology that provides the physical means whereby these objectives can be achieved.

The effective application of technology underlies the advances in efficiency and environmental mitigation and protection that the market-oriented industrialised countries, in particular, have achieved to date. In general, historical evidence suggests that technology has the capability or potential to cope with most of the problems and opportunities that arise – even if there are also examples where certain technological advances have themselves exacerbated the problems of humanity and its environ-ment (including the diversion of resources into weapons of destruction).

But rapid technological development is not inevitable, and the pace of development in recent decades has clearly been influenced by military and space research requirements. Support from these quarters may not be maintained at the same level in the coming decades, yet the well-being of the world's population is clearly going to continue to depend on maintaining invention, innovation and cost-effective applications of new technology.

This process is not spurred by subsidised energy prices, prices that do not reflect costs, or by relaxed attitudes on supply availability. The task of governments is to create an economic and commercial climate in which technological development can flourish. Thus, in order to flourish, technology needs to be placed in the context of an economy that enables and encourages its application. What are the requirements?

The most obvious is a competitive market system that encourages and rewards innovation. However, the private sector is not always prepared or able to underwrite the development risks, even of technologies that may be of great value in the more distant future. There can be many reasons for such caution: political instability, high interest rates, distorted pricing policies, inflation, disincentives arising from the excessive taxation of investible funds, or discouragement because of uncertain rewards arising from political uncertainties (shifting tax regimes for returns on investment, curbs on dividend remittances, and fears of expropriation).

Governments have an important role to play:

- by eliminating or reducing such distortions and disincentives;

- by assisting in the establishment of appropriate infrastructures, training, support of basic science and technology, international collaboration, and information on best practice around the world;

- by encouraging private research and development – while avoiding the problems and waste of money that have all too often occurred in the past when governments themselves engaged directly in research and development;

- by encouraging the development of ideas on future research and development requirements – for instance, in the field of mitigating environmental impacts of energy provision and use. But such encouragements should not go so far as to tempt governments themselves into the task of "trying to pick winners";

- by encouraging ideas within a broader programme of improved communication of information on the need for, and means of, improving energy efficiency.

The areas of opportunity are almost limitless, in both the further development of existing, well-established technologies and in the application of new concepts in basic science to prototype, development and through to the commercial exploitation stage. Figure 1.15 gives an indication of the timeframes of such developments, drawn, with minor modification, from the US National Energy Strategy, DOE, Washington, 1991. By definition, all of the technologies shown in this figure rely on established scientific concepts but longer-term perceptions require extensive scientific and engineering development, which means substantial sums of money, to bring to commercial exploitation. Nuclear fusion is a prime example. In the longer term its potential is immense; but in the shorter term funding is precarious in the face of equally promising but more immediately applicable technologies – some of which (the fast reactor for instance) are themselves suffering from severe funding problems.

There must be, on a global basis, a balanced portfolio of technologies with shorter and longer-term application times to ensure continual up-grading of technology in energy provision and use. However, it is necessary to take account of lead times in the development, introduction and diffusion of major new technology.

Technology and the Environment

In most OECD industrialised countries major steps have been taken to reduce adverse environmental impacts. It is not always recognised how much progress has been achieved over the past three decades in reducing pollution, and this is particularly true of energy-related pollution. It should also be added that it is not always recognised that these environmental gains have also generally undermined or offset efficiency gains.

The environmental achievements have mostly been confined to the developed world. Clean Air Acts have been passed, and the technology introduced to enable energy users to conform to new standards. Lead in city air, and dust or grit (particulate matter) from coal fires have been markedly reduced. Sulphur dioxide emissions from coal and oil burning power stations have also been greatly reduced. Pre-combustion coal cleaning can reduce sulphur emissions by up to 30%, work on advanced coal cleaning could yield up to 90% reductions. Through combustion control methods, such as fluidised beds, sulphur emissions could also be reduced by up to 90%, and with sorbent injection by up to 75%. More expensively, post-combustion methods (flue gas desulphurisation) can also reduce sulphur emissions by up to 90%.

The technology exists to curb the bulk of harmful emissions from energy production and use having local and regional environmental impacts.

There are also various means of reducing nitrogen oxide emissions through combustion control and by using catalysts.

There is a need on a global basis for the more rapid and wider implementation of best available technology. Much existing technology is not effectively used due to poor training, management, and mainte-nance; or to its unsuitability to local conditions for a variety of reasons, including lack of spare parts. Nevertheless, the record of technological innovation, managerial initiatives, and tighter environmental standards

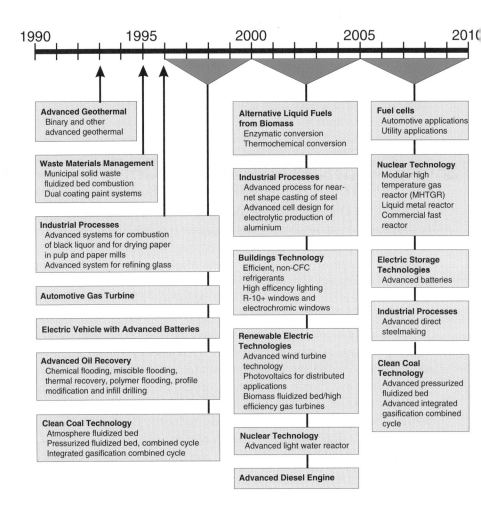

Figure 1.15   Time-frame for the Development of Existing and New Energy Technologies *(Source: US National Energy Strategy, DOE,Washington, 1991, with minor modification)*

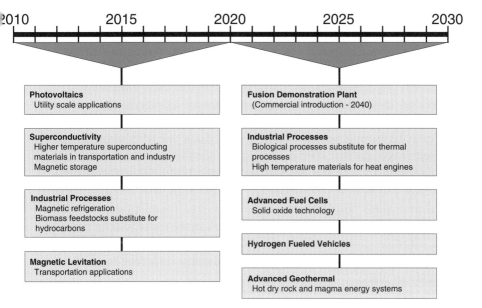

2010   **2015**   **2020**   **2025**   **2030**

Photovoltaics
Utility scale applications

Superconductivity
Higher temperature superconducting
materials in transportation and industry
Magnetic storage

Industrial Processes
Magnetic refrigeration
Biomass feedstocks substitute for
hydrocarbons

Magnetic Levitation
Transportation applications

Fusion Demonstration Plant
(Commercial introduction - 2040)

Industrial Processes
Biological processes substitute for thermal
processes
High temperature materials for heat engines

Advanced Fuel Cells
Solid oxide technology

Hydrogen Fueled Vehicles

Advanced Geothermal
Hot dry rock and magma energy systems

over the past two decades to reduce sulphur emissions is quite impressive in North America, Western Europe and Japan as Figure 1.16 shows.

Elsewhere in the world progress has been much less satisfactory in the reducing of even emissions of particulates, sulphur dioxide, nitrogen oxides and nitrous oxide. This is due to insufficient awareness of the causes and impacts of, and available remedies for, these emissions; cost barriers in tackling them; and the absence of effective government regulations and standards.

When attention is turned to global emissions of carbon dioxide and methane it is clear that they are rising and (at the global level at least) will continue to rise for decades to come. Technology to improve efficiency and policies to encourage conservation will mitigate these global emissions. But unless technologies are found to capture and re-absorb the main greenhouse gases much more quickly than can be expected, then global emissions reductions are unrealistic in the absence of policies, fuels and end-uses radically different from those presently in place.

TECHNOLOGY TRANSFER AND INTERNATIONAL CO-OPERATION

Energy technology will have a crucial role to play throughout tomorrow's world, but its potential contribution is even greater in the developing countries and in the economies in transition of the former USSR. It is in the developing countries that, over the next 30 years and beyond, the greatest increase in energy consumption is needed and will occur. It is in the economies in transition that the largest increases in energy efficiency can be made in the short term. Without increasing deployment of modern, higher efficiency technology neither the developing countries nor the economies in transition will be able to meet future energy demand in a sustainable manner.

Although many developing countries have an indigenous technological capability, the scale of the problem and the pressures of time are such that most of the technology required will have to be imported. Because of lack of resources, a significant proportion of this technology may have to be transferred on preferential terms. The basis for such preference could be mutual interest, as energy efficiency in recipient countries rises and both energy demands and environmental pollution arising from energy are constrained. This in turn could relieve pressure on finite energy supplies, shift the structure of energy demand to less polluting energy forms and cleaner processing, and open up wider opportunities for international trade. The end result could be greatly improved international relations and a reduction in international tension. There is scope for introducing incentives but not subsidies.

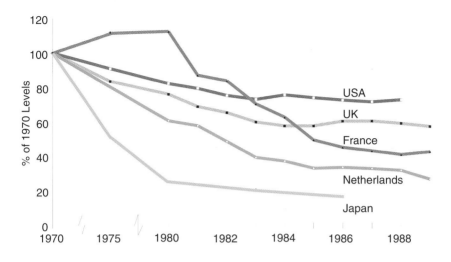

Figure 1.16   Sulphur Emissions for Selected Countries *(Source: Eurostat, OECD)*

The present realities are very different. Richer countries with the technology, and the industries which produce it, do not have much interest in giving such technology away freely. The value of intellectual property – covered by patents and reflecting past investment – requires protection and reward. Developing countries seek energy at acceptable cost – and do not necessarily see efficiency or environmental criteria as having the same high priority. The primary interest of industrial firms with appropriate technology is seeking to meet the requirements (in this context) of developing countries wanting energy at an acceptable cost. Many experts from developing countries believe that efficient technologies do not require subsidies, and indeed that as soon as anything needs financial adjustment then it is *prima facie* no longer efficient.

There are a number of internal contradictions and currently incompatible goals which need to be resolved. Much will depend on how far and soon changes at the local, recipient level in terms of institutional reforms, provision of local capital and attraction of foreign capital take place.

One emphasis in this complex process should be upon the transfer of appropriate technology, suited to local needs and supplied on terms which recipients can meet. There has been too much inappropriate technology supplied in the past, and on terms which have placed unnecessarily high economic burdens (especially of increased external indebtedness) on receiving countries. When local economies waned and global interest rates increased during the 1980s the inappropriateness of many aspects of the international banking system was sharply revealed.

The development of local capabilities and institutional strengths lies at the heart of ensuring the successful application of technology. The construction and installation of hardware without the development of local infrastructure and expertise is frequently a recipe for failure. The capacity of local users to run and maintain their technology is an important criterion of appropriateness. Transfers should be made wherever feasible within the disciplines of market mechanisms so that values and prices can be recognised and measured, rather than risk the waste which gifts are liable to incur.

The direct rewards for ensuring effective technology transfer and use could be immense. Mainly by using existing technology more efficiently Eastern Europe, for instance, could by 2020 reduce energy consumption in certain sectors of the economy by up to 50% from 1988 levels. Similarly in many developing countries, non-commercial energy consumption per unit of production would be reduced by up to 50% through the effective use of technology. But only so much can and will be given through grants and aid. World society is not suddenly going to become comprised of altruistic beings. Countries which seek investment and wish to buy modern equipment will need to take the necessary steps themselves to attract suitable investors and sellers.

Reduced energy consumption and constrained energy demand growth also mean cuts in emissions and wastes, of benefit in reducing both local and more widespread pollution.

> *The diffusion of more efficient and more modern technology is probably the most cost-effective contributor to curbing CO_2 and other greenhouse gas emissions from fossil fuel combustion, and the most favourable precautionary environmental measure at hand.*

THE DEVELOPING COUNTRIES

Due to growing population and energy demands of the developing countries, this report places a great deal of emphasis upon them. However, these countries do not form a simple homogenous group, clearly distinct from OECD member nations or the economies in transition. Three distinct groups of countries can be defined.

First, the newly industrialising countries (NICs) which since the early 1960s have enjoyed spectacular growth and economic success. The obvious examples are Hong Kong, the Republic of Korea, Singapore, and Taiwan China. For more than two decades from the mid-1960s per capita GNP grew by at least 6% per annum in these four countries – some four times the rate of increase achieved in the United States.

The second group of countries that can be identified are the rapidly industrialising countries. Among the more obvious examples in this

	1965	1975	1990
Newly Industrialising Countries			
Hong Kong	584	1080	1717
Republic of Korea	238	666	1898
Taiwan, China	n/a	n/a	2333
Rapidly Industrialising Countries			
Brazil	286	611	915
Chile	652	769	887
Mexico	605	870	1300
Indonesia	91	133	272
Malaysia	313	464	974
Other Selected Developing Countries			
China	178	351	598
India	100	131	231
Bangladesh	-	24	57
Bolivia	156	258	257
Burundi	5	7	21
Cambodia	20	54	59
Cote d'Ivoire	101	200	173
Ethiopia	10	14	20
Ghana	76	187	68
Kenya	110	158	100
Laos	24	44	39
Malawi	25	46	41
Mali	14	20	24
Mozambique	81	97	85
Nigeria	35	58	138
Myanmar	39	51	83
Singapore	2214	3589	5685
Peru	395	540	509
Nepal	6	9	25
Niger	8	25	41
Pakistan	135	137	233
Philippines	158	257	215
Rwanda	8	22	41
Senegal	342	332	156
Sierra Leone	109	78	77
Somalia	11	36	64
Sri Lanka	106	123	179
Sudan	67	87	58
Tanzania	37	55	38
Togo	27	60	51
Uganda	36	43	27
Vanuatu	197	371	293
Vietnam	97	132	100
Zaire	75	88	71
Zambia	464	534	379
Zimbabwe	441	594	531

Sources: World Bank: "Social Indicators of Development, 1991–92", 1992. Taiwan, China data from WEC National Energy Data 1992.

Table 1.5 Energy Consumption per Capita (kg of Oil Equivalent)

category are Brazil, Chile and Mexico in Latin America; and Indonesia, Malaysia and Thailand in the Pacific Region. These countries made particularly rapid economic progress during the 1970s, well above the world average, although some have suffered from the widespread economic stagnation of recent years. However, whereas the countries in this group have substantial natural resources, the rate of their depletion – and often the manner of their exploitation – have aroused widespread concern. Also, rapid population growth and urbanisation have created profound social and environmental problems. Issues of water quality, sanitation, over-crowding, inadequate housing, local environmental pollution arising from urban energy provision and use, and from energy supply more generally, have been and are profound. (For instance, large-scale hydro schemes in some of these countries have aroused severe criticism.) The need for the countries in this category to manage their industrialisation process better than more mature economies, protecting their natural resource base while combating poverty and environmental degradation, is particularly pressing. It is from these countries that the most frequent calls have come to "leap-frog" the development process through accessing the most modern technologies, thereby achieving a more sustainable course.

The third category of countries, which have not achieved the same level of economic development, is an even more disparate group. Within it are to be found huge countries with large natural and human resources, substantial cadres of well-educated people with technical know-how, and rapidly industrialising regions (such as China and India). The vast majority are less well endowed and suffer pervasive structural weakness. They generally have no strong record of past achievement, and have little hope for the future. Even these three categories fail to reflect the full variety. Thus South Africa represents an interesting hybrid of developed and developing country elements.

There are also large differences between the various extremes of urban and rural communities – from the significant local pollution and squalor in some cities of relatively high income developing countries to grinding rural poverty.

The rural poor suffer the most basic energy-related problems in many developing nations. In Sub-Saharan Africa fuelwood provides over 70% of the total energy consumed. It is usual for members of a family to devote several hours per day to the collection of fuelwood, frequently travelling in excess of 30 kilometres in order to do so. Further, inefficient cooking facilities (and a widespread unwillingness to use wood stoves) mean that the average family in Sub-Saharan Africa uses five times as much energy as a European family to cook the evening meal.

The problems of the developing countries essentially arise from a combination of population growth and poverty. There are no easy and quick solutions, and they raise issues which go well beyond the range of this report.

Table 1.5 shows energy per capita consumption for the newly industrialising, rapidly industrialising, and selected other developing countries
(lower income). There are wide differences within each grouping, but
with the exception of Indonesia the countries do fall into three defined
groups. However, of the 33 countries selected for inclusion in the third
group, 20 experienced declines in their energy per capita consumption
between the mid-1970s and the most recent estimate. In all, according to
World Bank Statistics of Social Indicators, over 50 countries have lower
energy per capita consumption now than 15–20 years ago.

Whereas the newly industrialising countries have energy per capita
consumption levels far in excess of the developing countries in general,
the picture for the rapidly industrialising countries is more complex. For
Malaysia and Mexico per capita energy consumption is well above the
developing countries' average, although in the case of Malaysia it is rising
much more rapidly than this average, while Mexico's per capita consumption has been stagnant over the past decade. Brazil remains above the
developing countries' average, but has moved closer to it since 1980.
Thailand remains below the average, but since the mid-1980s has been
rapidly catching up with it. Indonesia also remains below the average and
fell somewhat further behind during the 1980s. Table 1.6 summarises the
position for commercial energy.

Energy consumption per capita can be seen to have relevance as a
measure of social and economic development, and of structural change
(Figures 1.17 to 1.19). It also has relevance in the context of urbanisation,
a process which has proceeded especially quickly in the rapidly industrialising countries. Thus São Paulo in Brazil, and Mexico City, are
expected to become mega-cities of around 24 million people each by the
year 2000.

The process of urbanisation is, of course, a world-wide phenomenon,
as shown in Table 1.7. However, the fastest rates of urbanisation have
been in Africa, Asia and Latin America over recent decades, and this
process is expected to continue over the period to 2025.

Country	1960–70	1970–80	1980–1990
Brazil	3.6	5.8	0.7
Chile	5.1	–1.2	2.0
Indonesia	– 0.5	6.8	2.6
Malaysia	n/a	6.2	3.6
Thailand	11.9	7.2	6.5
World Total	3.0	0.9	0.4
Source: World Resources Institute (with UNEP and UNDP) "World Resources 1992–93", 1992. Table 4.1, p.51			

Table 1.6   Change in per Capita Commercial Energy Consumption
            (% Per Annum)

	1950	1970		1990		2000		2025	
	millions	millions	%	millions	%	millions	%	millions	%
Europe	221	307	+39	364	+65	387	+75	422	+91
former-USSR	71	138	+94	195	+175	217	+206	260	+266
Latin America	69	163	+136	324	+370	417	+504	645	+835
Asia	226	503	+123	931	+312	1292	+472	2589	+1046
Oceania	8	14	+75	19	+138	21	+163	29	+263
Africa	33	83	+152	223	+576	361	+909	914	+2670
North America	105	166	+58	204	+94	222	+111	260	+148
World Total	**733**	**1374**	**+87**	**2260**	**+208**	**2917**	**+298**	**5119**	**+598**
More Developed Regions	448	699	+56	876	+96	945	+111	1068	+138
Less Developed Regions	285	675	+137	1385	+386	1972	+592	4051	+1320

Source: World Resources Institute (with UNEP and UNDP): "World Resources, 1990–91", 1990. Table 5.1, p.67.

Table 1.7 Urban Population by Region, 1950–2025 (Millions of Inhabitants and Percentage Increase on 1950)

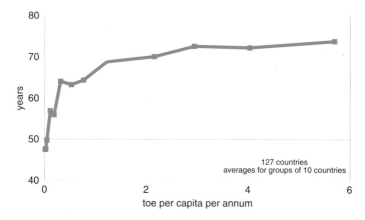

Figure 1.17   Life-time Expectancy *vs* Energy Use

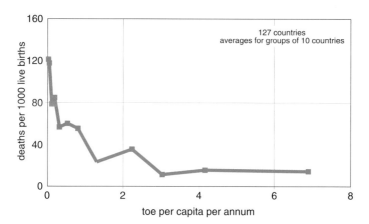

Figure 1.18   Infant Mortality Rate *vs* Energy Use

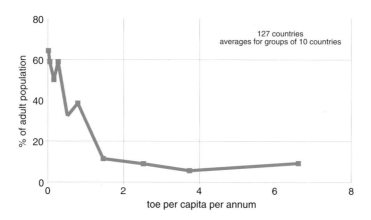

Figure 1.19   Illiteracy *vs* Energy Use

While the implications of urbanisation are most obvious for water quality, sanitation, and housing there are also energy implications. The provision of energy by large-scale electricity power generation is relatively attractive in urban centres, by contrast to the more diffused supply required in rural areas where smaller-scale, more local provision is generally more appropriate. This requires resources and assumes efficient pricing and billing – there is a good deal of informal, unmetered "diversion" of electric power in many of the urban centres of developing countries. Large-scale power generation and transmission also requires modern processes and clean-up technologies if pollution is to be avoided. While, as is well known from the experience of such mega-cities as Mexico City, air pollution from road vehicles can reach an horrendous scale. This is one of the reasons why ambient temperatures in major urban centres can be 3°C and more higher than in surrounding areas.

In the rest of this report there will be frequent reference to the developing countries, without wearisome repetition and qualification of varying prosperity, needs and priorities. For the world as a whole, only eight countries are expected to account for half of global population growth, and a significant proportion of global energy demand growth, over the next 30 years: India, China, Pakistan, Bangladesh, Brazil, Indonesia, Mexico and Vietnam. The scale of present and future problems is such that it is not surprising that most developing countries regard many local issues of much higher priority than global environmental concerns.

The major themes considered in this chapter – full-cost pricing, effective competition, technological innovation, and appropriate institutional arrangements for each of these tasks – recur in later chapters. They form an important foundation for promoting social development, and meeting the large and diverse needs of the developing countries. They will have an important role to play in curbing future energy demand, covered in the next chapter. They will encourage greater and more diversified energy supplies, discussed in Chapter 3. They are critical for moving more quickly towards realising the large potential for raising energy efficiency in both provision and use, and encouraging conservation, analysed in Chapter 4. They have close relevance for mitigating environmental impacts, discussed in Chapter 5. But for the successful introduction and widespread diffusion of technology, greatly advanced on the world's average standards at present (which are much inferior to best available current technology), will require a time-frame going well beyond the year 2020. This is why it is felt to be particularly necessary to examine world energy prospects beyond 2020 and for which an overview forms the epilogue to this report.

CHAPTER

2

ENERGY DEMAND TO 2020

The preceding chapter stressed the significance of world population growth for future energy demand growth, and the importance of energy in providing services which are crucial for satisfying basic human needs and supporting social development. These forces, and more widespread material aspirations and desires for comfort, mobility and communication, are likely to push energy demand upwards.

There are also some countervailing forces at work. The tendency for energy intensities to decline has been highlighted, especially as industrial economies approach maturity and people become more prosperous, while economies which have industrialised more recently have generally done so along a lower trajectory of energy demand per unit of GDP. In the developed industrial nations populations are, in general, no longer increasing, while concerns about the efficiency of energy provision and use – and about local, regional and global environmental issues – are growing. Consumer and policy responses are, so far, mixed and tentative towards these concerns. Some consumers and countries are taking action ahead of others, and this may promote more widespread and earlier action. But it should never be overlooked that demand is a product of customer actions – it is not God-given, or imposed by governments, or by the energy industries.

Case	A	B₁	B	C
Name	High Growth	Modified Reference	Reference	Ecologically Driven
Economic Growth % pa	High	Moderate	Moderate	Moderate
OECD	2.4	2.4	2.4	2.4
CEE/CIS	2.4	2.4	2.4	2.4
DCs	5.6	4.6	4.6	4.6
World	**3.8**	**3.3**	**3.3**	**3.3**
Growth Per Capita				
OECD	Moderate	Moderate	Moderate	Moderate
CEE/CIS	Moderate	Moderate	Moderate	Moderate
DCs				
Asia	Very high	High	High	High
Sub-Sahar. Africa	Moderate	Low	Low	Low
Most Others	High	Moderate	Moderate	Moderate
Energy Intensity Reduction % pa	High	Moderate	High	Very high
OECD	−1.8	−1.9	−1.9	−2.8
CEE/CIS	−1.7	−1.2	−2.1	−2.7
DCs	−1.3	−0.8	−1.7	−2.1
World	**−1.6**	**−1.3**	**−1.9**	**−2.4**
Technology Transfer	High	Moderate	High	Very high
Energy Efficiency Improvement				
OECD	High	High	High	Very high
CEE/CIS	Moderate	Moderate	High	Very high
DCs	Moderate	Moderate	High	Very high
Institutional Improvements (World)	High	Moderate	High	Very high
Possible Total Demand (Gtoe) (1990 = 8.7 Gtoe)	Very high 17.2	High 16.0	Moderate 13.4	Low 11.3
CO_2 Emissions from Fossil Fuel (GtC) (1990 = 5.9 GtC)	11.5	10.2	8.4	6.3

Table 2.1   Main Characteristics of the four WEC Energy Cases

THE FOUR ENERGY CASES

To support its analysis, the Commission has developed four Cases, each representing different assumptions in terms of economic development, improvements in energy efficiency, the pace of technology dissemination from the industrially developed to the developing countries, and resolution of institutional issues which impose barriers to beneficial change. The four Cases have the main characteristics outlined in Table 2.1.

These Cases and the assumptions behind them are illustrative. They are not predictions of what will happen. Each, however, illustrates future possibilities. To a degree the world (in the sense that huge numbers of energy consumers, large numbers of policy-makers and many countries through co-ordinated action or otherwise) can choose which of the paths, indicated by the Cases, it wishes to follow. Other variations of the four Cases could be chosen, although taken together they are believed to cover the broad range of likely outcomes for global energy demand and supply to 2020.

The four Cases, though illustrative, are also numbers driven (numbers that in turn reflect assumptions which, though they seem reasonable to the Commission at this point of time, inevitably relate to the unknowable future). The key numbers are also summarised in Table 2.1.

It will be noted that a restrictive range of underlying economic growth rates (GDP) has been assumed, although the global average masks considerable divergence between the low rates assumed for North America and Western Europe on the one hand, and the developing countries on the other

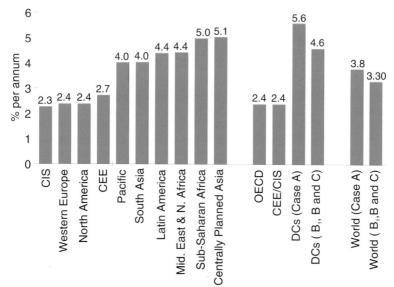

Figure 2.1   GDP Growth Rates from 1990–2020
(Case B for Geographic Regions)

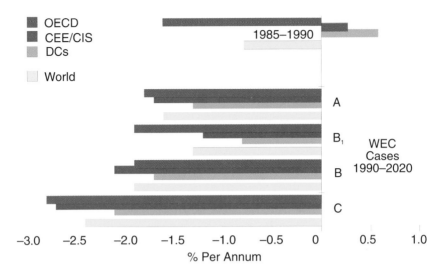

Figure 2.2 Regional Distribution of Energy Intensity Changes

(Figure 2.1). This divergence becomes particularly marked in Case A, where the developing countries are assumed to achieve 5.6% per annum GDP growth, as against 4.6% per annum in the other three Cases. A further assumption has been made that a relatively few, large developing countries will account for the bulk of energy demand and energy demand growth – namely China, India, Indonesia, Brazil, Mexico, Bangladesh, Pakistan, Vietnam and Philippines.

- Case A assumes a slightly higher rate of global economic growth, due to the developing countries achieving a performance well above the global average and more than double that of the OECD area.

- The reduction in energy intensity *in all four Cases* is assumed to proceed more quickly at the global level than has ever been achieved historically, although the difference between Cases B_1 and B lies in the delayed and slower reduction in energy intensity within developing countries assumed in Case B_1 (Figure 2.2).

- Whereas the four Cases indicate a feasible global energy demand by 2020 of between about 11 and 17 Gtoe, the more likely outcomes would seem to lie between around 13 Gtoe and 16 Gtoe. There is little sign in current energy policies around the world or the behaviour of energy consumers that the conditions required to bring about Case C are realistic as of now (Figure 2.3).

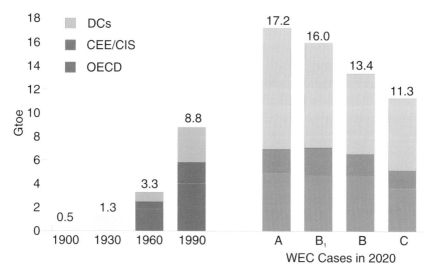

Figure 2.3   Energy Demand 1960, 1990 and in 2020 by Economic Group

- It is only Case C which approaches annual carbon dioxide emission levels from fossil fuel combustion in 2020 close to those of 1990 (Figure 2.4).

- None of the four Cases described can properly be termed "business as usual": they all assume some improvement on past rates of performance.

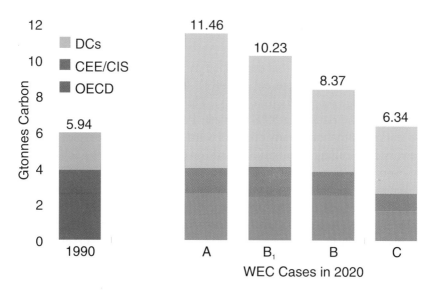

Figure 2.4 CO_2 (as Carbon) Emissions 1990 and 2020 by Economic Group

These projections are deliberately referred to as "Cases": they are not fully-fledged scenarios. They show how much energy would be consumed given certain assumptions. For a given population assumption, change in economic growth and energy intensity are taken as parameters, from which energy demand and energy per capita are derived. The four Cases indicate how difficult it will be to stabilise the current level of annual global carbon dioxide emissions from fossil fuel use even by the year 2020. The Key features of the four Cases are discussed in the following sections.

Case A

Global energy demand almost doubles from its 1990 level by the year 2020. The rise is 8.4 Gtoe, of which the developing countries account for 7.4 Gtoe. This partly reflects the rapid economic growth in many developing countries. One result is that annual CO_2 emissions from fossil fuel combustion by 2020 are nearly double their 1990 level.

Energy efficiency gains are more rapid in the CEE/CIS countries than at any point over the past 30 years; more rapid in the developing countries than previously achieved except in the late 1960s; and more rapid in the OECD countries except in the early 1980s. As a 30-year average, therefore, this report has assumed a faster rise in energy efficiency (reduction in energy intensity) in this Case than ever previously achieved. This implies not only more rapid turnover of capital stock and technological dissemination, but also effective measures to promote energy efficiency.

Case B

This Case lies closest to that developed by the World Energy Council for its 14th Congress in Montreal in 1989[1]. It has been updated for recent experience (see Appendix for details). This Case, while assuming global energy demand rises over 50% between 1990 and 2020, suggests a more modest evolution than many other forward estimates. This in part reflects the very challenging assumptions made on energy efficiency gains, which are even more testing than in Case A.

The rise in global energy demand in this Case is 4.6 Gtoe in the 30 years to 2020, of which the developing countries account for 3.9 Gtoe. New renewable forms of energy evolve more slowly in this Case than in any of the others, while the greater use of fossil fuels implies annual CO_2 emissions from this source in 2020 being some 44% higher than 1990 levels.

---

[1] "Global Energy Perspectives 2000–2020", WEC, 1989.

Case B$_1$

This Case is a variant on Case B, to take account of the possibility that energy intensity reductions in the developing countries and CEE/CIS may be delayed and slower than assumed for the other Cases. There are arguments for and against this delayed and slower evolution. However, its critical importance is reflected in the impact this single change of assumption has on global energy demand – pushing it up from the 13.4 Gtoe of Case B to the 16 Gtoe of Case B$_1$.

The rise from the 1990 level of global energy demand in this case is 7.2 Gtoe by 2020, of which the developing countries account for 6 Gtoe and the CEE/CIS for 0.7 Gtoe (a 40% increase from 1990 levels, and much the largest of the four Cases).

Much of the demand expansion is supplied by fossil fuels, which in this Case assumes annual CO_2 emissions from fossil fuel combustion in 2020 are over 70% above their 1990 level.

Case C

This Case uses the same economic growth assumptions as in Cases B and B$_1$, but the outcome in terms of global energy demand is markedly lower. The logic of this Case rests on a massive drive to raise energy efficiency reinforced by profound environmental concerns. An earlier and success-ful set of programmes to reduce energy intensity are combined with accelerated development and use of new renewables and natural gas. One element promoting these programmes could be fears in many energy importing countries for the longer-term availability and price of oil (and eventually natural gas).

Global energy demand in this Case by the year 2020 is about 28% above its 1990 level, a rise of 2.5 Gtoe. Energy demand rises 3.2 Gtoe in the developing countries, and falls 0.5 Gtoe in the OECD countries.

Because new renewables, natural gas and – to a smaller extent – nuclear power availability meet the demand expansion in this Case, global annual CO_2 emissions from fossil fuel combustion in 2020 are only some 6% above their 1990 level.

However, this Case has the most testing and far-reaching assumptions of all four Cases:

- A rate of reduction in energy intensity far in excess of anything achieved historically.

- A very low increase in energy demand in the developing countries, both in relation to what is implied by rapid population growth and what many would regard as socially and economically acceptable in terms of energy consumption per capita.

- Policy requirements for promoting energy efficiency and conservation, and for accelerating the development of new renewables, which will be politically challenging.

The assumptions and outcomes of the four Cases are provided in Tables 2.2 and 2.3.

	Historic Growth Rates (% pa) Year 19..						Assumed Growth % pa to 2020			
	60–65	65–70	70–75	75–80	80–85	85–90	A	B₁	B	C
OECD	5.3	4.5	3.0	3.4	2.5	3.4	2.4	2.4	2.4	2.4
CEE/CIS	5.0	5.1	4.1	2.3	2.4	0.8	2.4	2.4	2.4	2.4
DCs	4.1	6.5	6.2	5.4	3.6	4.1	5.6	4.6	4.6	4.6
World	4.9	5.1	4.0	3.9	2.8	3.4	3.8	3.3	3.3	3.3

Table 2.2 Historic and Assumed GDP Growth Rates of Economic Activity

	Rate of Change of Energy Intensity (% pa) Year 19..						Assumed Rate of Change (% pa) to 2020			
	60–65	65–70	70–75	75–80	80–85	85–90	A	B₁	B	C
OECD	0.2	0.1	−1.3	−1.5	−2.1	−1.6 ·	−1.8	−1.9	−1.9	−2.8
CEE/CIS	0.1	0.0	0.3	0.9	−0.2	−0.5	−1.7	−1.2	−2.1	−2.7
DCs	−0.6	−2.3	−0.8	0.4	0.2	0.1	−1.3	−0.8	−1.7	−2.1
World	0.0	−0.5	−0.9	−0.9	−0.7	−1.1	−1.6	−1.3	−1.9	−2.4

Sources: UN, The Penn World Table (Mark 5), and WEC.
Notes; These figures are on an internally consistent basis, but may not match precisely figures in circulation for a single region which are on a different basis.
Developing Countries in aggregate.

Table 2.3 Historic and Assumed Rates of Change of Energy Intensity

CO_2 EMISSIONS

A matter of widespread concern will be the implication that anthropogenic CO_2 emissions from fossil fuel use will continue to rise, albeit at widely differing possible rates, in seeming contradiction to the objectives of the UN Framework Convention on Climate Change. The Convention seeks to stabilise greenhouse gas concentrations in the atmosphere at a level which prevents dangerous anthropogenic interference with the climate system. This report seeks to take a realistic view on prospects for the stabilisation of annual CO_2 emissions and their atmospheric concentration, without wishing to undermine the achievements of the UN Conference on Environment and Development in Rio, during June 1992. None of the four Cases considered here permits stabilisation of either annual emissions or anthropogenic concentrations within the next 30 years.

POPULATION

It has been mentioned that in all the four Cases examined the critically important projection of population is the same. The current UN projection is taken, which assumes 1.4% per annum growth to 2020, as compared with an historic growth rate of 2% per annum between 1960 and 1965 declining to 1.75% per annum between 1985 and 1990. The assumed modest decline in the rate of population growth reflects evidence of declining fertility rates. However, as made clear in Chapter 1, it is recognised that population forecasting is uncertain even in the absence of large-scale disasters and wars. Official projections of global population could easily be out by 10% by 2020, and 30% (perhaps even 50%) by 2100. This sensitivity of population projections is of more than passing interest. If, by the year 2100, world population was well below 12 billion and global energy demand not much above 20 Gtoe then it is possible to calculate energy per capita consumption levels for people in the presently categorised developing countries several times higher than current levels with some hope of realism. With significantly higher population and lower energy demand assumptions the calculations quickly begin to seem far-fetched.

One point of significance is that in the short run the relationship between population growth and energy demand increases can readily be exaggerated. The impact is likely to be deferred as many of the increased numbers in the world by the year 2020 will be below the age of 15 years (over 30% of the total) and not major energy consumers.

DEVELOPING COUNTRIES' ENERGY INTENSITY

Another important question is whether energy intensity in many developing countries will rise (or not decline) due to economic development for many years to come (as reflected in Case B_1). There are researchers who claim that in countries as disparate as India, Thailand and the Philippines energy intensities have declined rapidly over the past 30 years. Others believe that energy intensity may continue to rise in developing countries (eg UNEP/UNIDO). It is possible that by not fully including traditional fuels (fuelwood, crop waste) in primary energy the declines in primary energy per constant GDP have gone unheeded. Another field of potential debate is whether higher economic growth rate assumptions imply higher energy demand in traditional terms or higher environmentally related expenditures. And so on.

In many cases, therefore, different assumptions could give more or less the same results as the Cases used here. The main purposes of these Cases were to try to cover the range of probable energy demand by 2020, and the conditions which would lead to them. Some very testing assumptions have been made here on energy intensity in particular, and that therefore prospective global energy demand may have been understated (especially in Case C) rather than exaggerated.

GENERAL TRENDS IN ENERGY INTENSITY

Given the uncertainties surrounding the main parameters underlying energy demand projections no attempt has been made to carry out detailed and intensive study of energy use at the disaggregated level, nor work on individual uses. They are not necessary for the purpose of indicating broad trends, and a number of research studies looking at individual uses – though more limited in time horizons and geographical coverage – have recently been published (eg L. Schipper and S. Meyers: "Energy Efficiency and Human Activity", 1992).

Although the energy intensity of an economy is a convenient aggregate measure of the "bottom line" efficiency of energy use in producing economic output, at the individual country level a lower energy intensity is not necessarily "better" than a higher one. There may be sound social or economic reasons why one country may have a higher energy intensity than another – ranging from climate and population density to the existence of cheap indigenous energy resources, which may make it appropriate for some countries to undertake more energy-intensive industrial production than others.

Nevertheless, this report has assumed faster reductions in energy intensity in its four Cases compared with the past. Why? Where energy intensity declines rapidly there is relief of energy supply pressures: economic needs are met with less use of energy, saving costs and reducing associated environmental impacts. The projections of energy intensity assumed here are challenging, but have reflected the following reasoning:

- Economic maturity leads to a reduction of energy intensity.

- Many developing countries, and some others, currently subsidise energy supply or allow it to be sold far below the costs of production. Price and institutional reforms are needed to ensure correct signals are given on costs and relative scarcity. Prices should be set to cover the full costs of production, including externalities such as environmental effects. The uneconomic use of energy will thereby be cut off and energy efficiency in provision and use raised. It is assumed that more energetic steps will be taken in this direction in the future under all Cases, but their speed and effectiveness are uncertain – as reflected in the Cases.

- There is likely to be growing concern with the environmental impacts of energy provision and use; with the congestion and consequential infrastructural and other expenditures incurred in the transportation sector; and with future energy supply prospects. This is likely to lead to tighter standards of energy efficiency and emissions; tougher regulations affecting energy users generally; and the introduction of taxes to curb what policy-makers have decided is undesirable energy usage and help achieve other policy goals in the energy-related field. Such measures are likely to depress energy demand – there is growing awareness of the economic value of using energy efficiently and effectively – not least in those developing countries that need to import much of their energy requirements and wish to extend energy provision most economically.

- There is expanding recognition that by raising the efficiency of energy use adverse environmental effects are reduced.

- There is strong likelihood that the world price of energy, and especially of oil and natural gas, will rise in real terms during the next 30 years and beyond.

Despite the challenging assumptions made in the Commission's four Cases, and the reasoning behind the energy intensity assumptions particularly, global energy demand will have risen substantially by 2020. There are two clear messages here for policy-makers:

- The world should be prepared for the probability that more energy will be consumed than widely anticipated.

- Some Cases show that, in the event of early world-wide agreement on effective policies which are implemented, significantly lower demand could be achieved than now seems likely – but global demand would still increase by at least 30% even if it fell in many of the more developed countries. Thus if the UN Framework on Climate Change signed initially by 154 countries and the European Community in May 1992 is interpreted as requiring stabilisation of atmospheric greenhouse gas concentrations over the next few decades, then so far as CO_2 at least is concerned this is far out of reach. Realistic prospects for global energy demand to 2020 mean fossil fuel use and CO_2 emissions from this source will probably rise substantially. The stabilisation of atmospheric CO_2 concentrations at

1990 levels within the next few years would require at least a 60% reduction in annual anthropogenic CO_2 emissions from now on. Instead, even the lowest energy demand Case considered in this report (Ecologically Driven Case C) does not have atmospheric CO_2 concentrations stabilised until 2070 (with declines thereafter – see Appendix).

CHAPTER

3

ENERGY SUPPLY
TO 2020

FOSSIL FUEL RESOURCES

Present estimates of proved recoverable reserves of fossil fuels, together with the ratios of these reserves to current world use, are given in Table 3.1.

World total ultimately recoverable resources (defined as the potential output assuming high, but not prohibitive prices, and no insuperable barriers to exploitation) can only be roughly estimated. The World Energy Council has from time to time sought to provide best possible figures (the current estimates are given in Table 3.2).

These figures would extend the resources to current production ratios shown in Table 3.1 by factors of about 2 to 5. Even given the considerable uncertainty in them – for instance they do not take account of recent adjustments to conventional resources estimates for the Russian Federation, which may now account for 17 or 18% of the world total (or push that total up by some 20 Gtoe) – these figures show that the world's fossil fuel resources are indeed finite. It is of course, true that many previous forecasts of impending scarcity of coal and oil made over the past century have proved incorrect. It is also true that R/P ratios for oil have tended to rise since 1980, and for natural gas remain about static since the mid-1980s. Thus the world has a considerable time to effect the transition

	Estimate of Cumulative Production to1990 (Gtoe)	Estimate of Proven Reserves in 1990 (Gtoe)	Estimate of 1990 Reserves to Production Ratio (Years)
Coal (Excluding Lignite)	n/a	496	197
Lignite	n/a	110	293
Oil	86	137	40
Natural Gas	40	108	56
Source: WEC Survey of Energy Resources			

Table 3.1   Proved Fossil Fuel Reserves and Reserves/Production Ratios

	Gtoe	%
Coal and Lignite	3 400	76
Conventional Oil	200	5
Unconventional Oils:		
Heavy Crude	75	2
Natural Bitumen	70	2
Oil Shale	450	10
Natural Gas	220	5
Total (approx.)	4 400	100
Source: WEC, 1992 Survey of Energy Resources; WEC 1989 World Energy Horizons 2000–2020; Masters C.D. et al, World Resources of Crude Oil and Natural Gas, 13th World Petroleum Congress, 1991; Masters C.D. et al, World Reserves of Crude Oil, Natural Gas, Natural Bitumen and Shale Oils, 12th World Petroleum Congress, 1987		

Table 3.2   Ultimately Recoverable Fossil Fuel Resources

away from heavy dependence on fossil fuels to alternative forms of energy supply, if supply exhaustion is the only criterion. The real challenge is to communicate the reality that the switch to alternative forms of supply will take many decades, and thus the realisation of the need, and commencement of the appropriate action, must be *now*.

In the meantime the following realities have to be faced:

- for many decades to come the world will have to rely upon fossil fuels for most of its energy supplies;

- the demand for coal, oil and natural gas is likely to rise for the next few decades;

- coal is the only fossil fuel likely to be available in substantial quantities much beyond the middle of the next century;

- China and India have huge coal resources and huge energy needs. A number of other developing countries have large coal resources. The pressures to develop these are immense and seen locally as a very high priority;

- fossil fuel resources are unevenly distributed around the world (Figure 3.1);

- import dependency for fossil fuels will grow as existing producers run through their resources, with growing concern over supply availability and price;

- although energy demand growth will occur mainly in the presently categorised developing countries, problems in transporting gas large distances and, for many, barriers to developing nuclear power capacity indicates coal, oil and smaller-scale renewables will be the main supply options;

- the lower the price of oil, and the longer this holds down other energy prices, the longer will be deferred the development of alternative hydrocarbon sources, substitutes, and adjustment processes more generally.

As scientific understanding of the forces causing climate change grows, it is possible that major responsibility may be more firmly attached to fossil fuel combustion. This could lead to calls for a decisive shift out of coal, and probably oil. Those voicing support for such shifts would regard discussion of ultimately recoverable fossil fuel reserves as largely meaningless – unless a way could be found to capture carbon dioxide emissions from fossil fuel combustion and fix them in stable sinks. However, voices expressing strong dissent can also be anticipated: from countries with substantial coal and oil resources and without substitutes at similar or lower cost; and from those who believe adaptation

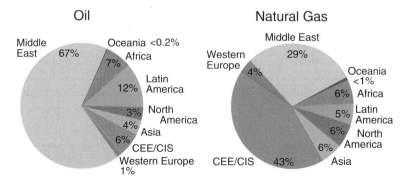

Figure 3.1 Distribution of Oil and Gas Proved Recoverable Reserves in 1990 *(Source: WEC Survey of Energy Resources)*

to climate change – including changed crop regimes and population movement – may not merely be desirable, or achievable at relatively low cost, but also unavoidable given currently realistic assessments of further rises in annual global anthropogenic CO_2 emissions over the next few decades.

NON-FOSSIL ENERGY SUPPLIES

If a significant decline in the world's relative dependence on fossil fuels is going to occur over the next century then a major drive will be required to:

- achieve the early rehabilitation of nuclear energy;

  or,

- advance the introduction and diffusion of renewable energy supplies, on a much larger scale than hitherto generally contemplated or likely to emerge from the operation of market forces alone;

  and *almost certainly both within that time scale.*

Nuclear

Today there are about 420 commercial nuclear power plants in operation world-wide with a total generating capacity of about 340 GW, with plants still under construction which are expected to add another 70 GW or so of capacity by the year 2000.

There is no prospect of a shortage of uranium in the period to 2020. However, supplies of uranium in readily accessible, significant sized and high concentration pockets are few. Overall, uranium is relatively scarce in the earth's crust, at about 4 parts per million on average. Therefore, a significant expansion of nuclear power – even the five-fold expansion widely canvassed before the incidents at Three Mile Island and (much more disturbing) at Chernobyl – would out-run readily accessible supplies. These supplies include both deposits previously exploited but mothballed due to lack of current demand, and known high concentration pockets that could be opened up quite quickly. Therefore the expansion of nuclear would highlight the need to bring rapidly back on course the development of fast-breeder reactors and pursue fusion technology.

Nuclear power has immense technical potential. Present day reactors only utilise about 0.65% of the potential of uranium. With the present rate of use of uranium approaching 58 000 tonnes per year the estimated known resources of 2.4 million tonnes of uranium recoverable at less than US$80/kg are equivalent to 41 years of current requirements, assuming that they could all be exploited. This is extended to 64 years if uranium resources recoverable at less than US$130/kg are taken into account.

However, this is assuming present reactor fuel cycle practices – an inefficient "once through cycle". The use of reprocessing and recycling of uranium and plutonium in the fuel would decrease the use by about 1/3 (increasing the number of years at current requirements by 50%). The use of breeders would not only make even larger amounts of uranium available but could increase the utilisation substantially.

Table 3.3 provides figures for uranium resources recoverable at up to US$130/kgU, estimated as "known" resources plus "undiscovered" resources together with the Gtoe equivalents when used in thermal and fast-breeder reactors.

If this total resource estimate is accurate, then its value is nearly twice the estimate of ultimate fossil reserves shown in Table 3.2; if it proves economic to utilise lower grade or more expensive reserves, the resource base would be larger than indicated; and, as mentioned, use of fast breeders would extend availability still further. Beyond this there is the longer-term possibility of indefinitely large energy supplies from nuclear fusion.

However, what really counts is the development status of the energy source, the price at which different kinds of energy can be recovered, and impediments to development and exploitation. Also the impact of any drive to move towards more environmentally friendly resources. That will depend *inter alia* on the interaction with demand, and the regulatory and energy policy framework. But, above all, it will depend upon whether public concern with operational safety and hazards of waste disposal can be satisfactorily resolved.

In the past the use of nuclear energy has been mainly by the developed industrialised countries. However, several of the Commission's regional reports (see Part II) have indicated intentions by developing countries to develop nuclear energy as part of their overall energy supply plans. At least eleven developing countries have nuclear plant in operation or under construction, and a further five have some form of plans for nuclear

	Mtonnes of Uranium	Equivalent Gtoe in:–	
		Thermal Reactors	Fast Reactors
"Known"	3.7	37	1 850
"Undiscovered"	13	130	6 500
Total (rounded)	17	167	8 400
Source. Based on "Uranium Resources, Production and Demand", 1992, NEA/IAEA with estimates for unreported resources.			

Table 3.3   Nuclear Energy Resources

	OECD	CEE/CIS	DCs	World
Plant in Service	80.7	13.6	5.7	100
Plant Under Construction	44.2	42.8	13.0	100
Planned Capacity	35.6	34.7	29.7	100
Source: Nuclear Engineering International				

Table 3.4   Distribution of Nuclear Energy by Economic Group (%)

construction. Table 3.4 suggests that, in the future, the developing countries (which already include several countries at an advanced stage of industrialisation) will make a greater contribution to nuclear output.

The table shows the shares between the three main country groups of nuclear plant in commission, of plant under construction and of planned new capacity. The word "planned" should here be treated with caution; it means that new capacity has appeared in some form of plans, but the status may vary widely between probably to go ahead and indefinitely deferred. Nonetheless, the existence of such plans at least indicates that the country considers itself capable of building and operating nuclear plant.

The issue of proliferation, though it relates more precisely to weapons and weapons capabilities, is indeed a serious one as events in Iraq and other countries have shown. This is an issue receiving serious attention by the UN Security Council and the International Atomic Energy Agency. Developments in the Democratic People's Republic of Korea are under particularly close scrutiny. These concerns will continue even if nuclear power does not progress, and will not be affected by the growth of nuclear power except at the time where nuclear fuel is reprocessed and breeder reactors are needed. Nevertheless, they do highlight the need for insistence on mandatory inspection by qualified international bodies, and effective sanctions where breaches in processes or procedures have occurred or seem likely to occur.

This report has indicated that a very large number of new reactors are likely to be required. In addition to this would be the potential need to replace the substantial nuclear capacity becoming decommissioned between now and 2020. The ability to put this totality of nuclear capacity in place will be heavily dependent upon the availability of technological, scientific, managerial and construction resources at that time.

Renewables

Whereas in the very long term (beyond the next century) the various forms of solar power are believed to have the technical potential to meet the bulk of the world's energy requirements, the contribution of solar and other forms of renewable energy will be much more modest in the shorter term.

The Commission has been assisted in its deliberations on the prospects for renewable energy resources to 2020 and beyond by the work of the WEC's Renewable Energy Resources Committee. This Committee has carried out detailed work on the technical potential and limitations of the various forms of new renewable energy. It has also considered what it believes to be the more likely evolution of renewable energy supply to the year 2020, which indicates rather slow progress; and an accelerated supply of renewable energy if early, determined and multi-national efforts were made to promote the faster development and diffusion of newer forms of renewable energy. Even this latter, more "optimistic" view is significantly lower than some recent reports have suggested is possible (that, for example, renewable energy could contribute 25% of direct fuel use, and 60% of global electricity generation, by 2025 – T.B. Johansson et al: "Renewable Energy", 1993). It is difficult to believe that politicians and policies, energy consumers and behavioural patterns, technology and the capacity to manufacture it and put it into operation on the required scale, will change sufficiently within the required time-scale to realise the achievements set out by Professor Johansson and his colleagues.

The WEC Committee believed that total renewable energy availability by 2020 could reach either around 2.9 Gtoe (the more likely outcome) or 3.3 Gtoe depending upon whether or not strong government support was forthcoming.

However, traditional biomass – fuelwood, crop residues, dung – accounted for 60% of total renewable energy availability in 1990 and large-scale hydro for a further 30%. Thus these two forms took up 90% of the total. Under even a very "optimistic" scenario for newer forms of renewable energy, these two forms are expected to account for well over half the total even in 2020.

The critical issue, perhaps, is what will happen to the "new" renewables – solar, wind, geothermal, modern biomass, ocean and small hydro – by the year 2020. Here there is obviously a wide range of uncertainty, with only major, effective and internationally co-ordinated policy support to accelerate development capable of making significant inroads into total primary energy supply. At present, energy consumers' attitudes and behavioural patterns, political attitudes and policies, and the capacity to manufacture the necessary facilities and put them into operation are unlikely to change sufficiently to achieve this by 2020. New renewables will also have to be introduced during the economic lifespan of existing energy systems.

In the event of major policy support, the WEC Committee believed it possible to envisage a contribution of "new" renewables within the assumed total of 1.3 Gtoe.

The Commission has therefore taken as the "minimum" contribution new renewables are likely to make – globally – by the year 2020 some

	In 2020 "Minimum"		In 2020 "Maximum" with major policy support	
	Mtoe	% of total	Mtoe	% of total
"Modern " Biomass	243	45	561	42
Solar	109	20	355	26
Wind	85	15	215	16
Geothermal	40	7	91	7
"Small" Hydro	48	9	69	5
Oceanic	14	3	54	4
Total	539	99*	1 345	100
% of Total Energy Demand		3 – 4		8 – 12
In 1990 "new" renewables contributed 164 Mtoe (1.9%) to total energy demand.				
* Difference due to rounding				

Table 3.5 "Minimum"/"Maximum" Contributions from "New" Renewable Energy

539 Mtoe. As a "maximum", with the requisite policy support, some 1 345 Mtoe (Table 3.5).

However, in order to achieve production more than availability is required. Because of variable, and often low, load factors most forms of new renewable energy require "spare" capacity to produce sufficient energy when conditions are right. This is obviously the case when production is dependent upon the availability of sunlight, wind and water flows. The intermittent nature of such renewable energy (especially solar and wind) highlights the need to develop electricity storage systems if sustained energy demand requirements are to be met, and the fuller potential of renewable energy realised. In the next two or three decades the problems of inadequate storage, together with lack of manufacturing capacity, are likely to prove a significant constraint where there is insufficient back-up to grid-connected systems.

The need to diversify into alternative energy sources nevertheless becomes clearer as the time horizon advances beyond the year 2020. The following factors need to be borne in mind:

- Even given clear and widespread public policy support, the "new" renewables will take many decades to develop and diffuse to the point where they significantly substitute for fossil fuels.

- Full recognition needs to be given to the low base from which "new" renewables start. In 1990 nearly 18% of the world's primary energy came from renewables – but over 98% of this from total biomass and hydro. Solar accounted for 0.8%, geothermal for 0.8%, and wind for 0.1%. Even modern biomass accounted for under 8% of renewable energy provision.

- Nevertheless, in many countries lacking in indigenous fossil fuel resources there will be significant local opportunities to use locally available new renewable resources. This is particularly the case for the many smaller developing countries short of foreign exchange to purchase imported fossil fuel supplies, without the resources to develop nuclear power, and too far away from sources of natural gas to make their transportation economically feasible. Local availability of solar, biomass and geothermal resources will be of particular potential significance in such cases.

- Although this Commission is in general opposed to government subsidies, if accelerated development of new renewable energy is to occur it is likely to come about largely through active government support including subsidies through the research and development stages to the demonstration stage (but should not go beyond).

- Even on the most "optimistic" assumptions, the idea that they will or can substitute entirely for fossil fuel provision even by the year 2100 seems far-fetched.

- Higher energy prices in general, and full-cost pricing to include environmental impacts for all forms of energy, are likely to facilitate the more rapid development and diffusion of "new" renewables.

- The utmost care must be taken to ensure that in endeavouring to promote "new" renewables further problems do not arise due to adverse environmental impacts.

Elaborating upon this last point, there is a need to consider the appropriateness of scale and environmental impacts in the area of "new" renewables as with other forms of energy provision. In building a better future, past mistakes must be avoided. The more obvious problem areas are:

- **Biomass – Modern.** Risk of loss of biodiversity (with adverse ecological impacts such as loss of habitats and reduction of flora and fauna species), unacceptable effluents and emissions, loss of alternative output, and visual impacts.

- **Tidal.** Risk of loss of estuarine habitats (adverse impacts on invertebrates, migrating and resident bird populations, fish, shipping, siltation) and visual impacts. There may, however, be some more attractive though localised opportunities to harness fast-flowing sea currents close to coasts which do not involve the destruction of estuarine habitats, and which can be effective at a smaller scale than ocean thermal schemes.

- **Ocean Thermal.** Unknown impact of changes in temperature gradients, which could have widespread effects (ecological and climatic). These concerns are partly a function of the large scale of schemes that have been given consideration.

- **Wind.** Well-known concerns about visual impacts, noise and interruption of telecommunications although careful siting, smaller and quieter turbines, can greatly ameliorate these concerns. Limited geographical application due to need for relatively high average wind velocity. Pressure to site large numbers of turbines in exposed situations, to take advantage of high average wind speeds in specific locations for economic reasons, and to experiment with very large (high) wind turbines, must be balanced by due regard for environmental considerations (especially impacts on the landscape).

- **Solar.** Although solar schemes probably have the smallest environmental impact of all current forms of energy, care needs to be taken with size of concentrators and also with the films and silicon used in photovoltaics. Solar systems are not as well adapted to concentrated urban uses as more dispersed uses, and attempts to overcome this problem with huge parabolic mirrors and solar chimneys (which are not the main thrust of recent developments or current prospects) should be avoided.

In pushing forward with "new" renewable forms of energy it is imperative that consistent, sensitive environmental criteria are applied throughout the field of energy provision and use. The sort of problems that have already loomed large with many large-scale hydro developments need to be avoided. Attention should concentrate on those forms with the best prospects.

CONSTRAINTS ON SUPPLY

Constraints on energy supply arise from various sources. The main ones are detailed in the following paragraphs.

Uneven Distribution of Resources. Oil and natural gas are distributed particularly unevenly (Figure 3.1). The Middle East and North African members of OPEC account for 70% of probable world oil resources, the Russian Federation possibly for over 17%. The CIS contains virtually half the world's probable natural gas resources, and the Middle East nearly 40%. Most countries are dependent upon imports for their coal, oil and natural gas supplies. Uneven distribution of resources also increases transportation costs, which can amount to 25% or more of the cost of crude oil, for instance.

Low Energy Prices. Low energy prices hold back the development of alternative supplies even if they benefit most energy users in the shorter term. This report does not advocate high energy prices *per se*, but prices which cover all costs. This would imply some increase in prices which would help extend available resources, and encourage the bringing on of alternative sources and substitutes. Higher energy prices may eventually create the conditions whereby cheaper energy services can be delivered.

Political. International conflict or trade disputes may interrupt supply; fiscal regimes and contractual terms may unilaterally change; experienced foreign partners in local joint ventures may be regarded as politically unacceptable; exploration terms may be commercially unrealistic for political reasons.

Financial. The ability of countries and companies to finance energy supply frequently depends on economically effective energy use, and on economic pricing to processors and end-users. The developing countries are placed in a particularly difficult position feeling unable to afford "proper economic pricing" of energy yet seeking to attract international capital and mobilise local capital. There are also other investments competing for funds – hospitals, schools, housing – and criteria for allocation are not simple and straightforward.

Institutional. In recent decades many forms of energy supply have effectively been monopolies, usually created at the behest of and protected by the State, and either wholly or partly distanced from the market disciplines of competition. Failure of some monopolies to achieve acceptable levels of efficiency, customer responsiveness and financial returns has led to steps being taken in some countries towards privatisation and the opening up of markets.

Technical. The ability to absorb and utilise the necessary technology and commercial skills; to mobilise energy resources and to convey them to the point of need. This links to the importance of being able to manage resources.

Time. Time is required to change perceptions, policies, institutions, infrastructures and technology. Time is a significant resource in marshalling and communicating argument, evidence and opposition to prevailing policies and actions. Perhaps most significant in the present context, in the absence of emergency conditions and policies, are long lead-times for the introduction and diffusion of new technology. Even the full exploitation of existing technology is a time-consuming and only partially achieved process.

Environmental. There is the need to control the adverse impact of energy provision and use on the environment – locally, regionally and globally.

In general, the fully developed Western market economies can cope with current issues in energy supply. Their wealth and technological know-how, coupled with the flexibility of the market system, generally allows them to deal with perturbations of supply. However, concentration of oil supplies in a limited number of countries – especially in the Middle East – raises particular concern from time to time. Past oil price hikes under emergency conditions have been disruptive, particularly because they were sudden. In the future, disruption of oil and gas supplies from other producing areas could also prove disruptive.

Poor, import-dependent countries are highly vulnerable in the event of supply interruptions. As Table 3.6 shows, the number of vulnerable countries and people is likely to increase sharply over the next three decades. The poorer, less developed countries are vulnerable in other ways. Some are heavily dependent on traditional energy supplies – especially fuelwood – which are dwindling as population is rising. In some parts of the world, notably parts of Africa, the situation is rapidly approaching crisis point.

Many other developing countries suffer from institutional problems associated with lack of development. The problems may range from a political and administrative structure that is simply underdeveloped to economic and social policies that impede development. These include

	1990	2020
Industrialised Countries	700	1 000
Economies in Transition	100	0*
Higher Income Developing Countries	450	1 100
Lower Income Developing Countries	1 650	5 100
* Economies in transition are classed as industrialised countries by 2020. However, the bulk of the population in this category are defined as energy exporters. Net Energy Exporters accounted for 2.2 billion total population in 1990.		

Table 3.6   Estimated Population in Net Energy Importing Countries (Millions)

centralist control policies by governments that discourage private initiative and competition.

The problems also include policies of subsidising energy prices for understandable social reasons. As discussed in Chapter 1, such policies once engaged in usually lead to a misallocation of resources, inefficiency, excess demand in relation to other resources and services, and chronic socio-political barriers to a reversal of policy. For energy companies operating in such environments competition is constrained, supply options distorted, normal investment criteria undermined, and financing and technology heavily influenced by political considerations.

These constraints are not the sole reasons why there are failures in getting energy supplies to the people who need them. People may simply not be able to afford even what is on offer: and that raises a further set of issues beyond the scope of this report.

These issues are not confined to the developing countries. In a growing number of developed industrial countries in recent years there has been a reappraisal of the nature and structure of energy supply, and the decision taken in some countries to move away from monopoly provision. The early results of such moves suggest there may be greater scope for competition in production and supply than many had previously thought feasible.

However, these changes have occurred in developed market or mixed economies, and where effective legislation is in place to curb monopoly and restrictive practices in the private sector. Many of the elements present have evolved over the years, and cannot be readily translated to good effect to many developing countries – or transferred overnight to countries which have long experienced other regimes.

Many of the issues discussed in this report are of an international nature, and require frameworks which recognise and facilitate growing interdependence. There is a need for more, and more effective, supranational institutions to meet the requirements of this evolution.

Appropriate investment and pricing policies, together with institutional reforms, will also go some way towards alleviating environmental problems. Encouragement of private initiatives, development of capital markets, and opening up economies to joint ventures with foreign companies (both from developed and other developing countries) will also assist progress.

THE FINANCING OF FUTURE ENERGY SUPPLIES

The capital requirements of future energy supplies are uncertain, but will inevitably be large. Historically, capital expenditure has largely been devoted to expanding supply availability. Only recently have expenditures begun to be directed in substantial amounts to efficiency and conservation-related investments, and specifically to mitigate or avert environmental impacts.

Significant changes are also taking place in the sourcing of finance. Whereas in the past few decades, in most countries, the electricity power generation sector has obtained substantial funds from the public sector, utilities increasingly recognise the inhibiting dependence on this source of funds when responding to the market. In many countries coal, oil and natural gas exploitation, transportation and distribution has been wholly or in part conducted within the public sector, despite the existence of major international players in the private sector, but again structural shifts are occurring and traditional public sector sourcing of funds is drying up. There is therefore widespread acceptance that private sources of funding will be increasingly sought.

This search, if it is to prove successful, will involve not only the existence of rules governing private investments but accept the need for competition, greatly reduced State intervention, the development of capital markets and the overall need to create investor confidence. In these emerging conditions the traditional role of State-owned utilities will have to change, because arms-length arrangements between what are essentially different parts of the same government make for difficulties. The involvement of private parties with a financial stake will both assist the provision of finance and encourage competition, with governments rolling back their involvement, providing regulatory frameworks which have as their primary goal the maintenance of competition and encouragement of efficiency. Any tendency to seek retention of control of pricing through such "command and control" systems as price review boards and tariff commissions should be resisted.

Possibly of even greater significance for the promotion of competition and efficiency is the extension of customer choice. Widely available for oil products, there are extensive constraints on competition in electric power generation, the distribution of gas and electricity, and end-consumer connection. There are, in many countries, constraints on accessing off-peak tariffs and the imposition of cross-subsidisation, leading to packages of services which inhibit new entrants. Thus in the emerging markets competition will be brought to the fore, and access to funds will become based upon normal market criteria of risk and profitability rather than political criteria.

Investments in the future will, where the necessary reforms have occurred, be made on the basis of attractive returns resulting from expectations of higher efficiency and lower costs, rather than hand-outs and jobs. In most of the developed market economies public utilities have long had to raise most of their capital by selling financial instruments in the capital markets. This is an important source of financial and economic discipline. A key aspect of this process is transparency of operations and proper independent accounting of corporate activities.

A major problem exists in the current absence of capital markets in many developing countries and some of the economies in transition – although the situation is fast-moving in the latter. The main reason is that capital markets are managed for political objectives, with widespread use of compulsory credit allocation mechanisms and reserve requirements. But savings ratios are believed to be relatively high in many developing countries already – 15% to 20% of GDP is typical of middle-income developing countries. Under present conditions few of these savings find their way towards investments in the energy sector for understandable reasons, and if they were to do so high and irregular rates of taxation, price controls, inflation and non-competitive financial institutions would act as further discouragement.

In Western Europe and North America (and in the two or three decades before the First World War in much of the rest of the world through overseas direct investment) the financing of public infrastructure has long been an important instrument in developing capital markets, with all the concomitant array of legal frameworks and institutional structures This has been severely inhibited in much of the world in recent decades. Governments have shifted the development of their capital markets by reserving infrastructure investments to the public sector and allowing inadequate financial rates of return. This has been a particularly important negative factor in many developing countries, where investments in infrastructure account for about 60%, on average, of total capital required.

Creating efficient and open domestic capital markets is now a priority. Raising funds locally, by offering shares to local investors, could make an important contribution both to the development of such capital markets and the financing of projects. The size and significance of the contribution will grow in concert with its success and the degree to which governments keep to their agreements. For foreign investors this could become a significant means of liquidating capital previously invested. Provided financial instruments are significantly liquid, and can be freely bought and sold, they can be successfully used to support long-term investments in the energy sector. Such financial instruments can provide an attractive alternative to holding government bonds and other securities.

There is therefore an urgent need, particularly in the many developing countries where these conditions do not exist, for the energy sector to mobilise financial resources. This requires the creation of investor confidence in order to attract external finance, joint ventures and equity participation by foreign interests. It also requires the development of domestic capital markets, with the necessary market institutions to support them and ensure adequate returns, liquidity, security, accounting and

auditing procedures. The energy sector in turn will be required to perform
with the efficiency required by investors as well as customers.

These changes will be required more than ever before in the coming
decades. Rising energy demand, based largely on the increasing need for
energy services in the developing countries, will require instruments to
expand supply availability. Growing concerns about energy efficiency,
conservation and the environment will also call for additional capital
investments. There will be pressures to expand the sources of primary
energy available to new, non-fossil forms as well as to ensure cleaner
fossil fuel supplies.

In 1987 the WEC published a report on the investment requirements of
the world's energy industries, 1980–2000. Considering only capital expenditure for supply purposes (ie excluding considerations of efficiency,
conservation or the environment) that report estimated that for the 20-year
period cumulative investments in total energy supply would need to be
US$10.2 trillion (at 1980 prices) under a low scenario and US$14.7 trillion
under a high scenario. Investments in electricity generation and supply were
anticipated to account for about two-thirds of these cumulative totals. The
developed countries were assumed to account for about 52% of the total, the
developing countries for between 21% and 26%.

Any estimate of the cumulative investment requirements of the
world's total energy sector over the next 30 years is bound to be wrong,
for precision is impossible. One benchmark for credibility is that,
historically, investments in energy have typically amounted to between 15 and 20% of total investments, and around 3 or 4% of GDP.
The following estimates imply energy-related investments at, or
slightly above, the top end of these ranges. In view of the various
forces at work this does not seem unreasonable. However, the relatively rapid expansion of energy demand in developing countries
(especially in some of the largest ones) accelerated by rising supply
efficiencies suggest that the geographical distribution of energy
investments will become significantly different from those provided
in the 1987 WEC study for the period 1980–2000 well before the year
2020. The presently categorised developing countries are likely to
account for a sharply rising value and proportion of total energy
investments, these countries possibly investing well in excess of
US$2trillion (at 1992 prices) annually by the year 2020, and well in
excess of 50% of world annual energy investments. These energy
investments are likely in large part to be concentrated on fewer than
ten developing countries. Thus taking account of the impact of
efficiency and environmental considerations (many leading energy
companies in developed countries are now spending around 25% of
their total annual capital expenditures on environmentally related
projects) a broad order of magnitude figure for the cumulative

	US$ Trillion*	%
Coal	4	13
Oil	6	20
Natural Gas	7	23
Electricity	10	33
"New" Renewables	2	8
"Other" Renewables	1	3
Total	30$^+$	100
* Trillion = 10^{12}		
+ of which specifically efficiency/ environment related US$ 7 trillion		

Table 3.7   Illustrative Allocation of Cumulative Capital Investment Expenditures (US$ trillion(at 1992 values) and %)

investment requirements (at 1992 prices) of the world's energy industry to the year 2020 would approach US$30 trillion. By comparison world GDP in 1989 was just over US$20 trillion.

Based upon the WEC's 1987 study, this total investment requirement might be allocated in a Reference Case as illustrated in Table 3.7.

These illustrative figures reflect some switch in priorities over time: rising investments in clean coal technology and the likely further exploitation of China's and India's large coal resources; interest in exploiting natural gas as a relatively clean fossil fuel; and expansion of investments in new renewables.

The WEC's Committee on "Renewable Energy Resources: Opportunities and Constraints 1990–2020" has estimated that "new" renewables will require nearly US$900 billion investment if a steady evolution leading to modest expansion of availability by 2020 is to be achieved. With major policy support and some US$2400 billion of investment the higher availability indicated in Table 3.5 could be achieved by 2020.

The issue is not whether such sums can be raised – the lower case in Table 3.8 would take up at most 0.75% of global gross fixed capital formation to 2020 and the higher case 2% – but whether such investment would be profitable. Oil and gas are generally considered to offer profitable investment opportunities but new renewables are generally regarded as uneconomic for the time being without the benefit of subsidy. Unless priority is accorded to the provision of new renewables it is generally accepted that only slow advance can be expected. And there are other priorities.

For instance, another way of looking at the higher figure of U$2427 billion is to compare it with the very similar sum currently estimated as required to raise the energy efficiency and environmental standards of Central and Eastern Europe, the CIS and (low/middle income) developing countries to present average OECD levels. This may be regarded as a very high priority.

It is also likely that very substantial investments will be required to raise present average OECD levels also, given the potential to raise efficiency and reduce harmful environmental impacts. While on the supply side, heavy investments are anticipated in oil and natural gas exploration and development in particular. This will have a significant impact on the price of energy.

	Steady Evolution			Major Policy Support		
	2000	2010	2020	2000	2010	2020
Solar	52	134	313	65	265	1 205
Geothermal	15	20	35	20	60	110
Modern Biomass	50	100	150	66	140	260
Ocean	1	10	55	1	50	150
Small Hydro	21	50	100	36	88	150
Sub Total	159	374	833	223	738	2 280
Transmission	10	23	56	15	49	147
Total	169	397	889	238	789	2 427

Table 3.8 Estimated Cumulative "New" Renewable Investment (US$ billions)

THE PRICE OF ENERGY

There is a very high likelihood that some time between 2030 and 2080 supplies of oil and natural gas will be severely constrained, with the remaining reserves allocated to privileged users and top premium uses.

Perceptions of impending supply shortfalls will cast a shadow forward, well into the period between now and 2020. Past estimates of supply availability, and prophecies of "reserves running out", have been notoriously erroneous but finite resources have by definition a finite existence.

There are good reasons, as indicated above, why fossil fuel resources are likely to be much larger than today's proved reserves. Nevertheless, there are no grounds for complacency, for the following reasons:

- The finite nature of oil and natural gas resources will become abundantly clear within the next century although the impact of perceived scarcity on price will bring on additional supplies and substitutes as well as moderate demand.

- More countries will become energy importers, and the number of people dependent upon imported energy supplies will greatly increase (Table 3.6).

- The length of supply lines for oil and natural gas imports will greatly increase. For instance, North Sea oil and gas supplies will decline and alternatives will be sought from much further afield. Many countries around the world will seek oil and natural gas supplies from such CIS countries as the Russian Federation, Kazakhstan, Azerbaijan and Turkmenistan.

- Uncertain geopolitical conditions, and uncertainties surrounding investment and financing rules could either discourage supply-side investments or raise their costs.

- Costs of exploration and production will rise as smaller reserves are exploited, harsher conditions are met (climatic, geological or sub-sea), or enhanced recovery techniques are used.

- Environmental and other externalities will tend to raise supply-side as well as demand-side costs.

- Efforts linked to securing Middle East oil supplies through military intervention from outside are costly and likely to prove both unsustainable and unacceptable in the longer run.

In view of the above, the real cost of energy is likely to rise in the coming decades. No one knows how soon, how fast, or how far. In Chapter 1 above, it was mentioned that oil consumers in particular have enjoyed a period of remission on their prices since 1985. Weak demand and diverse producer objectives have had their effects, but these conditions are unlikely to rule permanently. In the late 1970s and very early 1980s, when real oil prices were about double their 1992 level, significant behavioural and technological changes took place. These changes were the product both of higher oil prices and the shock of price rises, fears over availability, and concern about further real price rises.

ENERGY CASES – THE SUPPLY ASSUMPTIONS

The energy supply side of the Commission's four Cases reflect the foregoing. Careful consideration has been given to changes in the fossil fuel mix, the prospects for electricity and gas, and the relative shift of sectoral demand (Figure 3.2). Nevertheless, all these assumptions do not change the essential illustrative nature of the Cases: they cannot pretend to predict the future. Table 3.9 sets out the breakdown in global fuel use for the historic years 1960 and 1990, together with the assumptions for the four Cases for the year 2020.

A more detailed breakdown of this energy mix by regions is given in Appendix C18–C23.

The main conclusions are:

	1960	1990	in 2020			
			A	B_1	B	C
Coal	1.4	2.3	4.9	3.8	3.0	2.1
Oil	1.0	2.8	4.6	4.5	3.8	2.9
Natural Gas	0.4	1.7	3.6	3.6	3.0	2.5
Nuclear	—	0.4	1.0	1.0	0.8	0.7
Large Hydro	0.15	0.5	1.0	1.0	0.9	0.7
"Traditional"	0.5	0.9	1.3	1.3	1.3	1.1
"New" Renewables	—	0.2	0.8	0.8	0.6	1.3
Total	3.3	8.8	17.2	16.0	13.4	11.3

Table 3.9   Energy Mix – Annual Past and Future Global Fuel Use (Gtoe)

- Case A requires substantially increased supplies of all forms of energy. The largest increases are assumed to come from coal, natural gas and oil (in that order). With the developing countries accounting for the bulk of the demand increase, and China and India looming large in this context, major expansion of their coal output will be required. Much of this will go to meet domestic demand. It is also implicit that natural gas will be supplied long distance, primarily by pipeline, to the Asian developing countries in particular. The transportation sector of the developing countries is assumed to expand rapidly, and to require the large increase in oil supplies. The continuing rapid growth of many of the developing countries is assumed to generate and attract the finance required to permit the required supply availability.

- Case B1 also requires substantially increased supply availability, mainly due to the rapid expansion of demand in many developing countries. This reflects delayed and slower reductions in energy/GDP intensity. In this Case natural gas and oil are the preferred options for many, but it is implied that developing countries with major coal resources (notably China and India) will continue to expand their exploitation.

- **Case B** reflects a more modest growth in the energy demand of developing countries, but still a requirement for substantially increased supplies of natural gas, oil and coal. China accounts for the bulk of the increased coal supply. The more modest demand pull, by comparison with the two previous Cases, and failure of governments to take the necessary action results in the slowest expansion of new renewables of all four Cases.

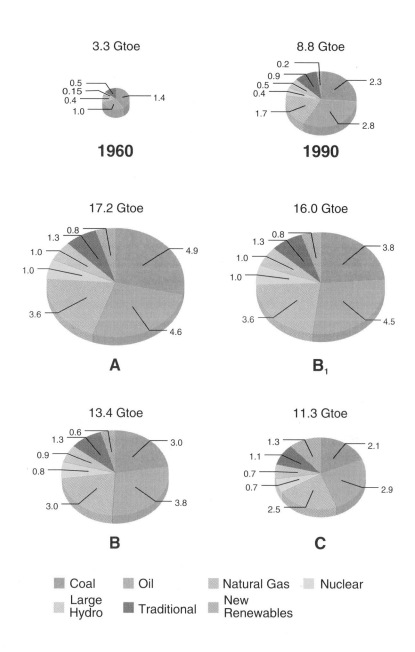

Figure 3.2 Energy Demand Mix and Total Energy Demand (in Gtoe) for 1960, 1990 and in 2020 for the four WEC Cases

- Case C, by contrast, is achieved principally by expanded supplies of new renewables and natural gas. Nuclear power and large hydro provide more modest expansions of availability. This Case implies not merely the testing assumptions on energy efficiency and energy use per capita (especially in the developing countries where population increases and development needs are likely to push up against the ceiling of this Case) mentioned in the previous chapter. It also implies very determined and effective action to reduce consumption of coal and curb the consumption of oil on environmental grounds, while accelerating the availability of energy from new renewable sources.

The technical feasibility of achieving these supply increases focuses primarily on the natural gas sector, and in all four Cases. Substantially increased gas finds, more widely spread, would be required together with large expenditures on transportation which will affect price and lengthen lead times.

Technical feasibility of production is less of a problem with coal, given the huge resource base and the potential for expanding lower cost production and world trade. The constraints are more likely to lie elsewhere – on the development and application of cleaner coal technologies, and whether potential climate change becomes a sufficiently significant issue throughout the world to cause resources to remain unexploited.

It will be noted that all four Cases assume an expansion of nuclear power availability. This is by no means a foregone conclusion. Much will depend upon decisions made about future nuclear power provision in a few key countries (notably the USA) and the avoidance of nuclear accidents in a few others (notably the Russian Federation, Ukraine and other countries of the former USSR operating RBMK reactors) over the next few years. High initial costs as well as safety are likely to remain a concern. Growing public and political acceptability cannot be assumed, even if without it future energy provision becomes in some respects more problematic.

	Cases			
	A	B₁	B	C
Coal	+2.6	+1.5	+0.6	−0.2
Oil	+1.8	+1.7	+1.0	0
Natural Gas	+1.9	+1.9	+1.3	+0.8
Nuclear	+0.6	+0.6	+0.4	+0.3
Large Hydro	+0.5	+0.5	+0.4	+0.2
"Traditional"	+0.4	+0.4	+0.4	+0.2
"New" Renewables	+0.6	+0.6	+0.4	+1.2
Total	+8.4	+7.2	+4.5	+2.5

Table 3.10   Contribution to Supply Changes in 2020 compared to 1990 (Gtoe)

CHAPTER

4

ENERGY
EFFICIENCY AND
CONSERVATION

INTRODUCTION

All the Regional reports produced for this Commission were agreed on
the need to give a very high priority to increasing the overall efficiency
of energy use. Indeed this was one of the most widely supported of all
aims in the energy sector.

Many detailed studies have shown the large technical potential for
meeting the needs and aspirations of society with much less energy use.
There are many examples of applications of energy efficiency or energy
saving techniques which are extremely economic, with rapid payback
periods. Much existing technology is not used to its full potential in
raising efficiency in energy provision and use. This failure to reach full
potential in the use of existing technology is largely the result of poor
management and poor training. Recognition of the true causes of this
failure will shift the emphasis away from the pursuit of new technology
to the better application of efficient existing technology, to general
benefit.

There are several reasons for seeking to improve energy efficiency. The Regional reports prepared for this Commission highlighted:

- improving economic efficiency and international competitiveness;

- reducing adverse environmental impacts.

Other reasons referred to were:

- reducing dependence on imported energy, especially oil;

- increasing the efficiency with which scarce domestic resources of energy are used;

- conserving finite global energy reserves, and inhibiting future energy price rises.

Underlying these general statements are a vast array of examples of processes, equipment and practices which use energy with glaring inefficiency. A common objective is the need to develop policies which provide headroom to eke out the scarcer finite energy resources and bring in alternative supplies and means of providing the services required. However, it should be recalled that during the process of social and economic development, countries which improve the efficiency with which they use energy – either through the application of technology or gains elsewhere in the economy – may thereby free up resources to consume more energy.

Although there is great scope for future improvements in energy efficiency and energy conservation, reliable estimates of what that scope is requires detailed bottom-up studies, and both technical assessments and commercial judgements as to what is realistically feasible. There has probably been a persistent tendency within the world's energy industry to understate the technical potential for improvement and substitution, and a persistent tendency outside the industry to be overoptimistic on the speed and ease with which such improvements can be introduced.

Technical improvements have the ability to tackle inefficiency and control pollution because of their ability to utilise key economic factors – especially capital and technology, coupled with relative openness and informed quality of public debate. This is stressed at various points in this report, and its importance for spurring international development and co-operation emphasised. But placing figures on possible savings of energy – say 30% to 50% by the year 2020 compared with the continuation of present practice – can only be indicative.

There are few known technological limits on the prospects for greater overall efficiency of energy use when changes of economic activity and lifestyle, possible alternative ways of doing things or providing services, and a sufficiently long time-span are taken into account. This report has assumed rapid improvements in energy intensity taking place continuously over many decades, as in Case C. An improvement (reduction) of 3% per annum in energy intensity over 30 years would lead to a reduction of 60% in the energy used to produce a unit of economic output.

In reality, however, what matters is not so much a numerical estimate of the large potential for improvement, but the rate of improvement that is achievable in practice. This involves consideration of the rate at which new technology can be developed; its rate of diffusion around the world; the investment capital needed to fund the penetration of the new technologies and the rate at which such funds can be developed; and of economic, institutional and human barriers to progress.

Growing environmental awareness and concern can be expected to highlight the scope for increased efficiency and conservation in the energy field. This will bring with it the likelihood that energy efficiency will ultimately rise under environmental pressures (though it may not always do so in the interim). These are the matters on which this report has concentrated.

ENERGY CONVERSION AND USE

The energy directly recovered from the Earth – coal, crude oil, natural gas, collected biomass, hydraulic power, heat produced in a nuclear reactor from processed natural uranium – is *primary energy*. Primary energy is generally not used directly. Instead it is converted into *secondary energy*. This has the advantage that secondary energy forms can be used in a much wider range of applications with greater ease – as electricity, motor gasoline, jet fuel, heating oil, etc. Secondary energy, having been converted in power plants, refineries, etc is delivered to consumers as *final energy*.

The process of energy conversion and transformation that ultimately results in the provision of goods and services involves part of the energy being transferred to the ultimate purpose, and part being rejected into the environment as "waste" heat.

Energy efficiency considerations focus on the efficiency of original extraction and transportation; on the primary energy conversion efficiency of central power plants, refineries, coal gasification plants, etc; on the secondary energy conversion efficiency into storage facilities, distribution systems and transport networks (eg of electricity grids); and final energy conversion into useful energy forms in end-use, and conversion devices (such as light bulbs, stoves and motor vehicles).

A great deal of work has been done in recent years to evaluate the efficiency, and scope for its improvement, of these various stages of conversion. More difficult is the evaluation of the energy services that result from the provision of useful energy. Energy services depend on many factors external to the energy system, such as the lifestyles and general social behaviour of end-consumers, and the structure of economies. The energy services of heating a room depend on insulation of the house, the outside temperature, pattern of occupancy, and the characterisation of the heating system itself. This same service also depends upon what is already provided, how it is priced, whether it can be afforded, whether improvements can be funded, the information available on how it can be improved and how well this is communicated, and on whether public policy is encouraging improvement or acting "perversely".

Similarly, the energy services provided by a motorised vehicle depend on its design (weight, related equipment, frictional losses, aerodynamics, etc), how effectively the vehicle is used in transporting people and goods, on the typical operational cycles (length of journey, traffic conditions) and on the availability of substitutes. The inherent efficiency of the internal combustion engine began to approach its limits in the 1960s. Engines built since range from 34% efficiency for spark-ignition automobile-type engines under optimum load/speed conditions to around 42% for large marine-type and direct injection diesels. The difference is due to the higher compression ratios, lower throttle losses and improved direct injection achievable in large diesels. In practice, optimum load/speed conditions are never achieved. The energy efficiency of a vehicle operating in traffic, with variable speeds and loads, is at least 30% lower. Short journeys, when the engine is cold on starting and never warms up sufficiently for optimal fuel combustion, create sub-optimal fuel use and high emissions. Stop-start conditions in heavy traffic also cause relatively high fuel use and emissions.

Engine efficiency is further reduced, often by a further 30% or so, by the carrying of oil pumps, air pumps, fuel pumps, electrical systems, heating, air conditioning and other related equipment. Friction and viscosity losses in the vehicle's drive train – not least conventional automatic transmissions which alone can reduce engine efficiency by 10% to 15% – cut efficiency still further. The average thermodynamic efficiency of the motor vehicle is, as a result of these factors, only between 10 and 17%.

Significant improvements in automobile fuel economy have nevertheless been achieved in recent years. The main gains have been made by cutting down on excess weight in the body, improving aerodynamics, and improving tyres. But even smaller automobiles of the conventional type are likely to weigh much more than their payloads for the foreseeable future. By contrast, "payload efficiencies" of fully loaded commercial aircraft are of the order of 30% to 35%, and heavy duty trucks, freight trains and ships can all achieve much greater "payload efficiencies" than the 10% or so of a medium-sized car.

Underpinning this sort of discussion of energy efficiency are a number of theoretical ideas and principles. If a power plant has an efficiency of 42% this is the conventional method of evaluating system efficiency, and indicates the amount of electric energy generated per unit heat of combustion. Thus 58% of the combustion heat in this case results in waste heat which is not converted into electricity. Because of the first law of thermodynamics, which holds that energy is converted (and neither wasted nor destroyed), this concept of efficiency is what is normally meant by energy efficiency. It is sometimes termed first law efficiency.

However, application of the first law of thermodynamics is severely inadequate for the task of assessing the minimum amount of energy required to perform a particular task by any possible system or device. It only provides a measure of efficiency of a given system or device. It is of limited value in attempting to estimate the actual effectiveness and the potential for improving the efficiency of the whole energy system. It is of use in comparing the performance of energy conversion facilities and devices of a particular type with each other – eg power stations, boilers, refrigerators, light bulbs. Thus not only does first law efficiency have value in comparing best available technology with a given application within a country, it also provides a good indication as to how far some countries may lag behind others in the efficiency of given devices. This is one basis for the arguments in favour of wider technology diffusion and co-operation advanced in this report.

The shortcomings of the first law of thermodynamics in this context have led to attempts to devise a broader measure of effective energy use sometimes referred to as "exergy". The objective is to assess potential improvements measured against a theoretical minimum "exergy" requirement supposing an ideal device were available for performing the specified energy tasks. It is assumed that a quantity of available work from energy is in an important sense "wasted". More "waste" occurs at each stage of conversion, transformation and use.

It is exploration of this broader concept of efficiency, requiring consideration of the whole energy system and its streams, which leads to statements such as the following:

> "The end-use efficiency for the USA as a whole gave the estimate of 2.5%. This means that, in principle, the same final services (heat, light, transport, cooking, entertainment, etc) could have been obtained by the expenditure of only 1/40 as much energy as was actually used.

Western Europe and Japan are significantly more efficient than the USA. Both regions are in the 4–5% range.

On the other hand, Eastern Europe and the former USSR, and the rest of the world use energy even less efficiently than the USA – perhaps 1.5% to 2%. For the world as a whole, it is likely that the overall efficiency with which fuel energy is used is currently no greater than 3% to 3.5%.

But there is no fundamental *technical* reason why end-use efficiency could not be increased by several-fold (perhaps by a factor of 3) in the course of the next half-century."

(R.U. Ayres, WEC Journal, July 1992 pp. 38–39.)

There is, nevertheless, no way of avoiding the imposition of upper limits on the theoretical efficiencies that can be achieved with a given conversion technology. There are practical thermodynamic and mechanical limits placed by available materials, finite heat conductivities, mechanical and other physical properties. There are examples of modern plant and equipment which have current net efficiencies close to their maximum theoretical efficiency. But there may be other processes which are more efficient in achieving a given task or providing a service required.

As energy is always conserved according to the first law of thermodynamics, all reductions in specific energy needs for performing a given task may be regarded as efficiency improvements. All reduction of energy needs due to changes in the nature or level of the required task is conservation. Thus the use of a more fuel efficient automobile for a particular trip is an example of efficiency improvement. Any reductions in energy needs for this given trip such as the improved use of the automobile (eg extra care with speed, gear changes, route planning), improved traffic conditions (eg traffic calming schemes, road user charges), etc would fall within the definition of conservation measures. Other conservation measures would include any alternatives to undertaking the given trip which use less energy, such as video-conferencing, making a telephone call or walking.

But many of the issues raised here involve new technology, materials, fuels, engine design, and vehicle design. They also suggest the need for changes in aspirations and lifestyles. Without different policies, pricing and incentive schemes, many changes are unlikely to come about quickly. Thus what is theoretically achievable over a lengthy time period is very different from what can realistically be achieved to raise the efficiency of a given system or device within the space of, say, 20 to 30 years.

THE SHORTER-TERM POTENTIAL

In the absence of radical shifts in energy policy and the behaviour of energy consumers, what is the shorter-term potential for efficiency improvements and conservation?

The essential mechanism for using energy more efficiently overall is to replace existing assets – buildings, plant, appliances, machinery and processes and economic activities – by new ones which meet the social or commercial aims of the user more effectively. Retro-fitting to modify or refurbish existing assets may also be feasible, though frequently less attractive.

There is a huge number of possibilities and only a selection of examples are given here under:

- manufacturing industry;

- agriculture;

- residential and commercial;

- transport;

- energy supply and conversion.

Manufacturing Industry

The industrial sector in the more advanced industrial countries is the most efficient energy user. It is easier to be efficient when operating on a larger scale and when energy is an explicit element of operating costs. Managers are required by competition to analyse costs carefully, and in industries where energy costs are a significant fraction of total costs managers are more alert to opportunities for savings. In industry it is rare for best practice technology to be more than about 20% better than average, whereas in the residential sector the variation is much wider.

Over half the energy consumed by industry in the leading industrial countries is as fuel for process heat, and over one-fifth (gross) is electricity for furnaces, electrolytic processes and electric motor drive. Most process heat is delivered in the form of steam, with an overall efficiency which has been variously estimated between 15% and 25%. The biggest users of process heat are the steel, petroleum, chemicals, and paper and pulp industries. Estimates of the efficiency with which process heat is used varies markedly between these industries, from around 10% (cement production) to 14% (petroleum refining) and up to around 20% (iron and steel manufacturing). Energy input per unit of manufacturing output fell sharply after 1974, particularly in the decade to the mid-1980s, due to structural change and changes in the output mix in almost equal parts. Technological change was estimated to have contributed about one-third of those changes.

The shorter-term potential for efficiency improvements in manufacturing industry in the leading industrial nations is regarded as around 30%.

Chemicals

Feedstocks account for about 5% of industrial energy. About a third of the energy content of chemical feedstocks is embodied in "final" chemicals, such as plastics. It has been estimated that in the USA feedstocks are currently used with an efficiency of about 30% to 35%.

Most inorganic and organic chemical production processes involve numerous sequential steps, including the making of intermediate compounds and their separation, in addition to the final desired product. The overall energy efficiency of the process will be an aggregate of the local efficiencies of each stage, and even if each stage is reasonably energy efficient, the overall efficiency can be quite low.

There are many options for improving efficiency, ranging from shortening and simplifying the basic steps to improvements in design of the chemical processes and better techniques. Examples are:

- Use of biotechnology to speed reaction times and reduce the temperatures and pressures used.

- Use of catalysts to improve yields, reaction times and to reduce temperatures and pressures. For example, the low pressure catalytic process for low-density polyethylene is said to reduce energy requirements to only 35% of those of the standard process.

- Improved process control, in particular via improved sensors and instrumentation. Studies indicate potential savings of 5–20% in particular industries, and potential for overall reduction in energy consumption of 10–15%.

- Separation/concentration can be made more efficient by improved distillation, membrane separation, supercritical fluids extraction, and freeze concentration (which methods can be 50% more efficient than other separation techniques and yield products of higher purity).

- The chemical industry already has sophisticated waste heat management, but studies indicate substantial further potential for improvement, in particular through optimal energy management: for example promising 32–48% reduction in existing energy costs in the United States.

Iron and Steel

Typically, energy costs are 20–40% of production costs. About 25% of the energy consumed in the steel industry is embodied in iron and steel. The basic modern integrated plant – taking iron ore to finished steel – uses the basic oxygen furnace (BOF). The processes involved are ore preparation, coking, iron making, steel making, casting, forming and heat treatment. Each of these has shown improvements in energy efficiency, which are continuing. For example:

- More energy efficient agglomeration processes for ore preparation.

- Dry coke quenching, cooling the hot coke by non-oxidising gas instead of by water. The efficiency of converting coal to coke has improved substantially in recent years: for example in the USA the energy used per tonne of output has declined from 7.0 GJ in 1980 to 4.1 GJ in 1989.

- Improvements in blast furnace efficiencies, eg by the use of top pressure recovery turbines, and in-process control of temperature and carbon content.

- Direct (continuous) casting: thin slab casting, thin strip casting, net shape casting and spray steel.

The other main modern steel-making process is the electric arc furnace (EAF), which is primarily a method for dealing with scrap (where EAFs are about twice as energy efficient as BOFs with integrated steel production). There is potential for improved efficiency, eg by scrap preheating, scrap beneficiation and the use of ultra high power electric arc furnaces.

In the future, more general changes are possible, involving for example direct reduction of iron or direct steel making from ore. The latter approach offers the possibility of a reduction in energy use up to 40%.

It has been estimated that bringing US steel making to current best practice would reduce energy use by about 30%, bringing it to about 14.8 GJ/tonne, some 16% better than Japanese production at 17.6 GJ/tonne. The energy efficiency of steel production in the developing countries varies widely. There is still some use of the old and outdated open hearth method, but this is expected to be phased out within a few years in most cases. Integrated steel plants in India and China use about twice as much energy per tonne of steel as do the more efficient US and Japanese plants. However, the production in other developing countries is very efficient, and/or improving rapidly. Examples are Brazil and Republic of Korea.

Pulp and Paper

Paper making typically consists of five process steps: wood preparation, pulping, bleaching and chemical recovery and paper making. Current technologies are mature; nonetheless technological improvements hold the promise for substantial energy improvements. Advanced pulping processes are in prospect: bio-pulping via the use of enzymes derived from wood rot fungi; chemical pulping with fermentation, and organic solvent pulping. Other technological changes which could reduce energy consumption are greater reliance on continuous digesters and displacement heaters in pulping, improvements in spent liquor concentrations, spent liquor gasification, mechanical de-watering in the paper-making process, improved presses to squeeze the water out of paper before drying (extended nip processes allow energy savings of 15% to 30%), and use of lower grade (less energy intensive) pulp.

Improvements are also possible by using better motor drive systems, co-generation, and recovery of process heat through the use of heat exchangers, recuperators and vapour compression systems. There is also considerable scope for increasing energy utilisation from the waste products of the industry: in particular hog fuel (bark, sawdust and other scrap), black liquor and forest residues.

The US pulp and paper industry reduced energy intensity between 1972 and 1985 by 36%, and additional energy improvements could achieve a similar further saving. Many developing countries have energy efficiencies well below the OECD average, with a corresponding scope for improvement.

Cement

Typically 30%–50% of production costs are energy costs. The manufacture of cement involves three basic processes: the mining and preparation of the raw materials, clinker production and finish grinding. The two primary manufacturing processes are the wet and the dry processes. The latter is more economic and energy efficient and is now the preferred process. As it replaces wet processes in various countries (at different rates), so world average energy efficiency improves.

Technological improvements which can save energy and which have been introduced or are in prospect are: better use of kiln waste heat to dry and preheat the feedstock; better instrumentation and product quality control; improved refractory materials for the kilns; improved grinding processes; use of off-grade fuels; reduction of clinker firing temperatures; and blending of secondary materials. In the developing countries there can often be scope for large savings by improving the efficiency and the quality of electricity supplies.

Technology improvements in the US cement industry could reduce energy use by as much as 40% if all cement producers operated at the efficiency of the most efficient plant. But technological improvements do not always save energy; for example, greater energy use to give improved environmental protection, and greater use of electricity for finer grinding if stronger cements are required.

Agriculture

Energy is used in agriculture for the manufacture of farm equipment and fertilisers, the provision of tractive power for the various activities of cultivation, application of fertilisers and chemicals, pumping and irrigation, crop drying, refrigeration and storage, transport of crops, and the utilisation of crop residues for energy production. All of these areas offer incentive for improved energy efficiency; three areas are considered here.

Irrigation

Irrigation reduces dependence on variable, uncertain or even locally inadequate rainfall and raises yields. Irrigation is most commonly done with either electric motor or diesel driven pumps. The causes of inefficiency and their remedies listed above for industrial pumps apply also to their use in agriculture. Reliability of the pumps and of their backup power systems is important; large amounts of crops can be lost if water is not provided at the right time. There is also scope for improved efficiency in delivery of water: eg in use of drip irrigation, the use of sensors to monitor the actual water need of plants, and computer scheduled irrigation.

Traction

Where agriculture is still heavily dependent on the use of draft animals, allowance must be made for the energy input required to feed them. Moreover, such animals become increasingly difficult to support as pasture is converted to crops in densely populated regions. A variety of improvements in nutrition, harness design, and other factors, can greatly improve the work output of draft animals. Mechanisation in developing countries by suitably designed and simple tractors helps to improve overall productivity.

Fertilisers

Nitrogen fertilisers are made primarily from ammonia. Currently, the energy required is about 33 GJ per tonne of fertiliser; with a theoretical limit of about 21 GJ per tonne and a practical limit estimated at about 28.5 GJ per tonne. The fuel component of this total energy consumption is usually provided by natural gas, which serves both as a feedstock and as a fuel. Further efficiency improvements are possible from eg purge gas recovery and various process improvements. New design methods such as pinch technology for heat exchanger networks in chemical plants, also offer both energy and capital savings.

Wider Issues

There are many wider issues that affect the overall economic efficiency of the agricultural industry, and so by implication its energy use: the proper pricing of agricultural products; the international impact of subsidised agricultural production by the developed countries; soil conservation; accounting for the value of soil and other environmental assets; and techniques such as improved pest management, intercropping, agro-forestry, and low energy inputs.

Residential and Commercial

Space Conditioning

This includes heating, cooking and ventilation and by implication brings in the whole subject of building design and building regulations. At present the majority of energy use for heating is by the developed countries in colder climates. In hotter climates, and especially humid ones, air conditioning systems are desirable but at present are common only in rich areas such as the United States and in the highest income households in developing countries. There is a very large scope for the increased use of energy for cooling, ventilation and dehumidification in developing countries, which are often located in hot climates. Such countries may often have low quality housing (uninsulated concrete block construction) which can greatly increase energy use for cooling. The overall energy efficiency of air cooling systems has been estimated as barely 5%, and the overall efficiency of energy use in space heating less than 1% in a "typical" North American house where the average efficiency of insulation is some 12% compared with the ideal. These figures do not take account of avoidable losses through heating or cooling unoccupied rooms.

Ventilation and cooling needs can be reduced. For instance, external heat gains can be minimised by shade trees, awnings that provide indirect light but shield direct sunlight, exterior or interior shades, reflective or tinted window coatings, insulated windows, light colour roofs, roof sprays, wall and roof insulation, ventilation by natural convection and use of the ground for cooling, and use of traditional heat shielding materials such as thatch. Internal heat gains can be kept low by using energy efficient appliances. Highly efficient mechanical cooling equipment can be used, as can direct and indirect evaporative coolers, air to air heat exchangers, gas-fired absorption chillers and engine driven chillers, and adjustable speed electric powered systems. These illustrate just some of the technical means currently available and in use.

The methods available for increasing the energy efficiency of heating are analogous to those for improving cooling efficiency: better insulation of buildings; use of free heat gain from appliances; more efficient heating systems; use of passive solar energy; use of heat pumps and co-generation systems where appropriate; development of a building's heat storage capacity; draught proofing; use of individual metering devices and thermostats, and so on.

Much of the attention to improving heating efficiency has been directed to the developed, high energy consumption countries in colder climates. Efficiency improvements in space conditioning are generally achieved by changes in the building shell such as better insulation; but these improvements are more easily and effectively made in new buildings than by retrofitting existing ones (though the latter is also an important means of efficiency improvement). The full achievement of better building efficiency is therefore limited by the rate of turnover of the building stock, which in practice is usually slow.

Efficient energy use is not simply a matter of the technologies available but of their dissemination and use. This is aided by the setting of suitable regulations by governments, getting builders and appliance manufacturers to achieve minimum efficiency levels that they would not be motivated to provide in the market-place when, as commonly happens, the latter is dominated by the commercial need to minimise first costs. Other aids are the widespread provision of information, incentives (financial and other), and the availability of consultants and others capable, for example, of conducting energy audits.

Cooking

Cooking is one of the most basic domestic and commercial services entailing energy use, and in many developing countries it can be the most important energy service. Whereas in the more developed countries, cooking is done by commercial fuels and increasingly by electricity and gas, in rural areas of developing countries traditional fuels – wood, crop residues and dung – are the primary fuels used for cooking. As incomes improve and commercial fuel supplies become more reliable, people are able to switch to modern stoves and cleaner fuels such as kerosene, LPG and electricity. These technologies are preferred for their convenience, comfort, cleanliness, ease of operation, speed, efficiency, and for avoiding the harmful health effects which commonly arise from the smoke and carbon monoxide produced by traditional wood burning stoves.

The efficiency, cost and performance of stoves *per se* generally increase as consumers shift progressively from wood stoves to charcoal, kerosene, LPG or gas and electric cookers. However, the overall system energy efficiency in these latter systems depends also on the cost and efficiency of the commercial energy delivery systems, for example the upstream costs of electricity generation, transmission and distribution. All these aspects are consistent with achieving economic energy efficiency provided there is an efficient commercial, marketing and pricing system which avoids subsidy of fuel supplies.

However, the use of traditional fuels will remain important for a long time to come, and much effort has been put into improved wood stoves for use in rural areas of developing countries. Trial and effort has shown that this is not an easy task, and early efforts were not successful. Indeed, it transpired that traditional stoves were well optimised for the local materials, pots, and other conditions, from many years of trial and error. More successful programmes have now been achieved, and showed that to do better required sustained technical input in design, quality control in production, careful field testing and follow up, and extensive input at every stage from end-users. Improved heat resistant materials such as metals or ceramics also proved important. In developed countries, studies of energy demand for cooking show a decline in energy intensity in recent years, arising from structural changes in the type of technology used (use of electric stoves and microwave ovens), behavioural changes such as the number of meals taken at home and the size of households, and efficiency improvements. There continues to be significant potential for efficiency improvements from technological shifts – still more efficiency improvements and increased use of microwaves. Deep-rooted preferences for traditional methods – part of a cultural norm – need to be recognised. Nevertheless, microwaves represent an efficiency gain over the average electric oven of the order of 7 to 10-fold.

Lighting

Modern electric lighting plays a very important social role in all aspects of life. As the conversion of primary energy into final electricity has an efficiency of about 30%, the overall efficiency for lighting is currently about 3% (and about 10% for fluorescent lights) if used with care. Unnecessary use reduces overall energy efficiency below 1%. The demand for lighting has continued to increase in the industrialised countries over the past 30 years as incomes have increased, and the trend to increased use of lighting can be expected to continue in all countries. It is therefore a fruitful area for improved efficiency, where many analysts believe gains of 60% to 70% are readily achievable, and up to 90% savings achievable with best currently available equipment.

For example, most residential lighting continues to be provided by incandescent bulbs. These bulbs have an efficiency of about 4% in converting electricity to visible radiant energy. Much more efficient and cost-effective lighting techniques are available; in particular compact fluorescent lights with long life, offering much lower overall costs of supplying lighting. Fluorescent lights have efficiencies of up to 35% and typically of around 20%. Constraints to the more rapid penetration of such technologies include lack of awareness and easy commercial availability or promotion, high first cost, high replacement cost of breakages, and often the general cost and inconvenience of retrofitting new lighting systems to existing domestic buildings, where rewiring and new sockets, holders and appliances may well be needed. Objections may also arise on aesthetic grounds, that the appliances and lamps do not comply with traditional values and preferences.

Further options to reduce electricity requirements include improved design and better control (such as varying the light levels according to function), more efficient reflectors and ballasts for fluorescent tubes, or behavioural changes such as turning off lights when they are not needed. However, people often ascribe a high convenience or security value to keeping lights on in a house.

Other Appliances

Other domestic and commercial uses of energy are water heating, refrigeration, washing and a variety of convenience appliances, commonly using electricity. All show scope for efficiency improvements.

Transport

Typically, about 80% of the fuel used in a representative vehicle travelling over a mix of urban, rural and motorway routes is unproductive energy, spent in overcoming internal friction in auxiliary items and in thermodynamic losses in the engine. The scope for reducing the latter is limited by the theoretical efficiencies of the operation cycles used in heat engines; and power which does reach the wheels must overcome rolling resistance and aerodynamic drag, especially at high speeds.

The technical characteristics and design of a vehicle may depend on many interlinking and conflicting objectives, including performance, comfort, safety, emissions, fuel economy and vehicle capital costs. The relative importance of these factors is determined by the manufacturer, competitors and the market as well as by regulations. In terms of fuel economy, relevant technical items in addition to engine type are vehicle weight, aerodynamics, tyres, steering and suspension, and transmissions.

All of these areas have shown substantial efficiency improvements in recent years. Much of the fuel economy improvement achieved in recent years is due to better aerodynamics. In 1973, baseline drag was about 0.45; now 0.3 is relatively standard for European cars. In a competitive private transport world, means of further improving efficiency cost effectively are studied intensively, and there is scope for improved fuel efficiency in passenger and goods road transport without sacrificing vehicle performance. Because of the many and conflicting requirements of transport users (and now, increasingly, of environmental protection regulations), the commercial application of new ideas is a complex and uncertain matter. Nevertheless, it is worth recalling that in vehicle mileage "marathons", of the sort conducted by Shell for many years, prototype vehicles (of limited road utility at present) have carried their drivers close to 10 000 kilometres on one gallon of motor gasoline. (The world record is 7 591 English miles, set on 17 July, 1992 by a French team, but over 6 000 miles on one gallon has been set by various Japanese teams over several years.) In a few countries there are significant numbers of vehicles running on compressed natural gas (CNG) and liquefied petroleum gas (LPG). In Brazil nearly 5 million vehicles run on ethanol (not without local effects), and hope has been expressed over many years that efficient electric vehicles with wide range may become available.

A switch to greater use of rail or other forms of mass transportation is widely canvassed as a valuable way to save transport energy, as is greater (shared) occupancy of private cars. However, given the very great flexibility and convenience of petrol or diesel driven cars and their ability to access directly departure and arrival points virtually anywhere, and given the huge investment in existing road transport systems, the scope for reducing road use in favour of rail is likely to be limited in anything under a very long time-scale without powerful interventionist measures.

Curitiba, in Brazil, has shown, however, what can be achieved by combining the production of an efficient bus network and land-use planning: 70% of Curitiba's population now uses the system and, although per capita automobile ownership is among the highest in Brazil fuel consumption per vehicle is among the lowest.

There is in principle great scope for increasing the energy efficiency of lorries in developing countries, where vehicle fleets are in general older, smaller and less technologically sophisticated than in the industrialised countries. However, developing country fleets are older because vehicles are operated to a much longer life before scrapping, since new trucks are expensive to buy and foreign exchange may not always be available. And the repair and patching up of old vehicles often becomes a fine art. While there is great scope for technological catching up in many developing countries, it may be necessary to ensure the development of modern road systems, efficient commercial fuel supply and repair and maintenance services, and efficient pricing policies if this scope is to be realised.

Energy Conversion and Supply

It is usually easier to tackle the energy efficiency of the supply side, as compared with energy use, since supply is less diffuse, and is the subject of intensive research and development by large firms which, on a world basis at least, are in intensive competition. Energy conversion includes oil refining, the supply of heat and production of synthetic gas; but the area which usually raises the greatest interest and controversy is the conversion of primary energy sources into electricity.

The development of commercial electric power stations is closely bound up with the availability and price in a particular country of fuel or primary energy resources, the commercial status of the industry, the environmental requirements, the social and commercial background, and so on. However, in practice, world commercial developments set the technology and efficiency standards for the main methods of electricity production (coal burning, nuclear, natural gas burnt in combined-cycle gas turbine plant, etc), and over time countries will be commercially motivated to take up the best available practice.

In recent decades, and in many countries, there has been fruitful experience with plant simultaneously producing heat and electricity (combined heat and power – CHP), and with district heating (DH) schemes supplying space and water heating to a number of buildings or whole towns from one or more heat producing plants. Both CHP and DH can contribute significantly to the conservation of energy and mitigation of environmental impacts. Carbon dioxide emissions from CHP systems are significantly lower than systems based upon separate production of heat and power. Efficiency improvements of up to 85% to 90% have been achieved in modern CHP plants built as extraction type or back pressure units, and particularly when constructed as combined-cycle units.

There is considerable potential for the expansion in use of CHP and DH schemes and their further improvement in efficiency (especially in Eastern Europe and the newly independent states). The major examples in Western Europe of CHP/DH schemes are Helsinki (Finland), Copenhagen (Denmark), Gothenburg and Västeras (Sweden), though schemes exist in several other countries. Paris (France) has the largest interconnected DH system, using steam as the heat carrier, to be found in Europe. In Eastern Europe Budapest (Hungary), Prague (Czechoslovakia) and Warsaw (Poland) have CHP/DH systems, but they have suffered from insufficient insulation, absence of regulating valves and thermostats, and prices far below the costs of supply. The Republic of Korea embarked upon a huge CHP/DH system in 1985.

With the growth in number of the world's urbanised population in future decades, such schemes could make a major contribution.

Great hopes are placed upon improving the efficiency of conversion, storage and transmission of the various forms of new renewable energy to enhance economic energy supplies. Only time will tell whether such hopes are soundly based, and will result in the emergence of a large-scale and economic supply source, but they should not be lightly dismissed.

Motor Drive Systems

Electric motor drive systems are often large and complex. The most common industrial systems include pumps, fans, compressors, conveyors, machine tools, rollers, crushers, and other direct drive systems.

Motor driven pumps, fans and other system components are usually deliberately designed to be oversized. There are many reasons for this: because operation parameters are uncertain, to allow for the build up of deposits over time, to handle starting stresses, to provide safety margins, and to allow for expansion of duty. In developing countries, oversizing motors is often important for preventing motor stall and possible burnout when the line voltage drops. More generally, these system components are often oversized because the increased energy and capital costs to the end-user are perceived to be less than the risk of equipment failure.

The avoidance of oversizing is often quoted as a potential way of saving energy. The above shows that the reasons for oversizing may be quite sound. Even so, there is clearly scope for innovation in reducing the impact of some of the reasons for oversizing, and for careful optimisation. For example, it pays to avoid oversizing sequential components if the cumulative oversizing then becomes excessive, or leads to the need for further throttling valves.

Some of the particular areas where there is scope for greater energy efficiency are as follows:

- High efficiency motors are readily available in industrialised countries, and offer economic and energy savings. However, it may be no use installing a motor which requires a constant and high loading to achieve its high efficiency if in practice its duty is for a low and intermittent loading. In some developing countries, poor quality electricity supplies (variable voltage) may make it difficult or impossible to utilise high efficiency motors.

- Pumps and fans are, overall, the most common motor driven equipment. Poor design and construction often leads to far lower efficiencies than are technically possible: eg due to excessive friction from rough surfaces, poorly finished edges, poor contours, internal leakage of fluid, and friction in the bearings and seals. Efficiency improvements can be achieved by remedying these defects – by improving maintenance, by optimising designs, etc.

- Adjustable speed drives can offer a number of advantages: more optimised designs with less oversizing, improved equipment lifetimes by allowing better operating duty and conditions, various technical flexibilities, and better control over manufacturing processes.

- There is considerable scope for optimising pipe and duct design, to balance cost against reduction in friction by increasing pipe size, and in relation to other parts of the system.

- Improved smart systems, controls and instrumentation all offer scope for greater energy saving.

BARRIERS TO GREATER ENERGY EFFICIENCY

There are many impediments to greater efficiency in energy provision and use, most of them also being barriers to greater economic efficiency. One challenge for effective policy measures is to provide a framework which promotes energy efficiency without simultaneously promoting forms of economic activity which also increase energy use. However, while reduction in energy use is an aim in itself where feasible, there is a more general aim of economically efficient use of energy.

This is of particular relevance to developing countries where energy demand will grow under pressure of population increase, and where modern and appropriate investments in technology should encourage economic and energy efficiency. It has been suggested in one study (J. Goldemberg et al, "Energy for a Sustainable World", 1988) that if developing countries adopted the best technology likely to be commercially available by the end of this century, these countries could enjoy a standard of living roughly equal to that of Western Europe in the late 1970s. Total energy demand was estimated as only slightly higher than the present average of 0.9 kW per head. However, these calculations implied a ten-fold rise in per-capita GDP in developing countries and some large increases in energy per capita consumption (eg 26 times in India). If this were to be sought as a goal by 2020 it would require a decline in average energy intensity of the developing countries even more rapid than the most optimistic assumption made in this report.

The main barriers to greater energy efficiency are institutional, informational, financial and technical.

Institutional

- poor information about, and lack of experience in the energy sector;

- ignorance of what is available in terms of technology and know-how to promote efficiency;

- bias in favour of encouraging energy provision and usages without similar bias towards efficiency;

- unwillingness to press for full-cost pricing;

- opposition to the imposition of earmarked taxes to promote energy efficiency from politicians and public revenue officials, because revenue raising is frequently given precedence over guiding taxpayers most effectively towards other policy goals. Recent government pronoucements in the USA and UK, for instance, suggest revenue raising still has higher priority than the promotion of energy efficiency;

- poor linkages between utilities and users, and between purchasers and users;

- intellectual property rights;

- unwillingness to promote public information campaigns and expose inefficiencies;

- ineffective regulation and labelling;

- electoral concerns.

Financial and Economic

- perceptions that costs outweigh benefits (despite the fact that payback periods are often in months rather than years, and that some efficiency improvements can be achieved at close to "zero cost" – even sometimes with net savings);

- difficulty in identifying and calculating savings with precision;

- value of and returns on, existing assets;

- financial accounting and budgeting methods;

- low energy prices, subsidies, and "perverse" incentive regimes which encourage marginal demand at minimal cost;

- threshold level of energy and cost savings (below which investments do not seem worth making even if in the aggregate substantial energy savings could be gained);

- multiple needs, seasonality, etc.

Technical

- non-availability of more advanced technology;

- non-availability of new materials and other substitutes;

- infrastructure;

- culture;

- reliability;

- scale;

- research, development and demonstration;

- technical and managerial expertise.

Among the most important barriers common in all walks of life are poor information as to how inefficiently energy is now used, how much more efficiently it could be used, the low costs of many efficiency improvements, and what is required in terms of energy management to put improvements in place.

OVERCOMING BARRIERS TO ENERGY EFFICIENCY

The most effective way of overcoming barriers to energy efficiency is an efficient energy supply market, which places major reliance on the proper pricing of energy. Ideally, there should be internalisation of all externalities in the price of supply. Full-cost pricing should be backed up by sound institutions, providing a framework of effective competition and accurate information exchange, and appropriate environmental regulation.

Another ideal is that if an energy user pays for all the costs of supply then it is the user's choice whether to use more or less energy: all the necessary incentives and disincentives have been provided.

In reality, energy users often forego beneficial opportunities to use energy more economically. Large returns often appear to be available on investments in improved energy efficiency, yet companies and individuals require rapid paybacks on such investments. Investments in new energy supplies are typically expected to show a real rate of return of around 10%. By contrast, companies tend to work for paybacks on investments in energy efficiency of one to three years, or at least 30% per annum. Individuals are at least as demanding: some surveys have found people wanted paybacks within a few months. Yet it is not that these investments necessarily involve high risks: investment in home insulation is in several respects low in risk and high in return, but still many are reluctant to pay for the necessary work.

There are several reasons for this situation which are readily understandable: lack of adequate information; shortage of capital to spend on items which may be regarded as of marginal importance; capital at a high marginal cost; transaction costs which may not be immediately evident to outsiders; or personal preferences. Householders may choose to synchronise energy efficiency improvements with moving house, or with major renovation or redecoration schemes. Where accommodation is not owned there may well be a reluctance to invest in insulation or equipment which has unequal returns to investing tenant and non-investing (or only partly investing) landlord. Whatever the causes, there are real problems in raising energy efficiency when a significant proportion of consumers do not have the financial means to invest in greater energy efficiency.

There are several reasons why it may be prudent to reinforce the operation of the market mechanisms including such market imperfections as inadequate pricing and information. Another reason is the growing perception in the developed industrial countries that it is sometimes – perhaps often – cheaper to invest in energy conservation than in energy supply. Compared with the cost of building new generating capacity, or bringing new sources of energy on stream, such investments are generally attractive. At the margin, saving a kilowatt-hour can cost less than generating one. Conservation has other advantages over developing new energy supplies. The technology is often simple and well-tested; planning permission is rarely needed; and the risks, both financial and technological, are low. This is not to suggest that investment in energy supply is unnecessary, far from it. Such investment is required to improve supply efficiency, upgrade existing equipment, protect the environment, and introduce new economic energy sources including alternative forms of energy. Above all, for more than 2.5 billion people who now suffer from lack of energy supplies the idea of investing in energy conservation rather than energy supply will seem grotesque.

There may also be serious market distortions, mostly within the category of institutional barriers to energy efficiency referred to earlier. The impact of prices may be blurred in various ways. Those who pay energy bills may not install the equipment which generates them. The builder of a new home or office even to modern standards frequently chooses not only the level of insulation (within building regulations which are unsatisfactorily low in most countries), but also the heating and/or cooling system. Reducing the running costs of using energy in the home or office may not increase the builder's profits. Instead his primary interests, and that of many purchasers, will be in maintaining a low initial selling price.

The structure of fuel tariffs may also be a disincentive. It is not enough to set prices overall to recover full costs. A first step is to ensure as far as possible that marginal additional purchases are supplied at the full marginal cost of production. But where marginal costs of production are very low by comparison with base-load costs and pricing, steps should be taken to discourage unnecessary consumption and waste at the margin if efficiency and conservation are accepted goals. Sophisticated tariff arrangements are therefore required, covering all sizes of customer, and the accelerated introduction of "smart" meters and cards in order that costs can be reflected accurately and clearly in charges. At present the simplest meters are not widely available in many countries.

Many of the approaches to overcoming barriers to energy efficiency require the establishment of an appropriate framework by government, and effective market regulation and support. Governments also have an important role to play in informing and communicating.

Taken collectively, and pursued systematically, these measures offer the prospect of significant improvements in energy efficiency. A first requirement is to inform customers better. One way would be for government or industry to promote greater understanding of the technologies for energy efficiency among technicians, skilled tradespeople, professional engineers and managers, and political and business leaders and executives.

From improving information to setting standards should be a short step. In the case of cars, where people should be aware of the fuel efficiency of the model they buy, minimum energy standards may not give significant extra value (although they are set by the government in the United States). In the case of appliances and even more in the case of buildings, where the effectiveness of insulation may be hard for a buyer to judge, it may be sensible to use regulation to drive up standards of energy efficiency. One measure proposed in several developed countries is to require all houses to be subject to an energy efficiency survey that would lead to an energy efficiency rating which would have to be disclosed to prospective buyers when the house is sold. More generally, governments may choose to adopt national, sectoral and industry energy efficiency targets, and programmes of achievement. Such a policy might be used to justify public investments in improving transport efficiency, such as better public transport and urban planning, better integration of road and rail transport, and greater use of high-speed trains for passenger transport. Governments may also lead by example. Governments (and local authorities) should ensure that their own offices and activities are managed to the best efficiency standards and use their purchasing power to promote energy efficiency.

Individual companies which want to improve their energy efficiency can start by appointing an energy manager, with responsibility for seeking out savings. Another approach is to conduct a regular energy audit, to establish where energy is being used and what savings are readily available.

In summary, there are many proposals on how to improve energy efficiency. In all of them, it is necessary to focus on the objective of overall economic efficiency. The question can reasonably be asked in response to most such proposals: are they consistent with free market principles? The purist would argue they are not. Many of the proposed actions involve government initiatives but it will be necessary to mobilise support at all levels of society, and rely on private firms and organisations to carry out much of the enabling action.

A more difficult question is whether government should go farther and intervene to subsidise energy efficiency. A number of schemes, some proposed, some in operation, channel government aid into investments in improving energy efficiency with a relatively long payback time. Governments may subsidise investments in energy efficiency by making access to capital for energy efficiency easier and cheaper. They may also increase research and development expenditure on energy efficiency.

Governments can also arrange for subsidy of energy efficiency investment indirectly. Under some schemes in the United States, utilities are allowed to recover the costs of investments that cut their customers' fuel bills; others go further and allow the cost of such investments to be included in a utility's rates base so that it makes a return, which increasingly is designed to be higher than the returns available on supply-side investments.

Such schemes are potentially profitable to utilities in part because of the nature of regulation to which they are subject, and have both advantages and disadvantages. They help individuals to realise energy efficiency opportunities they might otherwise not take up, and encourage some energy efficiency investment that would not otherwise have occurred. But they may not necessarily reduce overall energy demand. If energy prices remain unchanged, customers may simply find that, because their homes are better insulated, they can afford to keep the central heating turned up higher than would otherwise have been the case. Or they may simply let the utility pay for what they would have done themselves anyway.

Approaches of this nature are very culture dependent, and there is an element of compensation in the subsidy of energy efficiency for pricing policies that other countries would consider to be an inadequate reflection of long-run costs. It is not necessarily easy or appropriate to transplant methods from one country to another.

This report explicitly rejects a number of notions relevant to debates on energy efficiency. It has rejected the idea that there is a fixed relationship between energy input and economic output. Instead it has assumed significant and continuing declines in energy intensity in all four Cases examined.

This report has indicated there is large technical potential for meeting the needs and aspirations of societies with less energy use, especially in the developed countries. There are many opportunities for increasing energy efficiency at little cost and with short payback periods. There are also many opportunities for energy conservation.

Many of the really big gains from energy efficiency and conservation will, however, require time. Time for widespread asset replacement, new technologies and fuels, behavioural changes, improved pricing and policies, better information and communication. In particular, time to introduce substitutes for the services which existing energy forms and energy-using equipment provide. The realistic time-span is a matter of many generations of technology, and of many human generations. It was stated earlier that there has been a persistent tendency outside the energy industry to be overoptimistic on the speed and ease with which the technical potential for improvement and substitution can be realised and such improvements introduced. This report, by its full recognition of present inefficiencies in energy conversion, transformation and use (and the scope and technology for improvement), does not understate the potential.

Nor does this report fail to recognise the major contribution which raising energy efficiency and conservation will make to mitigating the environmental impacts of energy provision and use – the subject of the next chapter.

CHAPTER

5

ENERGY AND THE ENVIRONMENT

THE WIDER CONTEXT

Such is the current level of concern about local, regional and potential global environmental pollution in some quarters, that there is danger in getting environmental issues out of context. Without in any way wishing to understate the importance of environmental aspects, they should be seen in a broader context.

In seeking to advance into the future, and to achieve the environmental enhancement of the world, it is important to recognise the benefits which the application of commercial fossil fuels coupled with industrialisation have brought the world in so many ways over the past two centuries. A far higher economic well-being of vast numbers of people has been achieved than would otherwise have been the case. Societies have become more independent, and communication greatly improved. The material benefits, now so unevenly distributed around the globe, need to be extended.

There are great hopes around the world that the industrialisation process which gave such high material benefits to the mature industrial economies can be extended to the developing countries. These are accompanied by hopes of developing countries "leap-frogging" some of the problems associated with industrialisation, and avoiding many of the more severe environmental impacts associated with traditional energy provision, conversion and use. In the economies in transition there is the anticipation of improvements in efficiency, management, and the political and social context. As discussed in Chapter 1, advances in technology, appropriate pricing and effective competition have an important role to play here.

Nevertheless, the present situation is that even in the advanced industrial countries there are many cases of poverty causing poorer members of society to be deprived of affordable energy services, and/or spending a relatively high proportion of their income on domestic fuel and power bills. In such cases increased income support, where it is available, may increase access to energy but does not necessarily do anything to help investments in energy efficiency and hence the reduction in environmental impacts. It was stressed in Chapter 1 that over 50% of the world's present population does not have access to commercial energy, and thus are largely deprived of the services which energy provides and which are required to satisfy human needs. It was shown (Table 1.6) that in 20 out of 33 developing countries, selected mainly because they were of significant current population size, energy per capita consumption had actually declined in recent years – reflecting economic hardship. Over 50 countries in total have suffered in this way. With population expected to rise some 2.8 billion over the next 30 years, and over 90% of the growth occurring in the present developing countries, there must be real doubts whether energy per capita consumption will increase in poorer countries, and whether the basic needs of those people who already suffer deprivation will be satisfied any better in per capita terms in 2020 than they are now.

By raising energy efficiency in use, and by adopting cleaner and more efficient technology in the conversion and provision of energy, environmental impacts will certainly be ameliorated. Thus simplistic adoption of the economist's concept of opportunity costs – that the cost of having something (say a cleaner environment) is in other things foregone (for example, more energy to help meet basic needs of the chronically poor) – may mislead. Nevertheless, care is required to avoid giving the impression that privileged people are concerned for the environment because they can afford to make choices; underprivileged people who are not in the position to afford choices may not wish the privileged to make the choice for them of preferring better environmental conditions through depriving the underprivileged of energy. Whether put starkly like this, or in more complex and subtle ways, this is the essence of one of the major debates of our times: the trade-offs between seeking economic, energy efficiency and environmental gains. Gains in some areas almost always involve losses in others.

PRIORITIES

In an important sense, the foregoing discussion highlights the different priorities of the more privileged against the less privileged. No judgement is made between them, but their existence needs to be recognised and understood. Another area where priorities differ (one which comes through very clearly in the Commission's regional reports discussed in Part II), relates to local and regional environmental problems by comparison with potential global environmental issues. For developing countries the primary concern is with the local environment, regional environmental issues being secondary, and global ones a lower priority. Water quality and sanitation, housing and health care are the key issues. Air quality, and the impact energy provision and use have on air quality, is up among those key issues. By contrast, the debate on potential global climate seems relatively esoteric and long term – even to developing countries which have large numbers of people living in low-lying areas or where drought and famine are already a serious problem. For those who struggle to survive today, the evolution of carbon dioxide and methane concentrations in the atmosphere (never mind nitrous oxide and halo-carbons) over the next century understandably do not seem the top priority. Yet within 30 or so years the developing countries will be the major contributors to the problem, if it is scientifically confirmed.

THE COMMISSION'S PERSPECTIVE

The perspective of this report is a realistic appreciation of the multitude of links between the services which energy provides and people need; social, technological, financial, political and – not least – environmental. The real priorities of the poor are recognised. The unwillingness of many of the privileged to change their behavioural patterns is also recognised. But what is the Commission's overall stance on the environmental issues surrounding energy provision and use?

The supply and use of energy has both positive and negative impacts. Pollution is the principal negative aspect with local effects, such as the smoke from traffic and factory chimneys; regional effects such as acid rain and oil spills; and global effects, of which the main one could be the effect of greenhouse gases such as carbon dioxide and methane (some of which are emitted by fossil fuel provision and use) on climate.

Regional and Local Pollution

Reference was made earlier to regional and local pollution. Such pollution arising from energy provision and use includes acid rain deposition (sulphur dioxide emissions), city smogs (arising from particulate, sulphur and nitrogen oxides emissions from power stations, other chimneys and vehicles) and the burning of fuels in the home. The record of success in tackling local emissions is mixed: in London, the Ruhr and Tokyo substantial improvements have occurred over the years. In Los Angeles, Mexico City and Athens much remains to be achieved.

Local pollution is particularly acute in and close to the urban areas of many developing countries. Energy provision and use certainly makes a contribution to environmental degradation, especially of air quality and, to some degree, to pollution of the land and water also. The continued prevalence of leaded gasoline has been recorded in high levels of airborne lead in New Delhi, Kuala Lumpur, Harare and other developing areas. The high average age of vehicles and their generally poor state of maintenance and repair (especially of buses and public vehicles), and urban congestion raise emissions. UNEP has estimated the costs in lost time and additional petrol consumed as US$1 billion per annum for congestion in Bangkok alone (plus a further US$1 billion per annum for medical bills and other effects). Power plants and industrial processes are frequently older and neither efficient nor managed effectively, adding to particulate and other emissions. Biomass burning, especially in the home, causes severe respiratory problems in rural areas and the poorer quarters of urban areas.

Nevertheless, by comparison with the other causes of local pollution, energy provision and use while a contributor is still a minor player in most developing countries. According to UNEP, up to 50% of solid waste generated within urban areas is left uncollected in developing countries. More specifically, the World Bank has reported that 80% of refuse in Dar es Salaam, and two-thirds in Karachi, go uncollected.

According to the World Health Organisation over one billion people do not have uncontaminated water. Over 1.7 billion people do not have access to sanitation services – in Latin America as little as 2% of sewage receives any treatment according to the World Bank. The proportion of urban dwellers without sanitary facilities has remained static over the past 2 decades, according to UNEP, at nearly 30%.

The availability of normal-standard dwellings has actually deteriorated sharply over the same period according to UNEP. The percentage of households unable to afford such dwellings in selected cities (eg Cairo, Manila, Bangkok, etc) has risen from 35% to 75%. Overcrowding, sub-standard housing and squatter settlements have proliferated. About one-third of the urban population in developing countries live in urban slums and shanty towns. The number rose from about 200 million people in 1970 to some 450 million in 1990.

These developments, or lack of them, are reflected in chronic sickness, high infant mortality, undernourishment, poor education and unemployment. Over 35 000 children die daily in the developing world. About 75% die from pneumonia, and about 17% from whooping cough or measles.

Acute respiratory infections in children and women have as a major contributor the particulate released when wood and animal dung are used to fuel traditional stoves. The World Health Organisation has estimated that up to 500 million people (most of them women and children) are exposed to levels of particulate pollution ranging from 3 to 140 times the maximum recommended level.

This is the real world context in which the Commission's various regional reports have been set. It is not surprising that most regions, and all regions containing developing countries, have stressed that local and regional pollution is accorded far higher priority than global environmental concerns.

Nevertheless, within the context of what is economically and politically practicable greater efforts should be made to reduce local and regional pollution arising from energy provision and use by striving for improved efficiency; cleaner fuels, processes and appliances; full-cost pricing and tighter regulation; more effective competition; and better information and education. These measures are both easier for richer developed countries to take and a continuation of what most are already doing. They would, however, serve as a useful goal for countries with fewer financial resources, as they would reduce other health and social welfare expenditures.

Measures appropriate to reducing local and regional pollution are often, though certainly not always (due to reduced efficiency, higher CO_2 emissions, etc), also appropriate to tackling fears of potential global climate change.

Potential Global Climate Change

As already indicated, the Commission's regional studies indicate that global environmental issues do not yet receive high priority in developing countries – indeed they are very low down the list of current concerns. Yet within the next 30 years the developing countries will have become the main contributors to global pollution problems if the hypotheses about global pollution currently fashionable are proven scientifically.

Carbon dioxide and methane, the two greenhouse gases primarily focused upon in discussions of the enhanced global warming hypothesis (or potential global climate change as this report has chosen to call it), have been rising for the past two centuries. Attention focuses primarily upon carbon dioxide as it is believed, by a number of leading specialists, to be the most important contributor to man-made radiative-forcing changes. Nevertheless, there is recognition that there is probably a missing carbon dioxide sink, totalling around 100 gigatonnes of carbon, which may reflect increasing sequestration of carbon by trees and plants as atmospheric CO_2 levels have risen in recent decades. It is also suggested there is an additional large northern ocean sink (the debate is summarised in E.T. Sundquist: "The Global Carbon

Dioxide Budget", *Science*, American Association for the Advancement of Science, 12 February 1993, p 939). The significance of carbon sources and sinks can be gathered from Table 5.1, which though close to such consensus as currently exists, represents the estimates of only a few scientists and is surrounded by uncertainty.

If carbon emissions from fossil fuel combustion could be satisfactorily captured and reabsorbed, as the oceans are believed to achieve fully and soil/forests largely achieve (ie their natural carbon cycles are balanced), then debates over the future of fossil fuel demand would take on a different dimension (Figure 5.1). As it is, the huge magnitudes of non-atmospheric sinks and natural carbon emissions by comparison with carbon emissions from energy use suggest a more cautious evaluation of causes, effects and remedies than is often advanced. When sources and sinks are so finely balanced, it may be true that the small net anthropogenic contribution from fossil fuel combustion is sufficient to tip the balance. Alternatively, other forces may be at work (temporarily or permanently).

It must be recalled, however, that not all regions of the world face potential global climate change with trepidation. The Russian Federation, much of China (18% of its land area is permafrost), Scandinavia, Canada and Alaska would experience milder climatic conditions. Although thawing of the permafrost would create severe instability for existing man-made structures, and substantial quantities of trapped methane would be released into the atmosphere (at a global warming of 2°C the IPCC Impacts Assessments Group believed the tundra could disappear from the north of Eurasia), agricultural conditions and usable precipitation would improve. The IPCC Impacts Assessment on Climatic Change "Report of Working Group II,

	Sinks	Sources		
		Emissions	Absorbed	Net
Atmosphere	750	—	—	—
Forests	550	102*	100	+2
Soil	1 500			
Surface Ocean	1 000	90	92	−2
Deep Ocean & Sediment	38 000	—	—	—
Fossil Fuel Combustion (net)	0	6	0	+6
Other Anthropogenic	0	2*	2	0**
Total	41 800	200	194	+6**

*   Deforestation is believed to create some 2 GtC of carbon emissions per annum currently.
** Most estimates reveal unexplained differences in net anthropogenic annual carbon emissions, and hence net annual accumulation (which is believed to be around 3.5 GtC).
Source: IPCC "Climate Change", 1990. Fig. 1.1, p.8, updated

Table 5.1   Carbon Sinks and Sources (GtC)

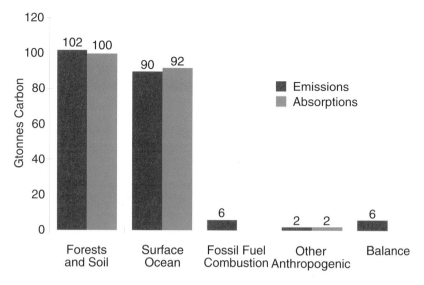

Figure 5.1 Carbon Sources

1990" has indicated that cereal production could increase in Northern Europe, and that potential productivity of high and mid-latitudes is likely to increase generally due to the prolonged growing season. In short, it is many of the now poorest developing countries that have the most to fear from potential global climate change – because they lie in tropical latitudes, are often afflicted by drought and famine already, or by inundations of coastal zones and deltas.

It is not the WEC's role to take a scientific view on such matters, except to consider the realistic context into which such possibilities can be placed from the standpoint of energy provision and use. The Intergovernmental Panel on Climate Change has conducted its own scientific assessment, setting out the key uncertainties, and its main findings as of 1992 are included in Appendix D.

Given the present large bounds of scientific uncertainty it is important to recognise that:

- Human fossil fuel burning accounts for 3% of total global annual carbon emissions (the emissions from soil, forests and oceans account for 96%, although each of these also provides a substantial carbon sink).

- Human emissions of methane from coal, natural gas and oil use are less than 20% of total global annual methane emissions, less than natural emissions from wetlands, and possibly less than those from either enteric fermentation or rice paddies.

- Nitrous oxide emissions from human activity are at worst half those from natural emissions. At best stationary and mobile sources of anthropogenic combustion account for one-eighth of the lowest IPCC estimates of natural emissions, and at worst between 8% and 20% of natural emissions.

- Even in the worst cases – carbon monoxide and nitrogen oxides – anthropogenic emissions from fossil fuel use are less than half total annual global emissions of these gases.

Fossil fuel combustion probably accounts for the major part of anthropogenic carbon dioxide emissions. Hitherto, mankind has made no effort to balance emissions by enhanced absorption. The large increases in atmospheric concentrations of carbon dioxide and methane over the past two centuries have coincided with major industrialisation, agricultural changes, population growth, and fossil fuel use. The Intergovernmental Panel on Climate Change scientific assessment "Climate Change (1990)" reported that atmospheric concentrations have risen over the past 200 years as follows: carbon dioxide from 280 ppmv to an estimated 353 ppmv in 1990; methane from 0.8 ppmv to an estimated 1.72 ppmv. Nevertheless, as the IPCC scientific assessment of "Climate Change (1992)" put it: "the unequivocal detection of the enhanced greenhouse effect from observations is not likely for a decade or more".

. ppmv = parts per million by volume.

In examining sources and sinks of these gases it is necessary to consider other possible causes. For a start, cement production and land-use changes need to be examined. The latter have been going on for many centuries, but particularly over the past two centuries in response to population growth and movement. Both are significant causes of net anthropogenic carbon dioxide emissions in addition to fossil fuel combustion. Rice production is a significant source of methane – as is the reliance of much of the human population on ruminant domesticated animals. The rubbish produced by human activity, and which goes into landfill sites, is also a major source of methane production and leakage unless effectively captured. Inputs of nitrogen through commercial fertilisers and nitrogen-fixing leguminous crops potentially increase emissions of nitrous oxide (N_2O) from soils, and nitrous oxide is a greenhouse gas. The nitrogen fixed annually by combustion plus the manufacture of fertilisers is probably about half the volume produced by plants naturally, and nitrogen in the stratosphere has a crucial impact on ambient ozone. However, the role of fossil fuel combustion in nitrous oxide emissions is very minor (much less than once thought) and thus other sources should be concentrated upon.

One of the problems facing both scientists and policy-makers is the uncertainty of the various linkages and their net impacts. In Chapter 1 reference was made to the role that air traffic movements may have in this context, as jet fuel combustion leads to formation of NO by "fixing" atmospheric N_2 and O_2 (as well as carbon dioxide and carbon monoxide). This has led to deep concerns about the possible effects if supersonic air travel was to expand.

Nylon production and nitric acid production are other sources of nitrous oxides. Volcanic eruptions (emitting large volumes of sulphur dioxide) and biomass burning are major sources of stratospheric and tropospheric aerosols, and the role of halo-carbons as greenhouse gases and stratospheric ozone depleters was the subject of the 1986 Montreal Protocol and its 1990 London Amendments. The purpose in mentioning these wider sources of greenhouse gas emissions, and wider range of greenhouse gases, is that if global climate change is occurring due to anthropogenic greenhouse gas emissions then comprehensive policy measures will need to be taken, and sensible precautionary steps should be introduced now. But sound precautionary steps and comprehensive policies should not be confined to fossil fuel combustion. If global climate change is such a serious issue then all anthropogenic sources must come under scrutiny and be curbed. Action will need to cover cement and nylon manufacture, agricultural practices, reliance on the products of domesticated ruminant animals and on rice, and land-use changes generally.

Nevertheless, it is likely that the pattern of primary energy mix will change only modestly between 1990 and 2020. While non-fossil fuel sources are likely to grow at a faster rate than fossil sources, this report's examination of a variety of Cases suggests that the absolute figures will show large increases in the volume of fossil fuels in most of the more likely Cases – a total of 3.0 Gtoe in an overall increase of 4.6 Gtoe in Case B. Even the most rapid development of new renewable energy resources envisaged (Case C) results in only a 12% contribution of these renewables to primary energy supply in 2020. In the absence of substantial government support and incentives, multi-nationally, the figure is likely to be a lower percentage than this. Obviously, the scope for much greater change over a longer period is larger.

Carbon dioxide emissions globally are likely to rise over the next 30 years. For Case A, which is dominated by energy growth in the present developing countries, carbon dioxide emissions could rise 97% in the 30 years to 2020. This conclusion underlines the strategic dilemma.

	1990	2020							
		A		B_1		B		C	
	GtC	GtC	%	GtC	%	GtC	%	GtC	%
Fossil Fuels	5.9	11.5	+95	10.2	+73	8.4	+42	6.3	+6

Note: Other anthropogenic CO_2 emissions – eg from cement, nylon, fertiliser manufacture etc. – are omitted, as are all other greenhouse gas emissions.

Table 5.2   Carbon Dioxide Emissions from Fossil Fuel Combustion in 1990, 2020 and % change from 1990

Economic growth and commercial energy provision are vital to alleviate poverty in the developing countries. If the overwhelming bulk of that commercial energy provision is fossil fuel based, and if fossil fuel combustion is the cause of unacceptable global warming and climate change, then the developing countries face the continued struggle of huge numbers of the unacceptably poor and deprived.

Table 5.2 illustrates how annual emissions of carbon dioxide from fossil fuel combustion will evolve in the four Cases examined.

It has been assumed in all four Cases that annual CO_2 emissions from fossil fuel combustion in the OECD area by 2020 will be at or (Case C) below 1990 levels.

Given the very challenging assumptions built into the four Cases and particularly into Cases B and C, it can be readily perceived that to contain the increase in global annual carbon dioxide emissions from fossil fuel combustion 1990–2020 to only 40% or so will not be easy (Case B). To curb carbon dioxide emissions to the extent of holding them by 2020 to around 1990 levels will be an extremely tough challenge which at present seems unrealistic. Only Case C outlines such a possibility, and then only with the most challenging assumptions of policy and behavioural changes and rapid technology innovation and diffusion.

If there is real substance in the linkage between anthropogenic greenhouse gas emissions and global climate change, and if in particular fossil fuel combustion bears the major responsibility for increases in atmospheric concentrations and emissions of CO_2 which could have major climatic effects, then there are few signs that the severity of the challenges are recognised. Neither energy consumers in general nor energy policymakers are gearing up quickly enough and sufficiently to meet them.

It should be noted that the results of Case A to 2020 (and beyond – see Epilogue) are broadly in line with the IPCC's Scenario IS92A, which is about the middle of the range of IPCC scenarios (see IPCC: "Climate Change 1992: The Supplementary Report to The IPCC Scientific Assessment", pp.76–83). However, the IPCC's lower energy demand scenarios are predicated on the UN's low global population projection of 6.4 billion by the year 2100 – widely regarded as unrealistically low. Thus this Commission has three Cases with illustrative energy demand projections well below those of the IPCC on comparable world population assumptions, reflecting in addition the very ambitious declines in energy intensities which at least two of the Cases assume.

The essential points are that even with precautionary steps being taken, rises of global annual CO_2 emissions from fossil fuel combustion are inevitable for many years to come; atmospheric concentrations of CO_2 will rise for at least several decades; and some rises in global mean temperature and sea level are unavoidable however much action is taken. Without effective, internationally co-ordinated and immediate action getting under way the scale of the task of tackling potential global climate change will grow and become ever more daunting. Adaptation must start now.

It is recognised that given the uncertainties surrounding the science of potential global climate damage (especially in understanding the full impact of its various feedback loops, though even basic data on greenhouse gas sources and sinks are far from perfect), and thus the difficulty in calculating the benefits of taking early action, there are problems in justifying precautionary policies and actions. Nevertheless, it is necessary to take precautionary action and, because of the uncertainties concerning benefits, this is more appropriate than attempting an orthodox cost-benefit approach.

It cannot be justifiably argued that the existing amount of pollution – whether emissions which may have global impacts, or those having more clearly understood regional and local impacts – is "economically optimal", in the sense that the costs of reducing pollution further exceed the identifiable benefits. If this were the case an economic cost-benefit appraisal might well be appropriate. The balance of costs and benefits would reflect society's judgement about the value of further reductions in pollution, but would also be consistent with continuing or increasing emissions which caused environmental damage. This is because the costs of tackling these emissions outweighed the benefits to be gained. Reference is sometimes made to the concept of "opportunity costs" – by spending money on tackling emissions some other benefits will be sacrificed. The problem with greenhouse gas emissions, particularly, is that their damaging effects have not yet been identified with precision or certainty, yet potentially catastrophic real damage from their polluting effects and consequential climatic changes may already be occurring and getting worse. But these damaging effects cannot yet be reflected in a cost-benefit calculus.

Given the as yet unknown consequences of continued and increasing greenhouse gas emissions and impacts, the ability to ascertain the "economically optimal" level of emissions and their mitigation, as required by a cost-benefit approach, is impossible.

As a matter of simple prudence, therefore, action based on the precautionary principle is advocated.

This stance is based partly upon the work of the Intergovernmental Panel on Climate Change, and in particular on its report "Climate Change 1992 – The Supplementary Report to the IPCC Scientific Assessment", which is a balanced account of the facts, arguments and continuing uncertainties. The precautionary measures should be based upon the following points:

- Intensified research on an international basis is required to reduce the recognised scientific uncertainties and improve the climate models in use, and the efforts of the IPCC in this regard are warmly supported.

- There is a need for rational abatement and adaptation strategies, and a key abatement strategy is the raising of energy efficiency wherever justified on cost/benefit grounds and increasing conservation.

- Adaptation strategies are required now, because if the concern with enhanced global warming and its climatic effects is well-founded then the world is already past the point where it can be avoided.

- The longer action is delayed the higher the costs of abatement and adaptation will become, if the concerns are well-founded, because of the long life times and cumulative effects of increasing atmospheric concentrations of some of the greenhouse gases.

- Government involvement is required, otherwise action will not be taken with the necessary speed and confidence in the results. Action will be required on a broad front, and although economic instruments are preferred to regulation, as a general rule historical experience confirms that the enactment of legislation has often been highly effective.

- Most of the precautionary measures under consideration here can be justified on other grounds: improving efficiency, conserving supplies of finite resources, and mitigating local and regional environmental impacts.

- Underlying these various precautionary measures should be the recognition that policy-makers and energy suppliers are primarily seeking to provide energy services – heating, mobility, etc – and a continual search is required for better and alternative ways of providing these services.

ENVIRONMENTAL REGULATION

The Commission recognises that uncertainty works both ways: on those who demand early action despite uncertainty, and those who adopt a *laissez-faire* approach because of uncertainty. Hence this report favours the middle course of acceptance of some recognised costs despite the uncertainties, in keeping with a prudent "precautionary" strategy. This strategy recognises the existence of potential environmental benefits arising from precautionary action involving real economic costs.

Trade-offs between different costs and benefits are accepted, where they can be ascertained, but within the context of placing resources where they yield the best results – not in response to arbitrary global target-setting. Nevertheless, at the present state of knowledge of some environmental issues this is *not* a "no regrets" policy. Costs will be incurred which may not be recouped in benefits. This is something which world society should recognise and accept.

The environment is traditionally a field which has been left to government regulation, the private benefactor or special interest groups. If complaints about local, regional and global pollution have justification then it can hardly be claimed that these combined efforts have been wholly satisfactory or sufficient. Indeed a report prepared in an era when "command and control" systems have been dismantled (in whole or in part) in many countries, would be odd to demand that environmental policy should be dominated by a "command and control" approach. Similarly, government regulations have often been ineffectual, contradictory, and even counter-effective as they have impacted on the environment and this cautions against over-reliance on a regulatory approach. Environmental policy should be oriented towards efficient, cost-effective responses backed by regulatory measures or taxes where necessary. Thus policy should encourage appropriate technological innovation and clean-up procedures, examine ways in which common law and property rights can be amended to assist environmental protection, introduce earmarked taxes (ie where the tax has a specific environmental goal and the revenue therefrom is used for specific environmental purposes, so that the taxpayer can see cause and effect and it is revenue neutral to the Exchequer), and experiment with economic instruments for environmental protection and enhancement (such as tradable property rights, emission permits, and emission reduction credits).

While several of these approaches are necessarily at the experimental stage, and where unsuccessful such experiments should be rapidly amended or withdrawn, their orientation is clear: the weighing of costs and benefits either explicitly or by imputation. The regulatory approach is fraught with a number of difficulties. The regulations themselves need the most careful drafting and application. The honesty, efficiency and thoroughness of regulators and other bureaucrats varies within and between countries and cultures. There are dangers in allowing exemptions for major polluters, or overlooking the regulatory breaches of many minor players in the pursuit of major companies in the public eye. There is a tendency to seek out a low common denominator in setting standards, and in consequence to discourage higher standards and faster progress than the regulatory norm. There is danger in target-setting, especially global target-setting, when what is required is that scarce resources are applied where they yield the best returns. A grave responsibility rests upon governments and regulatory authorities.

Much of the past and present environmental degradation is due (often unintentionally) to the activities of government and of official policy. It is imperative, therefore, for regulatory decisions to be as soundly based as possible. The Commission therefore advocates a greater reliance upon economic instruments and warns against over-reliance on a plethora of regulations and bureaucratic intervention. The best mechanisms and decision-making processes should be used, and there should be transparency of decision making coupled with independent peer group assessment of the supporting scientific and economic studies.

IMPACT ON THE VARIOUS FORMS OF ENERGY

How far environmental concerns and policies impact upon demand for the various forms of energy will be a function of many different forces. Among the more important are likely to be growth in scientific understanding of potential global climate change and its effects, the speed at which the best available technology is diffused and new technology becomes available to tackle those environmental problems for which no remedy is yet apparent, the availability of alternative forms of energy and fuels, and time. Given that no remedy yet exists for capturing and reabsorbing carbon dioxide emissions, fears of global climate change are clearly liable to have a significant impact on the role of coal and oil. In the first instance this is because of their relative contribution to carbon dioxide emissions.

These relative contributions worked through changing fuel mixes within different total energy use assumptions can make large differences in the carbon emissions which result. In the four Cases examined in Chapters 2 and 3 the range is clear. The global use of solid fuels in Case A by 2020 is 4.9 Gtoe, but in Case C only 2.1 Gtoe. This latter figure is

Coal 1.0	Oil 0.78	Natural Gas 0.6

Table 5.3 Relative Contributions of the Fossil Fuels to CO_2 Emissions for Comparable Units of Energy

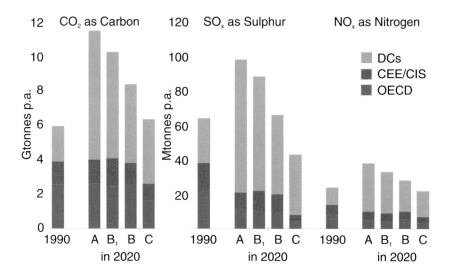

Figure 5.2 Emissions from Fossil Fuel Burning

lower than solid fuel use in 1990, when it was 2.3 Gtoe. Global use of liquid fossil fuels by 2020 in Case C is 2.9 Gtoe, about the same as 1990 levels. Thus carbon emissions from fossil fuel combustion in Case C in the year 2020 are virtually identical with those in 1990, despite substantial increases in natural gas use (Figure 5.2).

In the absence of major advances in technology permitting the reabsorption of carbon dioxide, of which there are – as yet – no signs, coal is the most disadvantaged fuel with oil in second place. However, given the anticipated major increases in global energy demand it can be seen that even natural gas, despite an inbuilt advantage, produces as much carbon as coal at a demand level only two-thirds higher.

Coal is also indicted because of its relatively high contribution to emissions of sulphur and nitrogen oxides as well as particulates. However, as previously discussed, modern technology can go a long way to mitigate these effects. The problem is that this technology is not widely enough applied. Oil is also under severe pressure because of the increasing demands of the transport sector, and emissions of nitrous oxides (nitrogen oxides and volatile organic compounds from road vehicles) which are the main components of city smog or tropospheric ozone.

Yet if a level playing field is introduced, whereby all environmental impacts are fully costed, then nuclear power and, to varying degrees, the different newer forms of renewable energy will also incur costs: relating to operational and technical safety, and the treatment of radioactive wastes, in the case of nuclear; and the variety of problems raised by "new" renewables discussed in Chapter 3. These environmental concerns will have to be carefully weighed against the local, regional and global pollution associated with fossil fuel use.

A particular unknown is the impact of future specific taxes and regulations on demand. In general terms, there is growing recognition that if carbon taxes were to be introduced to limit carbon emissions (and it should be questioned why just carbon if other greenhouse gases are indicted), their level would have to be significantly higher than usually predicated to have major and early impact. In terms of conventionally measured gross domestic product the costs of such measures to constrain carbon emissions have been the subject of widely varying estimates. These quickly amount to between 2% and 5% of conventionally measured GDP, and to a present value of implied consumption losses between US$1.25 trillion and US$5 trillion depending upon basic assumptions. These assumptions include more or less challenging carbon reduction goals, different time discounting factors and different periods forward.

CHAPTER

6

THE REALITIES AT 2020

In this chapter the realities with which the world is likely to be faced by 2020 are recapitulated.

Global energy demand is likely to have grown, from 8.8 Gtoe in 1990 to between about 11 and about 17 Gtoe in 2020 depending upon the various forces at work. The more likely prospects fall within the range of about 13.5 Gtoe to 16 Gtoe. Renewable forms of energy in total will probably account for little more than 20% of primary energy supply. This figure includes traditional as well as modern biomass, and both large and small hydro. "New" renewables (which exclude large hydro and traditional biomass) might account for, at most, about 10%. Even this expansion of "new" renewable energy availability will require major governmental support in many countries to ensure its accelerated development. Without government support, new renewables may only account for about 5% of primary energy supply.

The anticipated global energy demand rise is driven by various forces:

Upward Driving Forces
  World Population Growth
  Drive to Satisfy Basic Needs
  Need for Services Energy Provides
  Material Expectations and Desires

Other Driving Forces

Environmental Concerns
Shortages of Traditional Biomass
Supply Concerns for Oil and Natural Gas
Availability
Real Energy Price Rises (for Oil and
Natural Gas Particularly)
Greater Energy Efficiency
Wider Implementation of Existing Best Technology
Drive for Dissemination of Modern Efficient
Technology
Shift to Full-Cost Pricing
Balancing of Costs and Benefits (where Feasible)
Precautionary Action (where Science and Benefits
Uncertain)
Preference for Economic Instruments
Continuing Dependence on Fossil Fuels
Accelerated Development and Diffusion of
Renewable Energy
Safe Exploitation of Nuclear
Fundamental Changes in Underlying
Technology

These forces are to be seen within the broadest social context. Energy is not simply a matter of demand and supply, but of services which meet basic needs and promote social development. There will be numerous other forces at work, many of them seeking to offset the upward momentum of energy demand and reducing the environmental impact of energy provision and use.

Although energy demand growth rates will moderate, and CO_2 emissions from fossil fuel combustion in the OECD area stabilise in all Cases considered to the year 2020, the overwhelming impact of some 2.8 billion more people in the world and a desperate striving to satisfy basic needs will be the fundamental imperative.

The world will probably have around 8 billion people by 2020, rather than today's 5.4 billion. More people quite possibly with even less energy per head in hundreds of millions of cases. More people competing for less finite energy available – especially oil and natural gas. More people seeking alternative energy supplies – but will they have the money and other resources required to access them? More people looking to effective policies, financing and technology, and institutional change to satisfy their requirements. More people putting pressure on international relationships, communications, movements and trade. It is a paradox that, while global energy demand is likely to rise substantially, it is also likely that hundreds of millions will be little better off than their parents and grandparents are today.

There is simply not the time, within little more than a quarter century to 2020, to change this trajectory markedly. Supply concerns, as oil and natural gas supplies are drawn down, will grow as more countries and far greater numbers of people become dependent upon imported energy and supply lines get longer. As many of the remaining supply sources will be in countries or areas perceived as unsettled in geopolitical terms, these concerns will be exacerbated. Energy prices are expected to rise and there will be greater pressure to develop alternative supplies, especially indigenous and renewable energy sources and, probably, nuclear energy.

There will be growing awareness that the price of energy has in general terms been too cheap, and that the years since 1985 have been a period of remission since the period of warning 1973–1980. The desire to increase efficiency in energy provision and use, as well as to mitigate environmental impacts, will encourage the adoption of full-cost pricing. Such full-cost pricing will incorporate externalities such as social and environmental costs of energy provision and use. It will draw on orthodox cost-benefit analysis where this is appropriate because both costs and benefits are quantifiable. Where this is not feasible (generally where potential global climate change issues are at stake, and more locally where environmental assets are claimed to be incapable of meaningful valuation because "priceless") then prudence requires adoption of "the precautionary principle" to preserve environmental assets and prevent degradation or further deterioration.

But radical institutional changes will be required to ensure that governments create the right conditions for investment, whereby the resources of the private sector may be attracted. The scale and nature of the problems faced require the harnessing of all available resources and facilitating mechanisms to maximising effect.

The role of governments in the past – whether in creating and promoting effective competition, in proper pricing, or in environmental protection – has often left much to be desired. There is an important role for governments to fulfil in each of these areas if they set about their tasks in the correct way. Much will depend in the future upon wise and effective policies; the willingness of energy consumers to shift their behaviour patterns and accept the need to pay higher prices for energy and energy-related services; and upon technological innovation and diffusion. If technology is to perform its proper role then the conditions must be right for it to prosper and be rewarded, and the necessary time must be allowed. The right framework having been set by governments, the emphasis will pass to industry to innovate and disseminate the appropriate technologies, facilitated by the relevant financial and commercial institutions. The emphasis, in short, should be reliance upon the market system once framework conditions are satisfied.

Improved technology has a powerful role to play across the board – on the various forms of energy (coal, oil, natural gas, nuclear, "new" renewables, alternative fuels, hydrogen), their provision and use (including the plant, equipment, appliances and vehicles which use them). Much can be achieved in a century; not very much in a quarter century. That is one of the realities which will be apparent in 2020 to those who observe carefully. It is, of course, a reality today. But whereas in recent decades technological innovation has largely been driven by military and space research, the future is more problematic. Shifting geopolitical conditions, moves towards privatisation and shorter time-horizons, and reduced emphasis on basic research may slow the pace of innovation during the next decade or two.

The role that modern efficient technology can play in satisfying basic needs, advancing social development, reducing environmental pollution and promoting improvements in international relations has been stressed. This role cannot be realistically fulfilled by relying on technology imports by countries weighed down by lack of finance and by external indebtedness. Transfers of technology on a greatly expanded scale, based upon the principle of mutual interest, will be required. It will be in the general interest to raise efficiency in energy use and to reduce its environmental impacts; to reduce energy demand and constrain future energy demand growth; to reduce the pressure on finite energy supplies; and to provide headroom in the search for and development of alternative energy supplies. Nevertheless, there are strict limits on charity: countries wishing to receive such technology will need to create the conditions necessary to attract it and the finance to pay for it. The emphasis will need to be on incentives, not on subsidies.

The realities suggest that the international energy scene, and many national energy situations, will nevertheless be even more difficult in 2020 than they were in 1990. They will become even more stressful in the decades after 2020, unless action starts now to meet these future eventualities. However vague and remote these prospects may seem to many, the number of human generations needed to develop and diffuse the required technological innovations – each to several generations of new technology if they are to be successful – will be upwards of three. This means that what is started now will probably not reach its full flowering until the third quarter of the next century.

Over a realistic time-frame, with supportive and effective policies, much can still be achieved – especially in the areas of raising efficiency in energy provision and use; installing cleaner ways of processing and using fossil fuels; accelerating the development of "new" renewable forms of energy; seeking the generally acceptable use of nuclear energy; and in discouraging the more wasteful and environmentally harmful uses of energy.

REGIONAL
PERCEPTIONS
AND
PRIORITIES

CHAPTER

7

COMMON AND DIVERSE REGIONAL CONCLUSIONS

This part of the global report summarises the key perceptions, findings and proposals of the nine regional reports covering the world which were prepared for this study. The full regional reports were published at the 15th WEC Congress held in Madrid in September 1992. This chapter presents the regional conclusions and is followed by nine chapters summarising the detailed reports received from each region of the Commission. These are presented without major editorial amendment as they represent the views of the regions themselves. However, some additional comments are made in parentheses where appropriate.

It is stressed that the regional groups were asked to concentrate on the period to the year 2020. Some of the findings for that period may well not seem consistent with perceptions about a longer period, to say 2100. For instance, the supply availability of oil and natural gas may properly be regarded as adequate for 30 or 50 years, and this perception may well drive policy for longer than very far distant considerations would dictate.

Where feasible, the regional working groups were multi-disciplinary in their representation in order to reflect the broad context within which energy issues should be seen.

Each report does not necessarily represent a consensus of all the views to be found in each region. Although the regional co-ordinators consulted widely, in the end they had to take a view based on the results of this consultation; and many of the topics considered are subject to controversy, both within regions and globally. Not surprisingly, therefore, there were areas where regions disagreed with each other (in the main the areas of disagreement referred to well-known differences between the developed and developing countries). Moreover, for reasons of time and space or because of political sensitivity, not all regional reports dealt with all of the issues apparent to an informed reader. For example, little was said concerning nuclear reactors in Central and Eastern Europe and the Commonwealth of Independent States, some of which fail to meet adequate safety standards. There is controversy over whether, in relation to RBMK reactors in particular, necessary action is being taken either quickly enough or extensively enough.

Nonetheless, the Commission regards the regional reports as a valuable and authoritative input to this book and into the energy debate.

THE WORLD REGIONS

The eight original regions and their composition, as originally defined, are set out in Appendix A. However, Central and Eastern Europe and the ex-USSR were reported on separately, to produce nine regional reports in all. For the purposes of this report, the fifteen ex-USSR States are described as the Commonwealth of Independent States of the former-USSR (usually shortened to Commonwealth of Independent States).

The eight regions are:
- North America;
- Latin America and the Caribbean;
- Western Europe;
- Central and Eastern Europe, the Commonwealth of Independent States, Georgia and the Baltic Countries;
- Middle East and North Africa;
- Sub-Saharan Africa;
- South Asia;
- The Pacific.

The world, of course, contains countries in every state of development, and as explained in Chapter 1 it would be impossible to classify them with any precision. The terms used here are a standard and convenient shorthand, and inevitably result in oversimplification and distortion at times.

PLURALITY

For the most part the regions have been defined as containing countries which exhibit a broadly similar socio-political structure. Partly in consequence, they also have similar energy situations and problems. The main exception to this is the Pacific region, which contains an extreme diversity of countries – three OECD countries (Japan, Australia and New Zealand); rapidly developing and industrialising countries; centrally planned economies, most notably China; some less developed countries; and finally the Pacific islands. Sub-Saharan Africa also exhibits considerable diversity.

As might be expected, whilst the regional analyses show areas where the findings are in full agreement, there are also some very diverse characteristics and problems. It is clear that the circumstances, culture, skills and preferences of different countries have individual characteristics. Thus whilst the Commission's work can derive indications for policy and action from the regional and global analysis, their implementation should be subject to the decisions and judgement of individual countries.

MATTERS OF COMMON AGREEMENT

There are matters of common agreement among the regions, notwithstanding their different characteristics and problems.

Economic Growth

First, there is universal support for giving priority to economic growth, for many reasons: to meet the aspiration of peoples for a better standard of living and to relieve poverty; to provide the conditions in which population levels can eventually adjust to permit sustainable harmony with the environment; to provide the wealth needed to give adequate protection to the environment; to provide the wealth needed to allow investment in more efficient methods of energy production and use and to help energy conservation.

However, support for economic growth does not imply support for any particular life-style, and it certainly does not imply that present life-styles, especially of the rich nations, will continue or be relevant to all. Rather it implies the creation of wealth which allows people to have a choice of action, and so to have a greater ability to control their destiny. A number of regions have pointed out that where people exist in poverty, they do not have the luxury of such choice or control. The objective must be to provide the means to make the services which energy provides available at an affordable cost to those who need them.

Coupled with economic growth, regions stressed the need to remain competitive with other regions.

Adequate Energy Supplies

Adequate energy supplies are considered vital to support economic growth and to meet aspirations for a higher standard of living.

The Market Economy

There was general support for the principles of the market economy. However, this support was not of a simplistic nature. Markets always operate within a framework which is set by society, and in practice a totally free market does not exist in modern societies. In some countries a quite different approach continues to be pursued.

For the most part, the market framework is set out in legislation which varies from country to country but in general covers the following fields: child labour laws, trades union activities and employment conditions, the fiscal context (eg VAT, excise duties, company tax and more exotic items such as depletion or environmental taxes), planning requirements, building regulations, competition policy, contractual terms, environmental consid- erations, minimum efficiency standards, safety and licensing requirements, anti-fraud and public disclosure controls, the governance and supervision of companies, and international agreements such as GATT.

Governments also have more informal duties than simply setting the statutory framework, such as providing leadership and information in society. Societies often have difficulties in understanding and coping with the consequences of operating the market mechanism: this is evident in those societies which are now making the transition to this way of operation, but stresses also arise in the long established market economies.

The role of governments in a market economy may therefore be summed up as setting the statutory framework within which the market works, removing impediments to the efficient operation of the market, ensuring that market operation is consistent with wider societal objec- tives such as protection of the environment, disseminating information, and permitting the widest practicable understanding of relevant issues throughout society.

The Role of Technology

There was full agreement that continued technological development is vital for the satisfaction of peoples' aspirations for a better life, and for meeting their needs for energy services efficiently while protecting the environment. In general, the evidence is that technological requirements are met by the competitive market system. However, there are some areas where the regions perceived a role for government because the market is not regarded as working effectively. This is particularly the case in the field of long-term research and development. The main challenges which need to be tackled urgently concern technological transfer.

The Environment

All regions recognised the growth of environmental concerns and the importance of environmental protection. Overwhelmingly, the priority is to improve local environmental conditions and to reduce local pollution. For most regions, global pollution dangers have a much lower priority. All but one of the regions put climate change near the bottom of their list of priorities.

Energy Efficiency

All regions recognised the importance of improving energy efficiency. The motivations are first, to safeguard the environment; and secondly, to improve economic efficiency. Thus improved energy efficiency was not supported by the regions in the period to 2020 because of fears of an ultimate shortage of energy resources, and it would not be supported if uneconomic.

Electricity Use

It was generally recognised that the share of energy supply provided by electricity will continue to increase, because of electricity's properties of flexibility, versatility, cleanliness and efficiency at the point of end use. It is increasingly essential to the operation of advanced industrialised societies and is seen by developing societies as a key to meeting aspirations for a better quality of life. Moreover, electricity can be made from a wide variety of primary fuels and energy sources, including nuclear energy and most of the renewable energy sources.

Diversity of Energy Supplies

All Regions supported the importance of developing and using all the available energy sources with a view to diversifying energy supplies, thereby reducing risks to the security of supply or of unacceptable price rises in energy supply. However, such diversification is supported subject to its overall economic viability. Therefore in practice the policy of diversification amounts to taking action to ensure appropriate research, development and commercial application of new energy resources and technologies, with particular reference to the new renewable resources.

MATTERS OF DIFFERENCE BETWEEN REGIONS

There were areas where the perceptions of regions were quite different and lead to disagreements concerning policy. Primarily these arose from differences between the developing countries and the industrialised countries. They often referred to issues that are outside the immediate orbit of energy supply, but which were nonetheless perceived by the regions in question as vital to the solution of their energy problems. The main areas of contention were as follows.

Responsibility for Environmental Costs

Some developing countries regard the policies of the developed countries as unfair in that they do not take responsibility for the cost of environmental damage caused by those countries. In particular, the developing countries see the developed countries as responsible for much of the pollution caused to the global commons of air and water; and they see the problem of enhanced global warming and potential climate change as primarily the responsibility of the industrialised countries. The developing countries want to exercise their share of the rights to use the global commons. These perceptions are not uniformly shared by the developed countries. However the UN Climate Convention places heavy responsibilities in this regard on developed country signatories.

Closing the Development Gap

The developing countries see a need for the developed countries to take stronger steps to close the economic gap between the two. Some developing countries believe that this should entail the developed countries taking steps to reduce their energy consumption. The developed countries would not agree – they certainly favour becoming more energy efficient but, given the need for continued growth even in the developed countries, this is not synonymous with guaranteeing a reduction in energy use.

There is also pressure on the developed countries to make capital available to support economic development and to provide technology transfer under more favourable conditions. This is a key element within the terms of the UN Climate Convention. Another objective is the desire to reduce the technological dependence of the developing countries on the industrialised countries.

Trade and Free Access to Markets

The developing countries believe that trade imbalances and debt are a factor in holding back their economic development and consequently their ability to provide adequate energy supplies. The developing countries regard it as essential to have free access to the markets of the industrialised countries.

There are also complaints by the developed countries of barriers raised by the developing countries to free export of fuel, goods and services.

Intellectual Property Rights and Patents

The industrial countries place great importance on preserving intellectual property rights, which will usually be held by individual private firms and protected within the patents' system. This is seen as giving the necessary protection without which the firms will have less incentive to commit investment funds to research and innovation, which are necessary if technological development is to continue.

However, many developing countries see the insistence by the industrialised countries in retaining their intellectual property rights and patent rights as barriers to their ability to develop their own technological base.

Priorities

Different perceptions lead to different priorities. It is not surprising, therefore, that in some matters priorities between OECD, Central and Eastern Europe/CIS and the developing countries are markedly different. For instance, the OECD member countries give low priority to energy need, by and large, because availability is adequate and not perceived to be threatened over the next few decades. Similarly, technology is perceived to be readily available. The developing countries give highest priority to energy need and consequently to technology development, technology transfer, financing and institutional reform. CEE/CIS countries also give top priority to finance and institutional reform. All regions give high priority to efficiency and conservation and to pricing policies that will reflect costs more effectively. But developing countries and the CEE/CIS regions give low priority to climate change. Local environmental problems are seen to be more pressing and, for the developing countries, the need to provide energy services to the millions now without them towers above everything else. Table 7.1 gives a broad summary of the priorities accorded by regions to some of these issues.

SUMMARY OF REGIONAL PERCEPTIONS

The following summarises the issues arising from the regional reports that bear upon an agenda for action.

Economic growth is a top priority if aspirations for higher living standards, including the relief of poverty, security of energy supplies, achievement of sustainable population levels, efficient energy provision and use, and environmental protection are to be achieved.

Adequate and diversified energy supplies are vital, with new renewables playing an increasing role and the use of electricity expanding.

There is no shortage of ultimate energy resources for the foreseeable future, although distribution is uneven.

The developed industrial countries have achieved an effective energy supply through their market-based economies (even though with monopoly elements in some energy industries).

Technological development is a fundamental requirement, and in general is effectively provided by competitive market forces. However, long-term objectives may be satisfied more nearly by policy support of governments. Technology transfer is important and should be made via the market system, bearing in mind that a number of developing countries already have a technological capability.

Improved efficiency of energy production and use, and improved environmental protection, are important aims.

The market economy approach within an appropriate socio-governmental regulatory framework is supported.

These general conclusions are not dependent on the assumptions made on future economic development or future energy demand, and are robust.

	Energy Need & Population Growth	Technology	Financing	Institutional Deficiencies	Efficiency & Conservation	Climate Change
North America	4	4	4	3	3	3
Latin America	1	1	1	2	1	3
Western Europe	4	3	4	3	1	2
Central & Eastern Eur./CIS	4	2	1	1	1	4
Middle East & North Africa	1	1	1	1	1	4
Sub-Saharan Africa	1	1	1	2	2	4
South Asia/ Pacific	1	2	1	1	2	4
of which China	1	1	1	2	2	4
1: very important 2: important 3: of concern 4: no concern						

Table 7.1   Regional Key Issues and Priorities

CHAPTER

8

NORTH AMERICA

North America, consisting of the USA and Canada, currently has 5% of world population, and is responsible for 24.5% of world economic activity measured by volume. It is the most developed of all the regions. North America consumes 27% of world commercial primary energy use, and has 4% of world proven oil reserves, 6% of proven natural gas reserves and 25% of proven coal reserves.

As with the other developed regions, North America sees no problems of shortage of ultimate global energy reserves in the period to 2020, but is concerned with security of energy supplies. The region has the highest per capita income in the world, and as such can afford to choose and implement high local standards of environmental protection. In many parts of North America, the public is looking for an assurance of secure low-cost energy on the one hand and an unsullied environment and/or life-style on the other. For a host of reasons – and in particular because of mounting pressures in the region for a cleaner environment – the report considers it unlikely that North America's appetite for energy will be reduced in the near future; indeed energy consumption per capita may increase.

Both the United States and Canada are, for the most part, following a market-oriented approach to energy policy. There are some deviations from this approach in each country, particularly with respect to ensuring long-range energy security, but in general the two countries have displayed a flexibility with respect to energy policy which has allowed them to take advantage of the global market conditions that have existed in

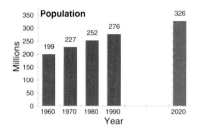

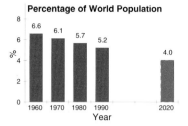

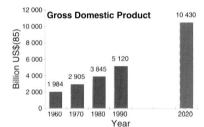

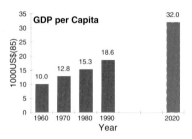

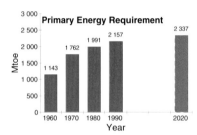

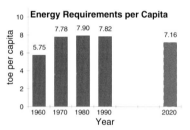

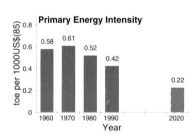

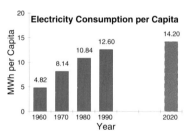

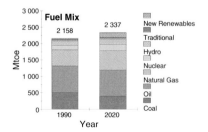

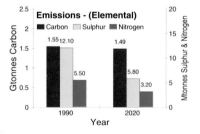

North America

Notes: *2020 population projection by UN*
All other 2020 data refer to WEC Case B
US$(85) means US dollars at 1985 value

recent years without significantly compromising their ability to meet long-range energy and environmental goals.

The policy initiatives most needed in North America are listed as ones that will:

- Diversify the energy mix in North America – primarily substituting indigenous fuels for petroleum in transportation.

- Preserve and renew the nuclear option.

- Enhance energy efficiency and conservation, particularly in transportation.

- Expand the economic use of renewable energy resources.

- Foster research, development and technological innovation relative to energy supply and use, including the impact of energy use on the environment.

- Establish realistic standards for energy-related emissions (accepted internationally).

- Ensure constructive dialogue between those primarily concerned with the supply of adequate low-cost energy and those primarily concerned with environmental protection.

The Region has set out an agenda for action under four main headings: environment/economy, demand/supply, technology and finally other subjects, covering finance, technology transfer and public consultation.

Environment, Economy and Energy Efficiency. The Report draws a number of conclusions on these closely related topics, especially in the context of the importance of economic growth:

"It is important that the energy policies adopted by the United States and Canada strengthen economic growth and competitiveness, not only domestically but throughout the world. At least moderate economic growth is fundamental to achievement of national and international goals such as providing basic social programs and an acceptable standard of living, improving the environment and preventing terrorism and war."

The public demand for higher environmental quality will have to be met in ways that do not seriously impair economic development. Aggressive conservation measures coupled with economic incentives are in hand to increase energy conservation and achieve higher energy efficiency in the use of all forms of energy. In particular:

- the mobilisation of public and private leadership to formulate explicit energy efficiency goals, specific programmes for that purpose, increased commitments to energy efficiency for government buildings and vehicle fleets, active corporate programmes and the development of demand-side programmes;

- energy efficiency to be given equal prominence with supply investment potential;

- government, government agencies and large corporations to use their purchasing power to promote energy efficient goods and services;

- utilities, in co-operation with manufacturers and distributors, to accelerate the purchase of high efficiency products through appropriate marketing programmes;

- energy awareness and education to be improved;

- utilities, financial institutions, architects, builders, etc to work together to expand consumer awareness of home efficiency options and to make additional financing available for efficiency improvements in new and existing housing;

- manufacturers to work together to develop uniform energy efficiency testing and labelling procedures;

- support for a global energy efficiency initiative;

- through governmental and private sector initiatives to promote demand-side management, integrated resource planning and appropriate research and development programmes in developing countries.

While energy markets dominated by natural or government-related monopolies cannot be totally deregulated, increased competition should be pursued to an extent consistent with the economic and political policies of each country.

There is a number of recommendations on this topic. Canada and the United States should continue their programmes to spur economic growth by appropriate application of energy policy and utilisation of energy. More emphasis should be placed on decreasing the negative environmental impacts of energy production and distribution, but with qualifications:

> *"This must be done in ways, however, that are compatible with the protective and remedial action being taken in other regions of the world and that do not seriously inhibit economic growth. Depressed economies will be able to support few, if any, environmental initiatives. Stagnant economies will be loath to burden constituents with pollution reduction and environmental clean-up costs over and above those built into existing budgets, all of which, around the world, are inadequate to cope with the environmental problems besetting humankind.... Moreover in all economies increasing attention must be given to internalisation of environmental costs."*

It is stressed that in all economies increasing attention must be given to developing mechanisms for internalisation of environmental costs. Energy efficiency and energy conservation programmes must be strengthened and should be the cornerstones of national energy policies, supported by government efforts, provision of appropriate incentives and removal of barriers which act as disincentives.

[In early 1993 President Clinton proposed imposition of an energy tax on all sources of energy, excluding "non-conventional" sources such as solar and wind (but including hydropower). Since the President's announcement there has been much discussion on the merits and weaknesses of the proposals, and a number of likely changes were quickly signalled to some Senators and Congressmen whose electoral interests were affected.

The proposals are based upon Btu values, and were originally expected to add $120 to the direct costs of an average family of four plus $200 in indirect costs. These estimates have been disputed. The tax is intended primarily as a revenue source, rather than as an environmental tax, and is intended to raise about $22 billion per year by 1997. Again this estimate of revenue has been questioned.

The proposals are at too early a stage, at the time of writing, to be more definitive.]

Demand/Supply. The flexibility required to meet future North American energy requirements will be significantly enhanced by intensive market-driven demand-side management and by various supply-side initiatives including advancement of coal technologies, deployment of evolutionary nuclear power systems, expansion of the use of natural gas, development of renewable energy systems and improvement of hydro-electric facilities. Both nations in the region are taking steps to ensure greater utilisation of indigenous sources when that is economically feasible. *[The US National Energy Strategy recommends exploration in the Arctic National Wildlife Refuge and offshore areas, although the environmental concerns are obvious. The potential of the Canadian tar sands cannot be overlooked. Improvements in extraction technology have resulted in substantial reduction in extraction cost per barrel: moderate escalation in oil price is likely to release the high production capability of these sources. Nevertheless, these heavy oils also raise some environmental concerns and in the Canadian context changed attitudes leading to sharp policy shifts can occur. Despite an impressive record in large-scale development of both nuclear and hydro resources, Canada has experienced set-backs in both Quebec and Ontario leading to more cautious and sensitive attitudes. There is uncertainty as to the direction and pace at which further large-scale hydro and nuclear development will take place.]*

The report notes that:

> **"In both countries, redundant and prolix regulatory and judicial processes have had, and will undoubtedly continue to have, serious negative effects on the energy sector. The problems of greatest concern are in the location and design of electric generating plants of various types, especially those powered by coal, water or nuclear energy; the siting of natural gas pipelines and electric transmission lines; and the location and operation of petroleum processing facilities."**

Electricity is the lifeblood of modern civilisation and in this region its use will continue to grow much more rapidly than the uses of other types of energy. Coal via clean technology and natural gas will be used in increasing amounts for the generation of electricity throughout the foreseeable future. Natural gas will also be increasingly used as a source of heat for industrial, commercial and domestic operations. Displacement of gasoline by other sources of energy (possibly natural gas, ethanol, methanol or electricity) in the transportation sector will occur slowly over a long period of time. *[Two-thirds of US petroleum consumption is in transportation and increased attention, some would say rather belatedly, is being given to the encouragement of more efficient vehicles and alternatives to petroleum. Even under the Clinton energy tax proposals, the level of tax on motor gasoline will remain very modest by West*

European standards. As the United States contains some 32% of the world's non-commercial motor vehicles in use, this issue is of more than local or regional significance.]

The report recommendations include: working to ensure a reliable supply of each type of energy; increasing domestic production of oil, gas, coal, renewable energy and nuclear energy; accelerating development and deployment of advanced supply and utilisation systems; simplifying and streamlining regulatory and judicial procedures; (for the United States) reducing dependence on foreign oil, in particular for transport; as far as possible allowing free market forces to determine the mix of fuels utilised in the transportation sector; and enabling electric utility companies to ensure an ample electricity supply including the deployment of both demand-side and supply-side options.

Technology. Technological development and technology transfer will have significant effects on the global energy economy during the next few decades. Industrialised countries such as Canada and the United States cannot afford "to rest on their laurels" in this matter. Large expenditures for energy research and development, including efforts to increase efficiency and conservation in both supply and end-use, and prompt adjustments to price changes will have to be made to keep North America in pace with the rest of the world.

The recommendations include: maintaining vigorous programmes for clean and more efficient fossil fuel burning and disposal of waste products, looking beyond current environmental standards; intensifying research on collecting and utilising carbon dioxide emission; improved planning of research and development programmes, including large-system studies; greater funding of high priority areas (efficiency/ conservation, renewable energy, nuclear power, clean-coal systems and better utilisation of electricity and gas); and more R&D effort on long-range programmes (particularly in the renewable energy and environmental protection areas) and to technology transfer and energy-related trade.

A recent joint study undertaken by the USEA Energy Research Committee and the Energy Council of Canada has recommended that, in view of the complex interaction of energy systems with environmental activities and economic programmes, studies of the potential local and global impacts of such systems should be undertaken.

Finance, Technology Transfer, Public Consultation. Except in times of severe recession, financing is normally available in North America for economically viable projects. It is recommended in the report that North America should join OECD countries in establishing and supporting institutions, either public or private, whose main mission is to facilitate financing for worthwhile and environmentally acceptable energy projects, no matter where they are located. Similarly the industrialised nations of the world should vigorously promote the transfer of energy technology and training to developing nations to help lift them to higher standards of living and thereby benefit the entire global economy. Public dialogue on the interrelations of energy production, energy utilisation, the economy and the environment should be encouraged and supported by national, state/provincial and local governments.

CHAPTER

9

LATIN AMERICA AND THE CARIBBEAN

The region has 8% of world population, and is responsible for 8.7% of world economic activity measured by volume. Population is rising and, if energy use per capita were to remain at today's level (which it will not), the region's energy use will rise by 60–85% by 2025.

The region consumes 6% of world primary energy and has 12% of world proven oil reserves (11½% of world production), 6% of proven natural gas reserves (5.8% of world production) and 2% of proven coal reserves (1% of world production). The region is responsible for 7% of total world energy production. There is growing co-operation across countries of the region through organisations such as OLADE.

The region's main conclusions and recommendations concern: economic development and life-styles; energy efficiency; energy use; security of supply; technology development; the environment; financing, institutions and pricing; and relations with the industrialised countries.

Economic Development and Life-styles. The social and economic developments in the region are relevant to energy use and energy policy but the majority of the population will continue to live under survival conditions.

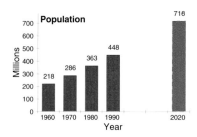

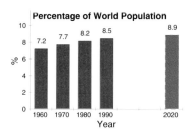

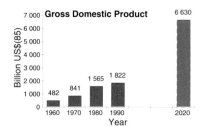

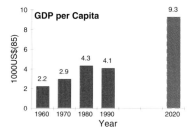

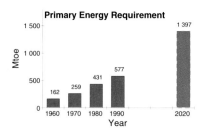

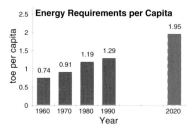

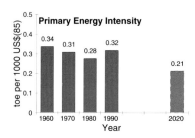

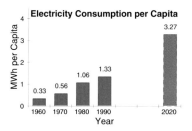

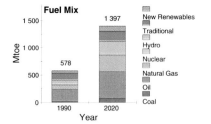

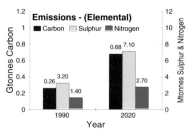

Latin America and the Caribbean

Notes: 2020 population projection by UN
All other 2020 data refer to WEC Case B
US$(85) means US dollars at 1985 value

This will be particularly so for most of the rural population and for recent rural migrants to the large conurbations and poor city dwellers:

"... forming ever expanding misery belts."

Urbanisation will grow and problems include inadequate land use, speculation, deficient public transport and highways, rising car use, lack of sewerage systems and potable water supplies, and financial difficulties leading to problems of urban planning. Extremely rapid growth in the last decade has forced unplanned urban expansion and provision of services has had to follow unplanned settlements.

The average age will rise and age groups will be more even. There will be an increase in population of working age and of working women, which means that 4–5 million new jobs per annum will be needed – if not, migration or destabilisation is possible.

Energy Efficiency. All of these changes will cause energy demand to rise. Energy use per capita is low, but the energy intensity is relatively high, partly because of inefficiencies but also reflecting an energy-intensive, low value-added industrial sector – an industrialisation process likely to continue if the region is to compete. The energy intensity is likely to rise; however, energy efficiency programmes are urgently needed to avoid further deterioration.

So economic, political, cultural and domestic activities must embrace energy efficiency policies. It is necessary to review all subsidies to reduce them, and to tap the technical potential for increased efficiency and economically competitive conditions. Energy efficiency programmes are likely to include identifying and developing specific investments, training of personnel and industrial firms, improvements of technologies, appropriate norms and regulations, and identification of mechanisms and incentives.

Changes in life-styles and consumption patterns could avoid following those of most industrialised countries and sensibly reduce energy demand without reducing living standards. But this requires a change of values and the possibility of choice – something that is hardly possible for the poor.

Energy Use. Oil will remain the main energy source to 2025, and the region will be a net oil exporter over this period. In the next decade, natural gas will grow fastest, overtaking coal use as the second most important fuel. Natural gas trade between producing countries and their neighbours will stimulate exploration of gas reserves.

Nuclear (which is seen as environmentally benign but with problems of acceptability) may grow. Growth rates of electricity will be higher than for primary energy. Hydro is the only important renewable energy resource, though geothermal, biomass and solar energy will continue to develop, but making only marginal contributions by 2025.

Security of Supply. For reasons of energy security, the region will try to substitute oil by nuclear, gas and coal and seek competitive regional oil supply systems. This will need investment in the infrastructure which is difficult to mount. The region believes it should widen its relations with the Pacific Basin and Europe to retain the freedom to establish its own energy policies.

Technology Development and Transfer. Technology development is one of the most important issues in the region. There is concern for the region's technological dependency, with a low own capability for energy technology. Export-oriented economic policies and opening up to international participation could widen the R & D base to more private participation.

Skills in the acquisition of new technologies are also important. There is a need for more higher education, and better quality of education and training at all levels.

The most important technologies for the future concern energy efficiency and end-use, followed by resource exploitation. Post-2010, energy conversion technologies will begin to impact.

The Environment. Next in priority come environmental concerns. These are important now and will become more so:

"Poverty is considered to be among the main sources of pollution in the region, in the sense that many environmentally damaging actions have their roots in it. Underdevelopment and environmental destruction constitute a vicious circle which limits the quality of life of an estimated 40% of the population of the region."

Local community environmental fears must be balanced against the development pressures of growing population, urbanisation, industrialisation and inadequate energy supply per capita. There is a lack of coherent environmental legislation and enforcement, and an inadequate institutional and human infrastructure. Even if these are improving fast in some countries of the region, much remains to be done.

Wood consumption in the region is still important if declining. It is the main energy source of suspended particles:

"It is estimated to be the main cause of respiratory diseases and conjunctivitis in more than 15 million women that still cook daily with this fuel."

Big hydro dams do have negative effects on local people, mitigated by low density of population, and can impact negatively on natural habitats over a wide area. Oil exploration has had some effects – eg deforestation. Refineries (including US ones) have dumped untreated liquid wastes in the Gulf of Mexico. Many improvements have been made but much remains to be done.

Finance, Pricing and Institutions. Up to 2020, financial constraints and debt are a problem. The security situation for electricity is likely to be critical since electricity growth rates are high and necessary investments were not made in the 1980s. The need is for investment of US$130 billion to recover. The financial deficit will be 50% of this and will force big changes – macroeconomic policies, wider participation of the private sector, better utility management practices, and stronger interconnections. Past investments in large-scale electricity power schemes are one of the main causes of heavy external indebtedness in the region.

Financial constraints will continue to limit the development of sound energy institutions. Other constraints are high interest rates, the stability of international energy prices and pricing policies:

> *"In general, subsidised internal energy practices have weakened the financial soundness of the energy industries."*

Other institutional limitations are: political interference, corruption, organisational inefficiencies including overmanning, bureaucracy, labour problems, limited technical human resources and lack of competence, and unnecessary, complicated and often illogical regulations. Insufficient technical development is a problem. Energy firms specialising in only one energy may lead to insufficient diversification overall.

Liberalising and opening up the economies will mean lessening the role of the State. With this and the huge financing requirement, the private sector will grow.

Relations with the Industrialised Countries. Many of the above issues raise matters of concern for the region in its relations with the industrialised countries. Population in itself is not seen as a problem ("population is the wealth of nations") but high population growth rates are, and achieving a more equitable energy consumption is definitely a major problem. So the industrialised countries need to cut their energy consumption, allowing developing countries to achieve a better standard of living by enabling their energy use to rise.

If the financial constraints are to be alleviated, it is necessary to improve resource allocation and recover investment, allowing greater participation by the private sector and foreign investors. But this needs greater economic growth and an increased inflow of resources particularly via exports.

This requires wider access to the markets of the industrialised countries, more diversification of exports and the ability to export higher added value products. The ability to export goods in this way is also necessary if the desired extra job creation is to be achieved.

The industrialised countries will control key technologies for the next 35 years, and so the technological gap between them and the region may grow. This would be destabilising and must be prevented. Technology transfer under reasonable conditions is needed, with access to relevant information, joint venture projects and avoidance of the transfer of obsolete technology.

The region and other developing countries are under pressure to improve their management practices, especially of energy, requiring further investments and use of scarce financial resources. Given the history and high capital consumption of the industrialised countries, their present international policies are seen as unfair by the developing countries:

> *"Latin America and the Caribbean have raised demands asking the industrialised countries to accept the principle of "co-responsibility" which states that the cost of environmental preservation should be distributed according to the damage already inflicted and still being inflicted today."*

This principle is nothing more than the "polluter pays" principle which the industrialised countries are applying to themselves. Up to now little progress has been made in this controversy and the parties remain polarised.

CHAPTER

10

WESTERN EUROPE

Western Europe (which includes the former Yugoslavia) currently has 9% of world population, and is responsible for 22.3% of world economic activity measured by volume. It is a fully developed region, and its member countries are all market economies. There is a wide degree of social, economic and political co-ordination through the European Community which has recently negotiated to join with the European Free Trade Area to establish the European Economic Area.

Western Europe consumes 18% of world commercial primary energy supplies, but has only 7% of world proven coal reserves, 2% of proven oil reserves and 5% of proven natural gas reserves. It is therefore an energy importing region and will remain so for the foreseeable future.

The report identifies no outstanding energy supply problems in terms of the present and likely future availability of energy to its people. World ultimate energy resources are regarded as sufficient to meet demand for the period to 2020. There are, however, underlying concerns which it would be foolish to overlook:

- Post-2000, the percentage of imported energy, already high, will rise still further. The threat of political insecurity of energy supplies and of the effects of global energy price instability are likely to increase rather than reduce.

- Reduction of local and regional environmental pollution is well in hand, but the problems are far reaching and costly

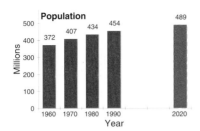

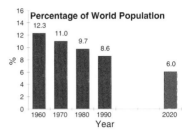

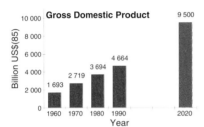

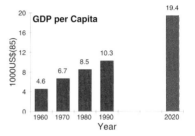

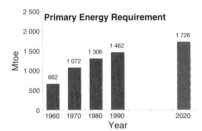

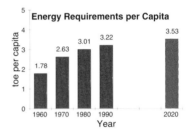

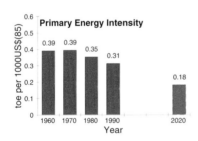

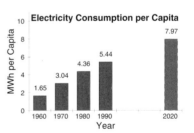

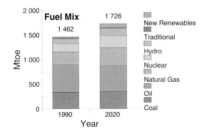

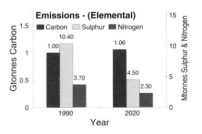

Western Europe

Notes: 2020 population projection by UN
         All other 2020 data refer to WEC Case B
         US$(85) means US dollars at 1985 value

and efforts must continue to find acceptable economic and political solutions.

- CO_2 emissions will continue to rise for the rest of this decade, and the region overall will not achieve the Toronto target of a 20% reduction by 2005 on either scenario examined.

The Western European report recommendations centre on environmental concerns, carbon dioxide emissions, energy efficiency, security of supply, research and technology, market mechanisms and economic growth.

Environmental Concerns. It is necessary to recognise growing environmental concern in regard to local and regional pollution and to continue the existing processes of improvement on both the energy demand and supply sectors. Environmental protection can be achieved primarily through government regulation and new market instruments. The cost must be reflected in prices.

Carbon Dioxide Emissions. The extent of the problem is uncertain, and the solution might be less emissions, or CO_2 sinks, or adaptation. The problem needs to be discussed in a global context, seeking appropriate world-wide agreements and considering trade-offs between regions. Nuclear and natural gas supplies should be favoured over coal, and the market would drive in the right direction. There should be more incentives and research into renewables.

Present scientific evaluation of climate change risks may justify only a minimum regret strategy. An energy or carbon tax is not thought desirable or even practicable: the countries of the region have different energy and fiscal structures, and different emission patterns, and construction of a tax equitable and acceptable to all countries would be extremely difficult.

> *"While awaiting the decisive answers during the ten to twenty years ahead, the only strategies to be adopted against the greenhouse effect are strategies of minimum regret."*

Changes in the energy mix and rising energy efficiency are the basic instruments to improve both security of supply and protection of the environment. The report emphasises the need for policies to favour less polluting fuels – nuclear and renewables – but recognises the problem of public acceptability in regard to both. In regard to CO_2 emissions, the Toronto target could be achieved by 2020 provided a change in energy mix away from fossil fuels together with substantial improvements in energy saving can be achieved.

"Measures that tend to decrease carbon dioxide emissions will be taken only if they contribute to other goals that are useful to the national communities, and if their cost is acceptable in the light of these goals: lower local and regional pollutant emissions, improved reliability of supplies, reduced import expenditures, and improved conservation of natural resources. The only expenditures that will be made will be those that will not be sterile if it proves that the risk of a change of climate is non-existent or slight. This strategy will, in the opposite direction, help to limit the risk of irreversible situations."

[Several WEC member committees in the region put forward alternative scenarios combining a sensible reduction of demand combined with energy savings through investment and a different energy mix which would reduce anticipated CO_2 emissions. These provided ways to meet the challenges of the next few decades but public acceptability of changing energy mix in particular, as the report points out, is an ever-present problem. It is noteworthy also that the "Report of the Commission of the European Communities, Energy in Europe", September 1992, asserts that, whilst primary energy demand in the Community will increase, and ongoing improvement in energy intensity will require additional efforts by both public and private sectors, the major challenge in Europe could come not from matters of traditional supply and demand but rather from growing environmental concerns, reflecting local, regional and global issues. As the regional report also states, these will require increased investment, the introduction of new market instruments and more effective energy efficiency policies.]

Energy Efficiency. In support of limiting adverse environmental impacts, energy savings should be promoted through regulation, pricing and tax incentives; and by such measures as the EC Commission's SAVE programme. It is necessary to aim at economic energy efficiency. The report examines a number of particular mechanisms for improving energy efficiency. For example, road transport efficiency should be improved, not by yet further taxes, but by better urban transport networks, long-distance integrated road and rail systems, by high-speed trains for transporting people, and by raising car efficiency standards.

Security of Supply. Both security of quantity and price are important. The region should aim at maintenance of viable indigenous supplies against short-term price fluctuations and expansion of nuclear while avoiding stop-go policies. The role of natural gas is expected to increase, and so a policy of co–operation with the countries of Eastern Europe and the newly independent states should be fostered with a view to encouraging the development of commercial gas supplies from that region. Indeed, co-operation with all fuel supplying regions (especially oil suppliers) to improve security of supply by diversification of resources is essential. The European Energy Charter should be implemented (see below).

[There will be a need within the next 30 years for Western Europe to import the bulk of its fossil fuel requirements. By 2020 Western European oil and gas reserves will have declined to a point at which only Norway is expected to have significant reserves of natural gas available and Western Europe may well enter a phase of declining oil production and rising oil import dependency. Thus, even before the year 2020 all the uncertainties of reserves and logistics are likely to reflect in uncertainty about price and availablity. The regional group found in its enquiries that there is widespread concern about the risk of oil price shocks arising from growing dependency on the Middle East. This led some of the energy professionals and economists within the group to believe oil prices could rise from US$20 bbl in 1991 to approaching US$35 at 1991 prices towards the end of the decade. This represents about half the ceiling reached in 1980 in constant dollars and some of the study's contributors believed that at least a doubling of current prices, to 1980 real prices, could occur by 2020.]

Research and Technology. There should be scientific and technical research for the long term (post-2020) into climate change, fast-breeder reactors, fusion, new renewable energy resources, and new technologies for the production and use of electricity. There should also be research in related economic and social fields: environmental cost internalisation and energy pricing, social attitudes on accepting energy projects, and the economic costs and benefits of energy savings. There should be help for developing countries:

> *"European energy industries should be prepared and should take initiatives in order to assist developing countries in appropriate energy strategies, in investments for energy production and savings, and in building and maintaining efficient and clean energy technologies."*

Market Mechanisms. The Western Europe report supports the need to base policy on the market and price mechanism within regulating frameworks:

"Policy responses should be based on reinforcement and extension of the market and price mechanism, rather than reliance on government intervention and regulation. The main steps to be taken are the introduction of full-cost pricing, including the internalisation of environmental costs, which together with selective government financial incentives will promote cleaner and more efficient energy provision and use. These steps are likely to prove more effective than energy or carbon taxes. Such taxes superimposed on existing ones are not required."

Economic Growth. The report emphasises the importance of economic growth in underpinning other policies:

"Economic growth is a precondition for the environmental alternative scenario as only growth may generate the funds needed for investments in research and new equipment. If economic growth were lower than assumed, there would be difficulties in achieving the environmental targets. If it were higher, the targets might remain realistic provided necessary investments are made at the right time."

The European Energy Charter

The West European regional report, and other regional reports draw attention to the European Energy Charter, which was signed at a ceremony at The Hague on 16/17 December 1991.

In fact, the Charter covers a wider area than its name suggests. The signatories included all the countries of Western Europe, all the countries of Central and Eastern Europe, all 15 of the ex-USSR States and the USA, Canada, Japan and Australia. The principles set out in the Charter are for wide-ranging co-operation based on open and competitive markets:

1.   **Developing of trade consistent with GATT, etc** by means of : **"an open and competitive market for energy products, materials, equipment and services"** with access to resources, access to markets, removal of trade barriers, modernisation, promoting energy transport, access to capital, access to transport infrastructure for international transit, and access on commercial terms to technologies.

2. **Co-operation in the energy field,** which will entail co-ordination of energy policies, access to data consistent with proprietary rights, transparent legal frameworks, co-ordination and harmonisation of safety and guidelines, exchange of technology information, know-how, training, and co-ordination of research and design and development.

3. **Energy efficiency and environmental protection,** which will imply creating mechanisms and conditions for efficient energy use, including regulatory and market-based approaches, promotion of energy mix to protect the environment cost-effectively via market-oriented energy prices, efficient policy measures, use of new, renewable and clean technologies, and achieving high nuclear safety.

As regards implementation, the signatories have committed themselves to the following (selected verbatim quotes):

> **"The signatories will strongly promote access to local and international markets for energy products for the implementation of the objectives of the Charter. Such access to markets should take account of the need to facilitate the operation of market forces, and promote competition."**

> **"In order to develop and diversify trade in energy, the signatories undertake progressively to remove the barriers to such trade with each other in energy products, equipment and services in a manner consistent with the provisions of GATT, its related instruments, and nuclear non-proliferation obligations and undertakings."**

> **"The signatories recognise that transit of energy products through their territories is essential for the liberalisation of trade in energy products. Transit should take place in economic and environmentally sound conditions."**

There are also clauses on non-discrimination, transparency, fair taxation, and a wide variety of technical, safety and other areas for co-operation.

However, the assent to principles is merely a beginning, and work is currently taking place to formulate the "basic agreement" which, with binding provisions, will implement these principles. Given the fundamental nature of the commitments in the terms of the Charter, it is likely in practice to be a long and arduous task to bring it to fruition; nonetheless, goals have now been set.

CHAPTER

11

CENTRAL AND EASTERN EUROPE

Central and Eastern Europe, consisting of Bulgaria, the Czech and Slovak Federal Republics, Hungary, Poland and Romania, has 2% of world population and in 1990 was responsible for 2.1% of world economic activity measured by volume.

However, the transition from centrally planned to market economies in the region has caused serious industrial recessions because of counter-inflation policies; and, for example, electricity use was down 10% in 1990 compared with 1989. The rate of recovery is not known.

Central and Eastern Europe consumes some 4% of world commercial primary energy use, and has a little over 6% of world proven coal reserves and well under 1% of world proven oil and natural gas reserves. The region will continue to import primary energy from other countries, especially oil, natural gas and nuclear fuel. The political changes of recent years have caused the region to look increasingly to the West for primary energy supplies, not least in the light of uncertainties in regard to imports from the East. A basic problem remains the shortage of hard currency and the residually low domestic energy prices which cannot fund purchase in Western markets.

The region's main conclusions and recommendations concern socio-economic policy, security of supply, energy and electricity use, energy efficiency, the environment and financing.

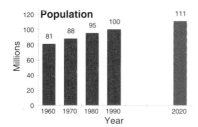

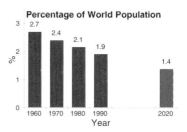

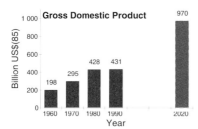

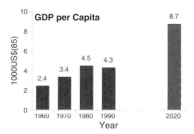

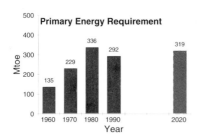

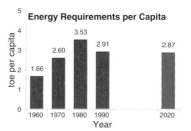

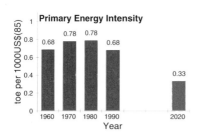

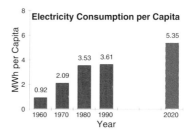

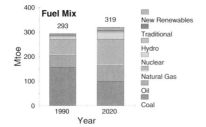

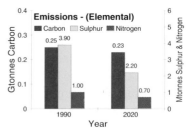

Central and Eastern Europe

Notes: 2020 population projection by UN
            All other 2020 data refer to WEC Case B
            US$(85) means US dollars at 1985 value

Socio-economic Policy. The main aim of the region is to move to a market economy and to catch up with living standards in Western Europe, though it is recognised that this will need a very careful social policy. Achieving this aim will require major changes in energy provision, use and pricing, not least in terms of efficiency and energy mix.

Security of Supply. The countries of the region follow the "energy safety" concept. The region is importing energy. The main problem is to make better use of indigenous energy resources and to assure various other sources of energy supply, not to depend on only one. All indigenous resources are taken into account but there are limitations because of environmental protection. The nuclear industry is used to some extent. The development of the supply infrastructure (pipe lines, transmission lines, communications networks) to enable imports from various directions is essential.

Energy and Electricity Use. The region has forecast an increase in primary energy use of 16–29% by 2020 over 1990, including an increase in nuclear power of 3.5–4.9 times, and increases in the use of electricity and natural gas, which is mainly imported from the ex-USSR:

> *"Electricity production will rise more quickly due to a general rising trend in productive efficiency as modern technology is introduced and living standards rise. The higher demand for electricity is expected to be met by development of nuclear power, combined cycle gas steam turbines and fluidised bed coal plants, and CHP plants."*

> *"There will be efforts to increase the utilisation of gas. It will need increased supply reliability. The networks should be meshed and reinforced. Multilateral negotiations are in progress. The development of the gas networks will need capital to finance the investments and time to build the new connections to transmit some 5 to 10 bcm per annum additionally and the related distribution infrastructure, by the end of the century."*

Energy Efficiency. Improving primary energy utilisation means primarily better technology: refinery effectiveness, coal cleaning, use of coal-fired combined cycle gas turbines (CCGTs), reducing network losses, more district heating and combined heat and power schemes. Electricity is regarded as the most convenient form of final energy for many purposes. Better efficiency of energy end-use is essential. The need is for better technology in industry, building and agriculture, and for the recycling of materials. Old and inefficient kitchen equipment, lighting, cars etc should be replaced by modern ones. This will take 5–10 years as factory output must be planned.

The establishment of full-cost pricing is essential:

> *"The fundamental condition of the increased energy efficiency is the pricing of all energy vectors."*

The key problem is to avoid social protests, for example by synchronising price changes in steps to avoid heavy inflation. In summary, it is necessary to:

- Use market forces to enable and start the energy conservation programme.

- Improve primary to final energy transformation and corresponding technologies.

- Reinforce and modernise the whole energy infrastructure.

- Increase the efficiency of energy utilisation to stay at the present level of primary energy use per capita.

The Environment. Central and Eastern Europe is the most polluted region in Europe as a result of the technologies used in the region and of emissions blown in from Western Europe. Environmental protection is a decisive factor, and immediate action is necessary at the European level because of trans-boundary pollution. There is a need for close international co-operation, standardisation and mutual assistance in know-how, including, particularly, management.

To reduce fuel use degrading the environment, the needs are: development of nuclear and hydro; fuel cleaning, clean coal technology, sulphur removal and NO_x reduction; cleaning of output water; reclamation of mining land; ash disposal. Even so, CO_2 emissions will rise.

Financing. Meeting energy supply, energy efficiency and environmental needs will require tremendous financial resources, of about US$200 billion over 10–20 years, in addition to the finance needed to modernise existing industry and repay debts. Further development of the energy sector is dependent on successful economic reforms. Some of these needs should be met by self-financing. Some will be met by attracting foreign investments, and may need government guarantees, especially for environmental protection and drilling and mining licences. There is a need for interim finance as an East-West bridge.

Overall, however, it may be said that whilst the political and economic picture in Eastern Europe has changed significantly even since the regional studies commenced in late 1990, the obvious observation is that the transformation of the formerly centrally planned economies has turned out to be a much more difficult and complicated process than many imagined and this has impacted on energy as on everything else. In energy, European integration is slow, with barely perceptible progress in electricity, oil and gas. Institutional change and transition to market economies is inhibited by general recession in Europe,and this worsens a lack of funds for investment in energy conservation and in the environment.

CHAPTER

12

THE COMMONWEALTH OF INDEPENDENT STATES, GEORGIA AND THE BALTIC STATES

The region has 5.5% of world population and in 1990 was responsible for 8.0% of world economic activity measured by volume, though this has now declined sharply. Following the recent political changes, and attempted move towards market economies, the economic and political position is uncertain, and it is not possible to make any firm forecasts of future activity.

The region consumes 17% of world commercial primary energy use, and is a net exporter of energy, in particular of oil and natural gas. However, the region is currently experiencing energy production difficulties, and there is a declining surplus of energy for export.

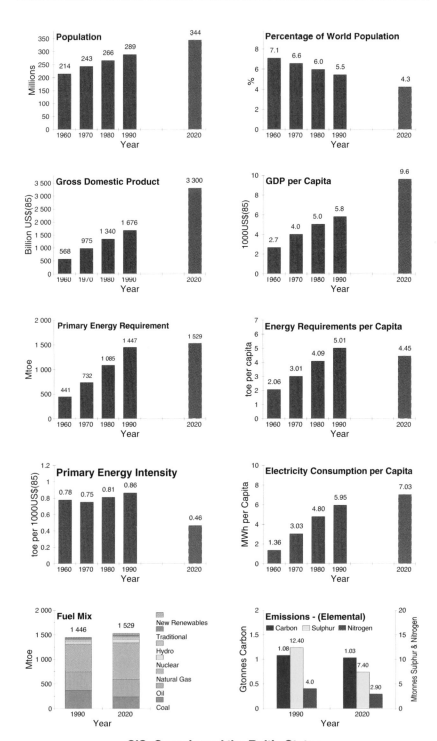

CIS, Georgia and the Baltic States

Notes: 2020 population projection by UN
All other 2020 data refer to WEC Case B
US$(85) means US dollars at 1985 value

Although economic activity has fallen because of the political up-heaval, primary energy use has not fallen in line. This arises from inefficient energy economies (energy intensities double the OECD average), caused by energy abundance, low energy prices not reflecting world prices, the slow spread of energy efficient technology and problems in exploiting scientific progress.

The region has 6% of world proven oil reserves, 38% of proven gas reserves and 22% of proven coal reserves. However, these reserves are concentrated in only a few of the independent States, notably the Russian Federation, and only three of the States (the Russian Federation, Khazak-stan and Turkmenia) are net exporters of energy. The transition to market (ie world) prices is proving difficult. The States have inherited a common physical energy infrastructure; it is now much harder to operate with split responsibilities and there are interstate tensions and problems on rights and obligations.

The region's main conclusions and recommendations concern transition to the market economy, energy resource base, fuel/energy foreign trade strategy, manufacturing industry support, energy demand-supply scenarios, electricity supply to meet social targets, expenditure to protect the environment, energy efficiency, energy supply technologies, and key issues and problems to solve.

Transition to the Market Economy. The transition to the market economy and wider spread of self-management practices is the most important process in the national economy. A stock exchange will be organised, which will regulate the efficiency of capital use in fuel/energy industrial branches, as well as commercial banks and banks for investment in new technology, and other structures of the market economy.

As industrial branches of the fuel/energy industry become more and more mature in their preparation for the transition to the market economy, it is planned to introduce privatisation and private ownership through stock holding companies, starting with the privatisation of small and medium-sized enterprises. The transition to the market economy will determine a rational system of price formation and of investment policy in the energy economy:

"Real economic liberty in investment policy can be achieved only through the separation of the functions of State and business management. The domain of State activity should include the estimation and selection of priority directions of State incentives and State budget financing. In parallel with this, the tax (and rent) policy, as well as depreciation, price, lending and financing policy, will be established."

[Whilst the developed countries, especially those which have recently undertaken transition of major industry from the State to the private sector, have difficulty in achieving a satisfactory balance between regulation and freedom in the market, the transition problem for the ex-centrally planned economies is an order of magnitude more difficult. Aid and advice from the West can and must be offered, but countries will need to gain from individual and hard experience.]

Energy Resource Base of the Commonwealth of Independent States. The States of the former USSR can be grouped into three in respect of their indigenous energy reserves:

- Three States which have a positive balance of fuel/energy resources: The Russian Federation (RF), Khazakstan and Turkmenia.

- Six States partially supplying their needs through indigenous energy resources: Azerbaijan, Estonia, Kirgizstan, Tadjikistan, Ukraine and Uzbekistan.

- Six States having virtually no energy resources of their own, or whose level of supply from indigenous resources is no more than 5%–10%: Armenia, Byelorussia, Georgia, Latvia, Lithuania and Moldavia.

Fuel/Energy Foreign Trade Strategy. The strategy for foreign trade in fuel/energy resources of the newly independent States is based on the necessity to maintain substantial, though somewhat decreased, volume of energy resources for export, as this represents one of the most important sources of hard currency earnings.

Of the States, the Russian Federation (RF), Khazakstan and Turkmenia have the greatest export possibilities. For the RF, the net surplus of coal and electricity production over demand will remain stable over the period up to 2020, the net surplus for oil will decline slightly, and the net surplus of gas will increase substantially, reaching some 350 million tonnes oil equivalent by 2020. For Khazakstan, coal production will exceed consumption by about 30–40 Mtoe. The major export resource of Turkmenia is natural gas, where production is expected to reach about 60–70 billion cubic metres per annum, or some 5–6 times domestic requirements.

Manufacturing Industry Support. The fulfilment of the fuel and energy resources development programme is directly linked with the preparedness of domestic manufacturing industry to supply the fuel/energy industry with equipment and materials. For the fuel/energy industry to increase its economic efficiency, it is necessary to improve substantially the technical and economic performance of the equipment supplied (more automation, shorter overhauls, faster production rates, fewer operation and maintenance personnel). For the more widespread penetration of non-conventional energy sources it is necessary for the machine-building industry to promote the development of corresponding technologies and equipment, and for the chemical industry to organise the output of appropriate materials.

Energy Demand. Energy demand is expected to rise, net of energy conservation, by 1.3 to 1.4 times the 1990 level by 2020 to 1.5 to 1.6 billion toe. Electricity's share of the market is expected to rise from about 25% in 1990 to 27% in 2000 and 31% to 32% in 2020.

Electricity Supply to Meet Social Targets. Fuel and energy balances for the region must have regard to social indicator targets; for example concerning per capita living space, food supplies, quality of life (reliability and adequacy of energy supplies and services), and public transport services. In consequence, the per capita electricity consumption is expected to increase from 5.5 MWh per annum in 1990 to 7.2–7.3 MWh per annum by 2000 and to 9 MWh per annum by 2020. The consumption of electricity in the commercial and residential sector will increase at faster rates: from 0.8 MWh in 1990 to 1.2–1.3 MWh per annum by 2000 and 1.7–1.8 MWh per annum by 2020.

Expenditure to Protect the Environment. At present three-quarters of the harmful emissions in the region, contributing to greenhouse gas emissions, and up to 80% of harmful emissions into the atmosphere from human activity in general, are caused by the burning of fossil fuels. In the period 1986–1990 considerable efforts were directed to the protection of the environment and, at a price of doubling of investments, a decrease of harmful emissions was achieved. For the period 1991–2005 the total volume of investment for environmental protection in the fuel and energy sector is estimated as 117 billion roubles at 1990 prices, including 28.4 billion roubles in the period 1991–1995. The environmental protection component of total energy cost in the year 2005 will be in the range 6–50 roubles per toe at 1991 prices. Studies are being made of a possible tax on CO_2 emissions but, in view of the good prospects for energy saving, such a tax is initially likely to be at a moderate level (120 roubles per tonne for coal, and pro rata for oil and gas).

Energy Saving. In order to use the potential for energy saving, it is planned to introduce new management systems in energy conservation as free market conditions are created. This will accelerate the use of established and progressive technologies, maximise the reduction of energy losses in energy production and supply, and create energy saving materials and equipment. In the early years, the main gain in energy saving will be from the penetration of energy efficient technologies; in later years, structural change in the economy will play the greater part. The possible expenditure on energy efficiency could be about 80–90 billion roubles by 2020, with a gain for the regional economy of about 55–60 billion roubles.

Energy Supply Technologies. The following developments are envisaged in the main energy supply technologies:

- Nuclear generation: As the basis for future nuclear construction, two types of nuclear reactor are being considered: the fast reactor with lead coolant, and the thermal heavy water reactor with pre-stressed concrete/steel containment and pressure vessels. These types of reactors are believed to possess appropriate inherent safety characteristics. The projected scale of nuclear output is for 400–600 TWh per annum by 2020, compared with 211.5 TWh in 1990.

- Clean coal technology: Environmentally clean three-stage combustion of coal is foreseen for thermal power stations with removal of ash and particulates, sulphur and nitrogen oxides. Other measures for clean coal combustion are the creation of advanced steam generators with new combustion techniques, and coal washing and preparation.

- Non-conventional renewable energy sources: These sources, and in particular solar, geothermal and wind energy, biomass energy and low-potential heat, present an important resource for the generation of electricity, heat and mechanical energy. A substantial increase in output from these resources, of some 20–25 times, is envisaged by 2020. The most important among them will be biomass, with solar and geothermal also making a large contribution.

- Natural gas production up to about 1.25–1.3 Tm^3 pa (just over 1 Gtoe).

- Oil output is expected to decrease through to 1995, but thereafter to reach about 500–530 toe.

- A moderate growth of hydroelectricity of 1.6–1.7 times is expected, mainly from new hydropower stations on mountain rivers.

- Overall, an increase in annual energy production, relative to 1990, of 120–240 toe by 2000, and of 240–350 toe by 2020.

[The regional report makes little mention of coal, even though this is and will remain of primary importance in energy production. For completeness, it may be noted that there are very large potential resources in the order of 6.8 x 10^{12} tonnes and proven reserves of 285 billion tonnes in the region. Coal consumption is estimated to rise from

the 1990 figure of a little over 700 million tonnes to 800–900 million tonnes by 2010.]

Key Issues – Problems to Solve. These fuel/energy supply strategies give rise to the need for a number of studies: optimising export-imports; creation of market infrastructure (corporations, stock holding companies, etc); extent of demonopolising of branches of the fuel/energy sector; scale of small energetics; transition to liberalised prices for fuel/energy; improved mathematical models of optimisation of fuel/energy balances within the new market context; and studies to provide a scientific basis for the concept of national economic development of the individual sovereign States and their fuel/energy systems.

[Some comment is necessary on the status of nuclear plant in Eastern Europe in the aftermath of Chernobyl, and implications for the future of nuclear energy in general. The report of the CIS, Baltic countries and Georgia makes no mention of Chernobyl as such but, as has been said, the expectation is one of continued nuclear expansion based on new thermal and fast reactor designs.

This region presently operates 46 thermal reactor units on 16 sites. Of these 20 are RBMK (broadly Chernobyl) type designs. There is a strong recognition in Russia of the need not only to rectify the mistakes of Chernobyl but to be seen to be doing so. Informed opinion is that, whatever the long-term ecological consequences of the Chernobyl accident are, the cause was fundamentally one of design, aggravated by operating practice. Improving the safety of the RBMK reactors is imperative because there is no short-term alternative to the 15 000 MW of power provided by RBMK reactors other than failure to provide heat and light to the populace. This has been done as far as is possible within the limitations of the existing design. The problems of the fossil fuel industries, coal, oil and gas preclude early substitution to these plant even if replacement finance were available, which it is not. Moreover, export of fossil fuels is and will be a vital hard currency earner into the long term and every nuclear station that runs releases exportable fossil fuel. In the opinion of the World Association of Nuclear Operators (WANO), what is needed now and into the future is not further analysis of the safety of these reactors but practical technology that will be used and that will improve safety on the ground.]

"The safeguards for control and mitigation of accidents have been found below current Western standards. A strong belief in the role of technology distracted attention from precautionary measures to counter unlikely technical and human failures." A Birkhofer

"In Russia we are well aware that it is not the future of our nuclear power alone that hinges on the safety of Russian plants." V N Mikhailov & E O Adamov

"We are at a critical point in time to deal with the very real threats from unsafe nuclear plants in Eastern Europe and the former Soviet Union. Unless more incentives are provided to start phasing out these plants decisions will be delayed even further, increasing the probability of another costly accident." Tony Churchill

[The European Commission has allocated US$400 million altogether between 1991 and 1993 to improve the safety of civil nuclear power installations in Central and Eastern Europe, with increasing stress on on-site assistance to back up generic studies, not least in the Russian Federation and the Ukraine. This approach is exampled by the nuclear plant at Kozloduy, Bulgaria, where since mid-1991 a WANO team drawn from across the world and funded by the European Community has worked with the station staff on site to improve safety practices. As with the plant in Russia and CIS, shutdown is not regarded as a practicable option.]

CHAPTER

13

MIDDLE EAST AND NORTH AFRICA

The region has 5% of world population, and is responsible for 4.1% of world economic activity measured by volume. The region consumes 3.4% of world commercial primary energy supply.

The region is notable for containing some 70% of the world's proven oil reserves and 35% of the world's proven natural gas reserves. However, these reserves are very unevenly distributed in the region, with much of the reserves in lowly populated countries and with some highly populated countries having few reserves. The region has negligible coal reserves.

The main conclusions and recommendations of the region concern: socio-political priorities; energy efficiency; the environment; prices and institutions; finance and technology; regional co-operation; and energy export dependence.

Socio-political Priorities. Together with Sub-Saharan Africa, the region has the highest population growth rate of any region, and meeting their needs is the main priority. Water is the main natural resource in short supply and often involves building desalination plants. There is a need to increase the provision of electricity and clean drinking water.

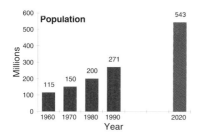

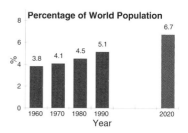

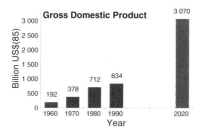

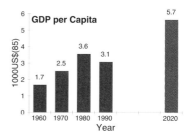

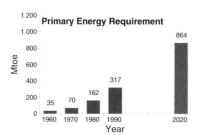

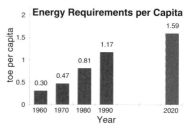

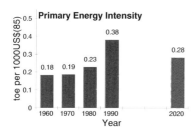

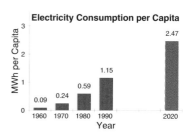

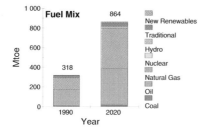

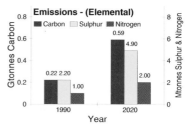

Middle East and North Africa

Notes: 2020 population projection by UN
          All other 2020 data refer to WEC Case B
          US$(85) means US dollars at 1985 value

Energy Efficiency. There is an urgent need for energy efficiency and conservation, and reduction in energy intensity. Energy management, conservation and efficiency especially in end-use would greatly reduce energy cost to the region's economies and release more crude oil for export.

The Environment. Awareness of the importance of environmental preservation is emerging, but the countries are more concerned with their local issues. Global pollution has been mainly caused by the industrialised countries, and the region is willing to contribute to any global environmental effort if it is supported with capital and technology.

The provision of electricity and modest supplies of commercial energy would save a lot of vegetation and help in better standards of living and environmental control.

Prices and Institutions. Other than for oil production and export, energy institutions in the region are modest and lack efficient control of the energy sector, particularly on the demand side. Energy supplies are heavily subsidised in the oil producing countries, at even below the low local costs of production, and lead to over use of energy. It is necessary to eliminate such subsidies, and to restructure the energy sector by improving decision making and providing a greater role for the private sector.

Finance and Technology. Other than for the major oil exporting countries, lack of capital is a main constraint in the development of the region and its energy sector. More than one-third of the region's population do not yet have access to electricity and utilise only very limited commercial energy resources.

There is a need for better interaction with modern technologies, and technological work within the region, rather than reliance on third parties and imported application of technology.

Regional Co-ordination. Electricity interconnections are missing and natural gas networking almost non-existent. There is an urgent need for the development of regional co-operation and integration, which would save a lot of capital and improve energy utilisation.

Dependence on Energy Exports. Because of the abundance of crude oil reserves the region's economic future will remain highly dependent on future oil prices and demand. It is necessary to diversify the economy of the region from almost total dependence on oil exports for income and foreign exchange earnings. Utilisation of the region's vast gas reserves for regional use will save crude oil for export.

The lower royalties available to Middle East and North African oil exporters since the early 1980s have had an adverse impact on the pace of economic and social development not only in these countries but, due to the reduced surpluses available for grants and aid, to the region more generally. However, with the region expected to account for a steadily

204 ■ Part II - Regional Perceptions and Priorities

rising proportion of global oil reserves in the future (a figure which is already 70% of the total) its future oil and natural gas production should be assured. The amount of capital required to raise the region's oil production in line with prospective supply requirements will be substantial, but the raising of these sums is not regarded as problematic given reasonable stability of political and economic conditions.

The region emphasises that dialogue between oil producers and distributors be established. Oil prices and supplies should not display in the future the type of volatility they had in the 1970s and 1980s and should reflect the real value of oil to the world economy as a scarce and depletable resource.

CHAPTER

14

SUB-SAHARAN AFRICA

The region, including South Africa, has 9% of world population, and is responsible for 2.5% of world economic activity measured by volume. It consists of 47 countries, most of which are low income and largely rural agrarian communities. There is a wide linguistic and cultural diversity across the region as well as sharp contrasts in life-styles and standards of living. The region is in a state of transition, with widespread aspirations for political reforms, and social and economic development.

The region consumes 2.7% of world commercial primary energy use, as well as a large amount of biomass energy, principally wood fuel. The region has 2% of world proven oil reserves, 3% of proven gas reserves and 6% of proven coal reserves. There is a massive hydropower potential, extensive uranium deposits and a consistently high level of solar irradiation. In spite of the extensive primary energy resources, the region's per capita commercial energy use is among the lowest in the world, at about 16 GJ pa.

The main energy issue affecting the Sub-Saharan African region is energy supply; that is, how to ensure adequate, reliable, environmentally acceptable and economically sustainable supplies of energy to a region which has not only the lowest per capita income in the world but also the fastest growing population, at over 3% per annum. The region indicates the need for new initiatives in the following areas:

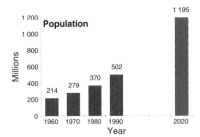

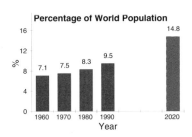

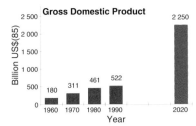

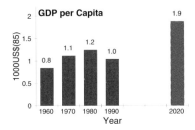

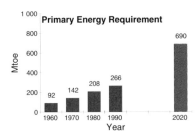

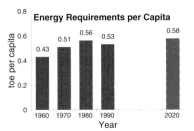

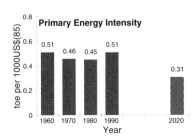

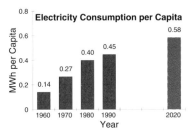

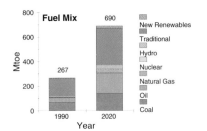

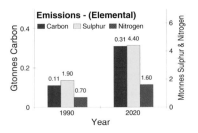

Sub-Saharan Africa

Notes: 2020 population projection by UN
All other 2020 data refer to WEC Case B
US$(85) means US dollars at 1985 value

- to increase the awareness of governments of the critical importance of adequate and reliable energy supply for economic development and social uplift;

- to sustain fuelwood supplies, and to plan and develop rural afforestation programmes;

- to redress adverse macroeconomic policies and correct institutional deficiencies;

- to inject massive new local and international capital and technology into the energy sector;

- to take economic advantage of numerous opportunities for regional co-operation in the energy sector;

- to introduce incentive energy policies and institutional measures that enhance energy efficiency, conservation and environmental protection;

- to reinforce the efforts to restructure the terms of international trade between Sub-Saharan Africa and, especially, the OECD countries and to increase the level of aid.

Energy Supply and Development. The main forces driving the demand for energy in the region are population growth and economic development to support improved standards of living. The region is already a net importer of commercial energy and more than half of the countries spend about 35% of their total export earnings on petroleum imports, making them vulnerable to price rises. Improving the supply of energy and attaining the planned transition in the patterns of energy use from wood fuel to commercial energy will require considerable new investments.

Furthermore, planning and development lead times for new supply facilities, the sheer magnitude of its infrastructural investment requirements relative to the economic capacities of most countries in the region, and the economic penalty of supply failures all serve to dictate an urgent and high level priority for the energy sector on the national and international agenda.

Wood Fuel in the Regional Energy Balance. The region depends on wood fuel to the extent of about 60% of total energy consumption. The more desirable end-use forms of energy, such as electricity, are still well beyond the economic means of the majority of its communities. Furthermore, considerations for commercial energy supply are far outweighed by the pressing needs for more basic services such as water, health, education and even food security. Hence wood will continue to be the dominant energy resource despite the range of environmental, social and economic problems associated with its use. Governments and development agencies need to undertake dedicated investments in rural reforestation and afforestation.

Macroeconomic Policies and Institutional Development. There are several causes of the inadequate performance of the region's energy sector: inappropriate macroeconomic policies, weak energy institutions, over-centralisation of ownership and control, grossly uneconomic pricing, and ad hoc and negative government interference.

There is now a need for new policy designs directed towards the evolution of a market economy, with diversity and competition, and with incentives for new private capital and technology – as well as transparency and accountability of public energy enterprises.

Energy Financing and Technology Transfer. The energy sector is a large consumer of national resources, demanding large capital expenditures, skilled manpower and steady foreign exchange outflows. Almost invariably, energy financing has been the exclusive prerogative of government finance ministries, whose own capacity to finance new investments is now simply inadequate.

> *"The practice of arbitrary price subsidies has also meant that the economic cost of services is not recovered, leading to the widespread technical bankruptcy of energy enterprises in the region and to inefficient use of energy resources."*

Constraints in energy financing as well as distortions in energy pricing have significantly contributed to the legacy of inadequate investments, uneconomic choices and to poor overall performance. Clearly, other sources of finance are needed.

Private equity and the transfer of private international capital are likely to be the best underwriter for the transfer of competitive technologies. Governments need to appreciate that these changes do not necessarily imply the surrender of the public interest, given an appropriate regulatory framework.

Regional Co-operation in the Energy Markets. The distribution of primary energy resources in the region is uneven. Too often, the size of the domestic market alone is too small to justify the economic exploitation, by one country, of an energy resource such as a major hydro site. This makes regional co-operation an imperative.

However, the policy and institutional defects already noted are inhibiting factors, and there are others: national investment planning which does not take account of opportunities in neighbouring States; pricing or exchange rate distortions which inhibit regional trade; application of punitive transit or wheeling charges or royalties; and other political and institutional problems and instabilities.

Taking account of the economic opportunities for co-operation will require political will from governments, regional political stability, mutual trust and fair trading practices as well as appropriate regional trading structures, such as joint development, ownership and operation of energy facilities.

Energy Efficiency, Conservation and the Environment. Throughout the region the efficiency of energy production and use is very unsatisfactory. Almost invariably the main cause is the lack of incentives, particularly through pricing. Electricity tariffs are, on average, a third of the prices in developed countries and access to appropriate energy efficient technologies is also constrained. However, many countries have started to reform energy pricing policies, aiming at recovering full economic cost.

The main environmental problem facing the region is the local degradation of land through deforestation which is mainly the result of land clearing for agriculture and through overstocking. Dams for hydropower projects have also flooded land otherwise needed for agriculture and settlements. Future hydropower and modern biomass developments will need to balance energy availability requirements against environmental impacts, in order to ensure such developments are not counterproductive (eg by damaging future income streams from tourism).

Meeting legitimate aspirations for economic development is likely to take priority over large investments or penalties purely for environmental protection. In summary:

"Energy efficiency, conservation and environmentally responsible action will only be possible when driven by appropriate policy and pricing incentives. There is a need to develop adequate policy instruments and pricing systems that promote the efficient use of energy in the Region. Considerable technical assistance is required to improve the operation and maintenance of energy production and supply facilities as well as in the design of country programmes for energy efficiency. Technical assistance is also required in the transfer of energy efficiency technology, particularly in the form of local demonstration plants."

The Energy Economy and International Trade. The energy sector is the single largest consumer of resources, in the form of capital and foreign exchange, in the region, and in some countries has accounted for up to 40% of foreign debt. Yet for these countries their main product, agricultural commodities, continue to suffer falling prices on the international markets and tariff barriers in the hard currency markets.

"There is a widely held view that agricultural subsidies for farmers in OECD countries, for instance, cannot be justified in the circumstances where economic restructuring, competitive market systems and price deregulation are being advocated for developing countries."

Furthermore, Sub-Saharan Africa is clearly not the favoured region for foreign aid. With 500 million inhabitants in 47 countries, the region received less aid in 1990 than a single country with 13 million inhabitants. In summary, overall:

"The structure and terms of international trade between the Sub-Saharan African region and the OECD countries are considered to be discriminatory, through excessive protectionism, transfer pricing and other negative practices. These can be reviewed and rectified. Furthermore the overall level of aid to the region should be substantially increased before there is any prospect of economic recovery and growth. In particular, given the emergent will for political reform and economic restructuring, the time should be ripe to review and pardon much of the foreign debt that has crippled the Sub-Saharan African region. The co-ordination and effectiveness of aid programmes should be improved."

CHAPTER

15

SOUTH ASIA

The region has 22% of world population, and is responsible for 4.5% of world commercial economic activity measured by volume. The countries of the region form a homogeneous group, with most of them classified as low income and largely rural and agrarian. Though the rate of economic growth is high, population growth is also high and the overall level of development remains low:

> *"A large majority of population remains without access to safe water, or adequate health facilities: poverty levels are high and as per the UNDP Report on Human Development (1991), out of the total poor of 1200 million in the entire world, the region has 575 million, and most of these are in India and Bangladesh."*

The region consumes under 4% of world commercial primary energy supplies, and remains very dependent on non-commercial energy use. It has a relatively small natural resource base: 1% of world proven oil reserves, 2% of proven natural gas reserves and 6% of world proven coal reserves.

The region's main conclusions and recommendations concern: economic growth and development; life-style and energy consumption; energy use; the environment; institutions, pricing and finance; security of supply; energy efficiency; technology; and regional trade and co-operation.

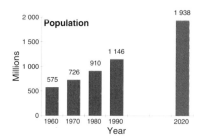

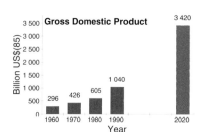

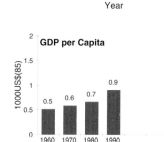

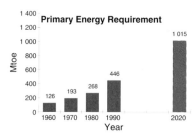

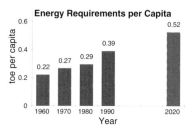

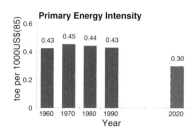

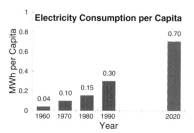

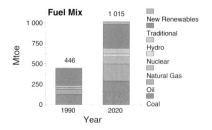

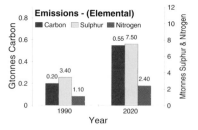

South Asia

Notes: *2020 population projection by UN*
         All other 2020 data refer to WEC Case B
         US$(85) means US dollars at 1985 value

Economic Growth and Development. The major problem for the region is the rapid growth in demand consequent upon the growth in population and the aspirations for improved standards of life. The present energy pattern is non-commercially intensive and unless the resources are made more productive even the present levels of use are not sustainable. Hence economic growth and development is a top priority:

> *"The region believes that economic growth and development would be necessary to eliminate the present levels of poverty and human deprivation. Economic growth and development thus offer the best way of limiting population growth and constraints on growth would be counterproductive."*

Life-styles and Energy Consumption. The regional per capita consumption of commercial primary energy is only one-fifteenth of the consumption of the industrialised countries, though this is supplemented by high non-commercial energy use. But increasing urbanisation, expected to reach 40% by 2000, will add to the demand for commercial energy from fossil fuels. In rural areas, deforestation for agricultural land, timber and in some cases, fuel, means that traditional woodfuel resources are depleted and more difficult to obtain. People are forced to burn lower quality fuels and spend more time in collection or money in buying them.

> *The region does not consider this difference in personal energy use to be sustainable: "This is important since in the long run the present level of inequality in the living standards and energy consumption between the developed and developing countries is not sustainable in an open international economy."*

Energy Availability. There are large coal resources and this will remain the most important energy source. There is a need to cut total costs, including environmental costs of mining and use, and to promote cleaner technology and efficiency of use. Pakistan aims at 50% of electricity production from nuclear by 2020; and India 30%.

The most important renewable energy resources are hydro and biomass, and these must be exploited commercially if they are environmentally satisfactory. There are opportunities for new renewable energy sources, especially in remote areas: biogas and gasifiers based on biomass, solar, wind and micro hydro. It is necessary to identify thrust areas, get correct (full-cost) pricing of alternative fuels including environmental costs, and spread information.

The Environment. There is growing concern about adverse environmental impacts, especially at local level:

"All of [the countries] exhibit growing environmental stress since the natural resource management responses have proved inadequate to combat the adverse impacts of development and economic growth. Though there is a general awareness that economic decisions affect the condition of the environment and that environmental quality affects the performance of the economy as well as the welfare of the people, often these facts are ignored since growth maximisation is an important economic and political objective."

Poverty and environmental degradation are inextricably linked and future strategies must concentrate on improving economic growth with steps to improve environmental and natural resource management. But it is hard for the region to apply the "polluter pays" principle, especially to internalise environmental costs when the poor cannot afford to pay full prices or taxes.

Though the region is not a major global polluter, enhanced energy use will double CO_2 emissions by 2010.

Finance, Institutions and Pricing. The major challenge is raising finance. The institutional structures and political conditions in the region are major limitations; governments control energy investments, supply and pricing leading to government interference, public sector dominance and lack of market discipline:

"Most of the energy sector units in the region are characterised by low operational efficiency, lack of cost recovery and unrealistic pricing structures, large and often rising system losses and inadequate attention to load management or technical dynamism ... often pricing policies are used to carry out welfare transfers."

The need is to reform the institutional structures, and to introduce full-cost pricing, including environmental costs, if meaningful energy demand management programmes are to be carried out. Even given these internal reforms, there will be a need for large-scale outside assistance, and better financing terms.

Security of Supply. The issues include dependence on fuelwood, where the private and social costs (which are hard to internalise) diverge; and dependence on foreign oil, where it is necessary to reduce dependence on the volatility of price and availability:

> *"A relatively small natural resource base, especially that of oil, has led to high dependence on imports and hence the economies of the region are extremely vulnerable to fluctuations in the international oil markets."*

Energy Efficiency. The region has low efficiency of energy use and management of natural resources, and the scope for improvement is huge. The region must now drive for increased energy efficiency for the environmental benefits, to save scarce capital for use elsewhere, and to avoid the increasing move from non-commercial to commercial energy constraining development.

Constraints include lack of information, technologies and incentives; unavailability of energy conservation services; and the lack of the necessary pressures to avoid wasting resources. Institutional reforms, including full-cost pricing, mentioned above, are essential.

Technology. Technological development is the best way to raise the quality of life and protect the environment. Technology transfer issues are vital, and the need is for a free flow of technology at reasonable cost. The region is a net importer of energy technology, and the constraints on development are finance, the industrialised countries' insistence on "intellectual property rights", and patents.

More R & D and technology transfer is needed on clean coal, renewable energy sources and energy efficiency.

> *"Today, technologies exist in the world which can lead to efficiency in energy use, but they are still not available freely and at costs which are affordable."*

Regional Trade and Co-operation. This will expand the resource base and gives economies of scale and optimisation for natural gas, energy efficiency, hydro, capital markets, coal, technology transfer and environmental protection.

CHAPTER

16

THE PACIFIC

The region currently has 34% of world population, and is responsible for 23.5% of world economic activity measured by volume, with China dominant in terms of population and as producer and user of energy. Together with South Asia, the Pacific region is the fastest growing in the world. The region is easily the largest and most diverse of the eight regions, culturally as well as economically, and contains fully developed industrial countries, rapidly industrialising countries, less developed countries, centrally planned economies, and the Pacific islands.

The region currently consumes 18% of world commercial primary energy supplies; and has 4% of world proven oil reserves, 5% of proven natural gas reserves and 24% of proven coal reserves. However, these reserves are unevenly distributed in the region, being mainly owned by Australia, China, Indonesia, Malaysia and Papua New Guinea with many countries heavily dependent on imports.

The region's main conclusions and recommendations concern: regional challenges and priorities; energy use; market economy and trade; security of supply; the environment; energy efficiency; technology; and international co-operation.

Regional Challenges and Priorities. Economic development is accorded a very high priority in the region and this will entail a rapid increase in energy supply. The regional challenge is to meet these aspirations within the constraints of environmental, financial and human resources. This will not always be easy:

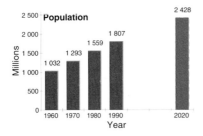

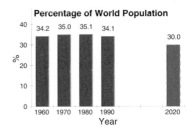

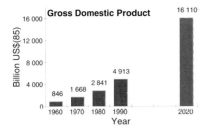

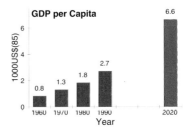

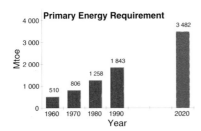

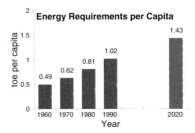

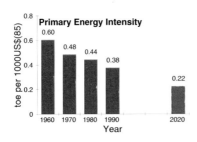

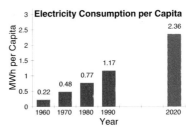

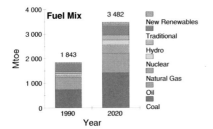

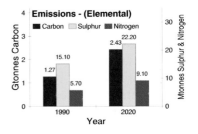

The Pacific

Notes: 2020 population projection by UN
          All other 2020 data refer to WEC Case B
          US$(85) means US dollars at 1985 value

"There are several countries in the region for whom the provision of even basic energy needs remains a priority, and where electrification of the remote areas is still a priority. .... For example, some 80% of Chinese living in rural areas live primarily on biomass energy forms, or on the simple burning of coal, with unacceptable local environmental effects."

To achieve these aims, the region believes it must keep economically competitive with other regions; it must recognise cultural and economic differences within the region; and it must prepare for unprecedented change with resilience based on commitment to education, to science and technology, a good infrastructure, a strong economy and willingness to innovate.

Energy Use. It is necessary to use the region's energy resources to their economic potential while keeping to environmental goals. The main energy supply will still be from oil, natural gas, coal, hydro, nuclear and biomass, and so must concentrate on improving the efficiency, cost and safety of their production, transport and use. As regards nuclear and renewable resources:

(a) "Many consider an expanded nuclear programme to be an essential part of their energy future."
(b) "The general view in the region is that [renewable] resources may not account for more than 8–10% of energy supply in the region by 2020, including and dominated by hydroelectric and biomass energy forms. However, actual penetration will depend to a large extent on political will since many of the existing barriers are institutional."

Market Economy, Trade and Finance. It is important to rely on market mechanisms wherever possible and to enhance them where necessary, by reform of pricing, regulation and, where needed, by reform of institutional structures. Financial resources will be strained. The region must compete for available funds and attract outside equity participation, and must also rely more on its own financial resources:

"In turn this will inevitably require that all forms of energy are priced correctly and that those prices reflect the full cost of producing, transporting and delivering the various energy forms."

The region has two other important requirements:

- Fiscal systems for energy which are neutral, stable, non-discriminatory and predictable.

- Free and efficient trade within the region and with the world, to support the extensive energy trade that will be needed.

Security of Supply. The best strategy is to increase energy choice, adaptability to change and international co-operation:

"A number of countries in the region have adopted the view that energy security is best achieved and maintained through initiatives that increase energy choices and promote adaptability to change, rather than through subsidising uneconomic offshore or domestic resource developments.... Consequently, in dealing with the security of energy supply objectives in the future, the challenge is to operate within a market-oriented energy economy for the development and transport of secure energy sources."

The Environment. Environmental goals are of equal importance with economic and social goals. It is necessary to work towards sustainable energy use by incorporating environmental considerations in economic decision making, while continuing to rely on market forces subject to suitable environmental standards:

"In the global market economy, the critical links between the present energy economy and sustainable economic development are energy efficiency and internalisation of environmental costs."

The high regional rate of economic growth has stretched resources and caused quite significant local and regional environmental impacts, the alleviation of which is the main priority. This is intimately linked to economic progress.

The region is also not unmindful of global issues, but it will be difficult if not impossible for it to meet arbitrary greenhouse gas target levels. As Mr Fujime of the Japanese Institute of Energy Economics said in June 1991, concerning Japanese energy policy:

"It has been said repeatedly that poverty is the greatest polluter of them all.....It is easy to forget that the war against poverty, and the associated need to lift the living standards of those living in poverty to an acceptable level, must continue to be waged both for humanitarian reasons and to assist in controlling local and regional pollution problems."

As regards these issues, China has 25% of world population, 80% of whom live in rural areas, with 75% dependency on coal and high CO_2 emissions. Around 800 million rural dwellers burn 300 million tonnes (mt) of coal at 10–20% thermal efficiency and also 300 mt in small industrial/power station boilers:

"If stabilisation of CO_2 emissions at the 1989 level must be achieved in and after 2000, it is necessary to slow Japan's economic growth rate by one-half, reducing the average annual economic growth rate from 4% (real, to 2000) to around 2%. It is a grave question whether policy measures calling for such a drastic slow-down in economic growth are acceptable."

Energy Efficiency. Enhancing economic efficiency of energy use is vital to achieve the best utilisation of resources and to protect the environment, and should be given a high priority. Energy efficiency should be improved by upgrading equipment, systems and building efficiency and use. The efficiency of new capital stock should be improved by strategies involving regulation, persuasion, and enhanced R & D for new and more efficient technologies.

"The dominance of China in this matter is such that it can be well argued that assisting China in achieving economic development with reduced greenhouse gas emission rates may be the single most beneficial action which mankind can take – with the potential improvement available eclipsing that obtained by further improving the performance of the developed world."

Technology. There should be a commitment to R & D and the management of technology and technology transfer to improve energy choice and to protect the environment.

International Co-operation. The region will need co-operation at the international level on developing technology and infrastructure, exchanging information and encouraging free markets and access to energy resources. The region must contribute to solving world energy problems such as global environmental constraints and the need of the developing countries for more advanced technology.

THE
AGENDA
FOR
ACTION

CHAPTER

17

THE MAJOR CONCERNS

This chapter summarises the major concerns identified in this report:

- continuing inability to access energy;

- resource and geopolitical constraints;

- increasing environmental pollution and degradation due, among other reasons, to energy provision and use;

- institutional rigidities.

These concerns would form the foundation for a sound future agenda for achievement of key economic, social, political, institutional and environmental goals pertaining to energy provision and use. This report's conclusions and recommendations, which would also form the basis of an *Agenda for Action*, are set out in the next chapter.

THE REDUCTION OF ENERGY POVERTY

Rapid and unconstrained expansion in energy demand could hit supply constraints – especially of oil and natural gas – well before the year 2050. Alternative supply options which rely on sources other than coal and nuclear probably cannot be made available in sufficient quantities within that time-frame.

It will require the expanding use of all energy resources – fossil fuels (including tar sands and oil shale), renewables and nuclear energy – to meet the requirements of a growing world population. It is likely that it will take until the second-half of the next century for alternative energy technologies to be developed and applied on a scale that will offer real hope for significantly increasing the availability of services from energy in poor countries, and real options in choice of supply everywhere.

Justifying the expanded access to energy places it in its broadest social and developmental context. Over half the world's current population do not now have access to commercial energy. In many poorer countries of the world the availability and use of energy per head has actually gone down over the past 15 years, reflecting poverty. With the population increases occurring in the developing world over the coming decades – despite uncertainties over the impact of armed conflict, inadequate water and sanitation standards, and the ravages of disease and famine – even the maintenance of energy per capita availability will be a challenge.

The problem of energy poverty is seen at its worst and most distressing in the developing countries. But energy poverty is arguably not confined to these. Even in the richer industrial countries poverty reduces access to affordable energy. Energy bills may be beyond the capacity to pay: poor people may feel they must simply do without, or pay a relatively high proportion of their income out on energy. This may not be a situation where increases in income support are regarded as appropriate or desirable. This may particularly be the case where home insulation cannot be afforded to a satisfactory standard, or energy efficient equipment be bought, and thus steps to reduce energy use and costs through higher efficiency will not be taken under prevailing conditions.

People need energy because of the services it provides. Without these services, a large proportion of the world's present and prospective population are unable to satisfy their basic needs.

The first item on the Agenda for Action is therefore the reduction of energy poverty by extending access to energy, and by improving the efficiency and reducing the environmental impacts of its use.

RESOURCE AND GEOPOLITICAL CONSTRAINTS – SUPPLY SIDE

Oil and natural gas availability are expected to come under pressure during the middle part of the 21st century if global energy demand follows one of the higher trajectories outlined in the Cases in this report. The higher the trajectory the greater is likely to be the demand for coal and nuclear. If policy-makers and energy consumers wish to follow a lower trajectory of energy demand – whether to reduce pressure on oil and natural gas supplies, to permit significant reliance on new renewables in the total fuel mix, or to reduce reliance on fossil fuels for environmental reasons – then the earlier appropriate action is taken the better.

In the much shorter term there will be an increase in the number of countries dependent upon importing fossil fuels, especially oil and natural gas, and supply lines will lengthen. These shifts will create uncertainty over supplies and upward pressures on prices.

The costs of exploring for, and extracting, oil and natural gas are also expected to rise as activity concentrates upon areas with harsher natural conditions (eg northerly latitudes), sub-ocean reserves and smaller pockets of resources.

Reserves of fossil fuels, particularly of oil and natural gas, are concentrated in a few regions and countries. Most of these regions and countries are perceived to be subject to geopolitical forces which may disrupt supplies or create price volatility.

Greater efficiency in the use of present fossil fuel resources will give headroom to extend supply availability and to use alternative fossil fuel resources such as tar sands and oil shales with clean conversion processes as a bridge to a wider range of primary energy supplies sources.

Because of the long-lead times involved from initiating R&D to large-scale commercial application, it will be necessary to devise research and development strategies on the basis of long-term price trends. The long-term price of oil is expected to increase, and short-term fluctuations or stability around a modest price level should not be allowed to blur this longer-term outlook.

The encouragement of new renewable forms of energy appropriate to local circumstances and resource availability will be of particular importance to the many developing countries that do not have indigenous fossil fuel resources. Many of these countries are far from supplies of natural gas and can afford oil import costs only with difficulty.

The second item on the Agenda for Action is therefore the need to expand the supply availability of acceptable traditional forms of energy and to diversify and increase the availability of non-fossil fuels.

RESOURCE AND GEOPOLITICAL CONSTRAINTS – DEMAND SIDE

The key resource constraints on the demand side are lack of finance, technology, know-how and management. These weaknesses are felt particularly strongly in the developing countries. They are areas where there is great potential through co-operation, transfers, joint-ventures and educational programmes to ameliorate the problems. If this potential for amelioration is to be realised then the background conditions must be supportive. Inappropriate ideological stances, political interference, institutional rigidities and other weaknesses need to be eliminated. The market system – supported by government action to ensure its effectiveness in terms of competition and pricing, and to encourage technological innovation and diffusion – is believed to be the best mechanism for progress.

Much has been said in this report about the potential and need for increased efficiency in energy provision and use. Energy consumers are frequently reluctant to take the necessary steps to curb their consumption, and energy policy-makers frequently shy away from introducing effective measures which may seem politically unpalatable. Energy processors and those with energy-using equipment are frequently constrained in the steps they can take to improve efficiency in use until plant and equipment can be replaced.

Various steps can be taken to reduce these constraints, including a range of economic incentives and disincentives (from tax credits, permits, accelerated depreciation and preferential loan schemes, to focused taxes and duties).

In recent years taxes intended to curb energy use and/or environmental pollution from its use have been much debated, especially carbon taxes. There are a number of practical objections to carbon taxes. To be effective their level would have to be set much higher than generally supposed. Carbon emissions are not the only emissions from energy use, not even the only greenhouse gas emissions. Taxation of energy more generally is severely problematic. Why should those using, or seeking to obtain, the services which energy provides be penalised by a general tax on energy? A general tax on energy penalises those forms of energy with limited environmental impact equally with forms having much greater impact. Can energy taxes be fine-tuned in such a way as to reflect accurately the environmental impact and other externalities of their provision and use?

If energy or carbon taxes were to be introduced then they should be structured in such a way that their revenue does not go into general government funds. Instead, such taxes should be revenue-neutral (that is, tax burdens elsewhere should be reduced so that there is no net increase in taxation). The revenue should be earmarked for spending in the energy-related sector: on helping to raise energy efficiency; encourage cleaner coal and other technologies; accelerate the development of additional energy sources, and alternative fuels, processes and equipment; introduce traffic calming schemes; improve the infrastructure of efficient collective transportation modes, and so on. This is something which governments have been extremely reluctant to do in the past; but should now be pressed to do with renewed vigour.

Numerous studies have found that carbon taxes are likely to reduce overall energy demand and the pattern of primary energy use. But they would have to be set at a very high level to have significant effect, which might be politically difficult. Several studies have suggested that at least a US\$300/tonne carbon tax would be required to have a significant impact on curbing fossil fuel demand and reducing CO_2 emissions from this source. There is also a widespread tendency to overlook the many taxes and duties already imposed upon fossil fuels, and which are therefore tantamount to a high carbon tax. Thus Italy, the UK, France and Denmark currently have very high "proxy" carbon taxes – with gasoline duties and taxes in Italy running at over four times the maximum level normally proposed for a carbon tax.

There is also doubt whether carbon taxes set at a politically realistic level would have a major impact on either electricity or transport demand, the two most rapidly growing energy demand sectors.

This report is therefore not opposed in principle to taxes on energy and energy use, but seeks to ensure there is a clear and well-understood link between cause and effect. Therefore the energy user, particularly the end-user, must bear the full burden of the "polluter pays" principle. It is not yet clear that governments have that as their overriding principle when considering such taxes.

The third item on the Agenda for Action is a package of measures to promote technological innovation and its diffusion; the raising of efficiency in energy use; the encouragement of energy conservation; the promotion of international co-operation and transfers; the support of international joint ventures and educational programmes; and the wider spread of the market system within a framework of effective government support and stimulation.

TACKLING ENVIRONMENTAL POLLUTION AND DEGRADATION

For most countries in the world – those in various stages of development towards industrial maturity – local environmental problems are the greatest concern and likely to remain so for at least some decades.

Despite improvements in tackling the local and regional environmental impacts of energy provision and use, too little has been achieved in relation to the scale and extent of these problems. Existing good technology is not being implemented rapidly and widely enough, while much needs to be done to achieve further innovation and diffusion of appropriate new technology.

Notable advances have been made in reducing emissions of particulates, lead and sulphur in many richer industrial countries. The reduction of sulphur dioxide emissions nevertheless has a considerable way to go even in these countries. One problem is that the current standard flue gas desulphurisation process involves the use of limestone (often extracted from areas of high landscape value) which is finally converted into excess supplies of gypsum. Overall environmental considerations suggest the use of regenerable flue gas desulphurisation processes.

In many poorer countries of the world emissions of particulates, lead and sulphur continue to rise. The result is city smogs, respiratory and other health problems, acid rain deposition and a deteriorating natural environment.

Less satisfactory progress has also been made in reducing or curbing a number of other emissions: nitrogen oxides (NO_x), nitrous oxide (N_2O), volatile organic compounds, carbon dioxide (CO_2), carbon monoxide (CO) and methane (CH_4). Anthropogenic emissions of these gases are rising generally, promoted by the overall rise in global energy provision and use and particularly by the rapidly growing oil-based transportation sector. These emissions have local, regional and – perhaps – global impacts.

This report has advocated the full-cost pricing of energy, to include environmental costs and other externalities. Where these costs cannot be gauged, particularly in the context of fears of climate change, precautionary measures have been advocated. The position adopted in this report on potential global climate change is fully consistent with that taken by the Intergovernmental Panel on Climate Change Scientific Assessment to date – including recognition of the uncertainties and inadequate understanding which abound.

It would be desirable to encourage an awareness of the need to conserve the world's resources in order to achieve sustainable development for the greater benefit of all. This is a key element in a precautionary strategy which assumes it is not acceptable to run down environmental assets. The consequences of doing so are not known, because ecosystems are too complex, and therefore precaution requires people to act as if running down natural assets will or could have major detrimental results. Similarly, precaution requires acceptance of the belief that actions may have harmful consequences which are irreversible – perhaps involving species extinction or the raising of the Earth's temperature. Some natural assets also serve as human life supports, and again precaution suggests that where no man-made substitutes are available these ecological assets should be conserved in the interests of sustainable development and the well-being of future generations.

These numerous, and often complex, concerns suggest that instead of considering carbon taxes or energy taxes *per se*, it is worth considering where the revenues from such taxes might first be spent. Where would the largest and quickest returns be made in ameliorating local, regional or potential global pollution. Where are the financial, technological and management resources least available for tackling these issues. Such considerations point primarily to the needs of developing countries and for institutional change rather than to the much more diffuse objectives of global target-setting.

The fourth item on the Agenda for Action is therefore the curbing of harmful emissions from energy provision and use. This will require a mixture of measures:

- raising efficiency in energy provision and use;

- encouraging conservation;

- accelerating the introduction of cleaner processes and energy-using equipment;

- promoting alternative forms of energy and fuels;

- discouraging energy processes and uses which result in harmful emissions;

- improved management and education in the efficient provision and use of energy;

- encouraging an awareness of the need to conserve the world's resources generally in order to achieve sustainable development for the greater benefit of all;

- concentrating efforts to curb harmful emissions first where the largest and quickest returns are to be made in mitigating local, regional and potential global pollution.

INSTITUTIONAL ISSUES

Despite the many debates on energy and energy-related environmental matters in recent years few countries have taken active steps to address the issues. Regulations are tightening in a number of countries; some have contemplated specific measures to shift behaviour through higher prices (while others through subsidies promote rather different goals); a very few have introduced market instruments of an experimental nature in the hope of addressing energy *and* environmental goals. Improvements have been occurring in energy processing and using equipment, in terms of their efficiency and cleanliness. Encouraging though all these developments are, they are not going either fast or far enough by comparison with the nature and scale of the problems they seek to address.

A major reason for this inadequate response lies in institutional rigidities. An important area of institutional change is the response of governments or groups of governments to perceived national and international constraints, opportunities and goals. The means is by adjusting framework conditions – policies, policy instruments and organisational structures. Actual implementation is left, or should be left, to the economic actors – enterprises, consumers, etc.

Institutional issues are procedural: they relate to the handling of conflicts between competing goals and actors and overcoming the perceived inadequacy of implementing instruments such as markets or prices. Institutional reforms are therefore directed at developing an evolving and appropriate framework of measures and mechanisms which anticipate and resolve conflict, develop consensus on goals and behaviours, promote the implementation of goals, and handle residual disagreement.

The current institutional framework suffers from rigidities which prevent adequate responses to the internationalisation of energy and energy-related issues and to the changing balance between societal goals. These rigidities are clearly apparent in the handling of efficiency, social and economic welfare, and environmental issues. The primary purpose and priority of institutional reform necessarily varies according to local conditions. In the developing countries the principal goals are the building-up of sound administration, education, information and communication as a basis for improved national performance and international integration. Unless these goals are achieved then the widespread availability of energy and its related services, at affordable prices, will either not occur or will be long delayed. In the economies in transition of Central and Eastern Europe and the CIS, the principal aim is – or should be – the introduction of market economy policies and structures as rapidly as social and political conditions permit. In the richer industrial countries a high priority is attached to removing market deficiencies.

The fifth item on the Agenda for Action is, therefore, institutional change appropriate to local circumstances and global needs; and the removal of rigidities which act as barriers to such change.

However, institutions cannot be expected to achieve desirable change by themselves. They are the instruments of politicians and of policymakers; they are intended to reflect the wishes of the wider public. This means that politicians and policy-makers must be prepared to support and implement new policy directions, and that the wider public in turn is prepared to give such new policy measures their understanding and support. Specifically, it requires energy consumers to give their active support to policies aimed at achieving wider and longer-term policy goals than may suit their narrower, short-term personal interests. This, in turn, will promote extension of the usual political considerations of the electoral cycle and electoral advantage.

It is this Commission's view that a new initiative is required which addresses the lack of energy availability in the developing countries, and at the same time encourages efficiency in the provision and use of energy; raises the quality of management and training in energy provision and use; heightens public awareness of energy-related issues; encourages local institutional reforms to help meet policy goals; reduces the adverse environmental impacts of energy provision and use; and provides a global institutional framework and resourcing of a scale and scope that matches the size and nature of the problems.

CHAPTER

18

CONCLUSIONS AND RECOMMENDATIONS

PRIORITIES

This report concludes, from the work of its regional groups and central studies of global perceptions, that there is a clear distinction to be made between the energy priorities of the developing economies, the economies in transition, and the industrial economies.

Despite their disparate nature and stages of development, the developing countries have the following priorities in common: economic growth and reduction of the incidence of poverty; access to adequate commercial energy supplies and the finances needed to achieve these; access to technology transfers wherever possible; and resolution of a wide variety of local environmental problems.

For the economies in transition in the Commonwealth of Independent States, and Central and Eastern Europe (CEE/CIS), their key priorities are: the modernisation and expansion of existing supply infrastructures; the promotion of the rational use of energy; transition to market-oriented policies and enterprises; the introduction of stable legal and fiscal regimes which foster investment and satisfactory returns thereon; and the abatement of local and regional pollution.

For the industrialised countries, the dominating issues are securing greater energy efficiency; the continuous improvement to the technologies deployed in their own countries and elsewhere; further abatement of local and regional pollution; and, in some of these countries, precautionary measures in relation to potential global environmental problems.

The challenge for the world's institutions is to rise above these different priorities and to secure broad progress on all fronts, rather than to allow sectoral or political differences to inhibit necessary progress.

One consequence of the huge increase of global population generally forecast, over 90% of it occurring in the presently categorised developing nations, will be rising global energy demand. This will involve the accelerated consumption of the world's reserves of fossil fuels, with coal depleting less rapidly than oil and natural gas. One result will be increased reliance on coal and ultimately a shift (probably well into the 21st century) to other fossil resources (such as tar sands, shale oil, synthetic gas, etc) which can only be developed at higher cost, with the application of improved technologies, but with the risk of increased environmental impact.

Such developments will therefore necessitate urgent steps to widen and strengthen the application of technologies which reduce emissions harmful at the local and regional level. They also indicate high priority should be given to the search after technologies which could recapture and reabsorb anthropogenic greenhouse gas emissions (particularly CO_2) that may have a harmful global impact.

The higher cost of fossil fuels and environmental considerations will place increased emphasis on energy efficiency, and should stimulate the development and implementation of the various alternative energy sources.

ENERGY MARKETS

To ensure that global and regional energy demand can be met in the most cost-effective way, energy markets will be required which function effectively. This will depend upon:

- Ensuring a high degree of market liberalisation, albeit within government regulatory frameworks.

- Ensuring the maintenance of an open international trading system, and avoiding regional bloc formation and national barriers which inhibit international trade.

- Identifying and implementing appropriate improvements to institutional arrangements, both national and international. It is particularly in the CEE/CIS and developing countries that such improvements are required in order to mobilise capital, create efficiency, and separate the State from day to day energy operations. These countries need to become customer-oriented and to ensure the protection of private and intellectual property. The right of access to, and use of, profits from private investment needs to be recognised in order to allow the effective functioning of markets.

- Moving towards the pricing of energy provision and use which covers full production costs, and their wider economic, social and environmental impacts.

- Reordering support and assistance from the industrialised countries to ensure optimisation of the use of such aid to cover, not only the transfer of technology but the training of managers and operators and the setting up of local equipment and other manufacture and maintenance.

RESEARCH AND DEVELOPMENT

The most important requirements for securing an adequate global energy supply up to 2020 will be:

- The efficient and responsible use of fossil fuels.

- Ensuring the safety in operation of nuclear energy.

- Expanding the availability of alternative fossil fuels and new renewables which, especially in the period after 2020, can be expected to start making a more significant contribution to total energy supply.

Fossil fuel reserves must be increased and husbanded. The contribution of nuclear with its high capital costs, long lead times and current public antipathy will be largely determined over the next 15–20 years as nuclear plants are decommissioned. It will then be seen if they are replaced by newer generations of nuclear plant, or by fossil burning plant. New renewable forms of energy will not make a major contribution on this short time-scale.

Research and development needs better direction. Some relevant considerations are:

- Although the long-term price of oil and therefore of other fuels will increase, prices in the shorter term may vary and blur the long-term outlook. This, however, should not deter long-term research and the development of energy strategies based on the longer-term price outlook.

- The technology for efficient energy application must be developed and implemented for world-wide application. This should be allied to sufficient commercial attraction to secure its widespread use.

- There is a need to improve the safety, capacity and efficiency of energy transport facilities.

- The development and introduction of more energy-efficient land transport vehicles, shifts towards the more energy-efficient modes of transport, the introduction of alternative and less polluting transport fuels, more stringent assessment of the need for additional transport infrastructure and application of innovative user-pricing schemes are required. In seeking to maintain and enhance mobility, radical improvements in means are required.

ENVIRONMENTAL QUALITY

The technology for abating local and regional pollution of energy provision and use has advanced to a point where the industrialised countries can steadily reduce the pollution to generally acceptable levels.

The new and even more challenging concern is now potential global climate change resulting from anthropogenic CO_2 and other greenhouse gas emissions. The developing countries and the economies in transition, as has been noted, regard their severe local environmental problems as a much higher priority for them. There is a need to bridge the deep gaps which currently exist in priorities and perceptions between the various groups of countries and people around the world, by effective communication and mutually acceptable actions.

To ensure that resources are used in an efficient and balanced manner as seen from both a global and a regional point of view, it will be important in seeking international agreement on greenhouse gas emissions that:

- Economic growth is seen and achieved as an essential part of any policy of sustainable development, necessary not only to meet people's needs and aspirations but also to generate the investment capital required to use energy more efficiently and to protect the environment.

- Steps are taken to account more effectively for the wider social and environmental impacts of economic growth and energy development, and to reflect them more adequately in the measurement of economic growth and priorities in energy provision and use, including the pricing of energy to cover environmental impacts.

- The claims of local priorities, based on local judgement and upon available resources, are recognised. This may require considerable assistance to flow from the industrialised countries to the CEE/CIS and developing countries, if local energy efficiency levels and other methods of reducing local emissions are to be implemented.

- Precautionary measures to reduce the emissions of greenhouse gases should be adopted since scientific evidence does not so far justify any other policy.

- Abatement policies should be based on the principle of expenditure optimisation across the globe, such that private and public funds are spent not on a national basis to secure national targets irrespective of global impact, but where the best global effect can be achieved.

- Adaptation policies will be required in the event of enhanced global warming and climate change due to anthropogenic greenhouse gas emissions becoming confirmed, and realistic prospects of fossil fuel demand indicate that if there is confirmation then adaptation policies are already unavoidable. Substantial increases in atmospheric CO_2 concentrations seem inevitable for many decades to come.

SUSTAINABLE ENERGY DEVELOPMENT

The top-down and bottom-up analysis of this study demonstrates clearly that the perception of what is important in the further development of the world energy system varies widely from region to region. In finding a path to sustainable global and regional energy development it will be of the utmost importance to address these widely different concerns in a realistic and balanced manner to reduce – as far as possible – the associated stresses between countries and regions. Without sufficient attention to this dimension of the world energy problem, there will not be sustainable development consistent with the expected population explosion in the developing world. The basic elements of global and regional policies to ensure a sufficiently balanced approach are:

- To ensure that the available resources are used in the most cost-effective and productive manner.

- To balance the measures selected to cope with the various priority issues in accordance with their importance and costs.

- To ensure that markets function as effectively as possible to obtain such balance and with acceptable global consequences.

- To ensure that governmental measures are mainly directed at providing the framework which permits markets to function and to avoid market distortions which prevent the development of the necessary longer-term solutions.

- To intensify research in order to improve scientific understanding of potential global climate change in support of the IPCC's existing efforts.

- To maximise energy efficiency and conservation wherever justified on broadly defined cost/benefit grounds as the primary measure to support economic development and assist with environmental protection.

The World Energy Council has instituted a programme of selective action and study to take further an understanding of the issues, and the formation of relevant and effective policies raised in this report.

EPILOGUE

EPILOGUE – BEYOND 2020

Any consideration of a period 30 years and more ahead is bound to be highly speculative. To go out to the year 2100 is to be reminded of how much has changed in the world since the 1880s, and how wide of the mark many speculations about the 1990s made then would have been. Thus what follows should be regarded as no less speculative and uncertain.

Beyond 2020 the world is likely to be confronted with two or three extremely challenging decades as growing uncertainty about oil and natural gas availability, pressure to take a clear position on the expansion of nuclear power, and insufficient progress on renewable energy provision stack up against the energy demands of a still-rising world population.

Faced with these challenges the rational and sensible response is to keep options open, not seek to limit them.

Much is made of the availability of geological reserves of oil and natural gas. This has long been a subject of controversy. Currently there is great complacency on this subject, but the passage of time may show this complacency to have been misplaced. The coming decades will see the growing import dependency of an increasing number of countries; lengthening supply lines; rising exploration and production costs due to tougher natural conditions or smaller pockets of reserves in easier natural conditions; and geopolitical uncertainties – including potentially rising tensions in the medium term.

Beyond 2020 the magnitude of the supply problems could expand, especially if higher global energy demand occurs and too little is done to develop alternatives. Under some higher global energy demand scenarios oil and natural gas availability could become extremely tight, and price escalation rapid, even before 2050. The problem is that no realistic demand scenario demonstrates severe resource constraints before 2030. Even if the resources are available the necessary exploitation may not be financed, although history would suggest that at a price such barriers are, at most, temporary.

It will be obvious that much of the incremental energy demanded as a result of population growth between now and 2020 will occur post-2020, to be added to the energy demands of the further 2 billion or so additional people expected to inhabit the world by 2050. By the year 2100 world population could well have reached 12 billion (about 87% of this total living in the present developing countries). The presently categorised developing countries can be expected to account for about 80% of global energy demand. Even then energy per capita availability in the developing countries is likely to be far less than in the rest of the world – perhaps only 50% or 60% of that in the OECD area by then. (If energy per capita consumption in the developing countries were to achieve *present* OECD levels by the year 2020, annual increases of over 6% would be required. For the developing countries to achieve *present* OECD levels even by the year 2100 would require annual increases of 1.7%.)

By the end of the next century close to three-quarters of the world's population is likely to be urbanised and the interim pressures on housing, sanitation, air and water quality, health care, and congestion are likely to have been intense. Energy systems geared to providing the comforts, motive power and mobility that people seek from energy may have led to some profound changes. The challenge to city transportation systems over that time-frame is likely to have called forth some imaginative responses. Urban heating and cooling systems could look – and be – very different from now. Rural life and the rural landscape could have markedly changed.

These are likely to be only some, of many, sources of instability and tension over the next century arising from the uneven distribution of resources – financial, managerial, technological as well as natural. Unless appropriate frameworks are developed, policies implemented, and recognition achieved of the international dimensions of instability and the need for action consistent with the fact of interdependence the outlook is profoundly worrying. Government aid and private charity from richer countries will not go far in meeting the requirements. Self-help, private financing, attracting capital, rewarding investors, reforming present institutions (or doing away with outmoded ones) and creating new institutions in tune with future needs will all be needed.

The further out in time one goes the greater, obviously, the need for solar and other environmentally acceptable and economically viable forms of renewable energy; and for publicly acceptable nuclear power. But reliance on thermal nuclear power will not be enough. The fast-breeder reactor and, eventually, nuclear fusion will be required.

Global energy demand prospects also become even more sensitive to small changes in basic assumptions the further out in time one goes: on population growth, economic growth, energy intensity, and energy use per capita. So much so that credible figures of global energy demand in 2100 range between 20 Gtoe and over 40 Gtoe – and if coal and nuclear power were to be accessed without constraint perhaps even higher. Such estimates – however rough and ready – could still be consistent with reductions in world average energy intensity of anything from 50% to (much more speculatively) 80% from 1990 levels. These reductions are likely to continue to come principally from technological innovations and the replacement of generations of capital stock. Focused energy efficiency measures and economic incentives to curb energy usage will support the general trend, as will continuing shifts in the overall structure of economies.

The practical value of such projections may be questioned, but they do illustrate likely problem areas and the need to respond to them well in advance. In particular, if concerns about potential global climate change are well-founded then the prospect of annual carbon dioxide emissions from fossil fuel combustion rising up to three times their current level and maintaining that level throughout the second-half of the 21st century is unacceptable. The only situation where that prospect would be acceptable would be if not merely clean conversion and use were universally practised, but also a way had been found to capture and reabsorb these emissions in a sustainable manner. In the time-scale of a century, under pressure for increasingly confirmed climate change and challenges to the survival of existing businesses, such technological developments should not be dismissed as unlikely.

Despite the declarations and signing of Conventions at the UN Conference on Environment and Development in Rio de Janeiro in June 1992, and despite clear evidence that the world's energy industry exhibits growing concern for social development and environmental protection – and belief in the enhancing role business can and increasingly wishes to play – the implementation of any agenda for action still rests firmly in the hands of end-consumers and policy-makers.

Yet changes must be encouraged. Action needs to start now, on a rapidly widening multi-national basis. Much greater emphasis and real achievements are needed on energy efficiency. The development of environmentally acceptable forms of renewable energy needs to be accelerated – which warns against rushing into excessive modern biomass development if this means loss of biodiversity and harmful emissions; constrains tidal power because of loss of key estuarine habitats; places question marks over ocean thermal because of ecological and climatic impacts; means great sensitivity in even small-scale hydropower developments; and requires very careful siting of wind farms. Great hopes are placed by many on solar power in its passive and many active forms. But even with solar power, if large-scale structures are contemplated, careful handling will be required. Above all, new renewable forms of energy need to become economic and readily accessible – and in general the world is a long way from that point at present. Upward pressure on prices of traditional fossil fuels, deepening environmental concerns, and supportive policy measures could, however, cause things to come out right – eventually.

In parallel, there is a need to continue to seek a way of exploiting the immense energy reserves of nuclear power which is publicly acceptable across the whole fuel cycle from procurement and processing through disposal.

A period of 100 years to 2100 or so, provides a realistic time-scale for substantial changes. It allows serious belief in absolute declines in global fossil fuel combustion having begun from mid-century; and global annual anthropogenic CO_2 emissions running at less than half 1990 levels by the year 2100. But only early, effective and collective action on a colossal scale would bring this about. Appendix E provides possible implications of this report's energy Cases for CO_2 concentrations, and for global mean temperature and sea level changes, if fears of enhanced global warming and climate change are finally confirmed and current mainstream global climate models prove accurate.

On a more fundamental level, however, the period post-2020, if not before, must see the implementation of new concepts of the energy "demand" and "supply" process. Indeed, the energy community is the captive of its own terminology in continuing to use these distinctive terms in ways which fail to recognise overtly or covertly the interdependence of procurement, provision, processing, transformation, transportation, distribution and utilisation as elements in a system which should be driven not by the exigencies of primary energy supply, trade or the energy market but by the end-point services which energy is the means of providing. The conclusion is to a large extent self-evident: the problems of energy cannot be divorced from the problems of global society as a whole, any more than can be the problems of food supply – and that will become increasingly so the further ahead one looks. The best action on energy will bring about, ultimately, the best results environmentally and socially. The energy industries have a key role to play in achieving these results.

This report has called for action now to start tackling the many challenges which the future holds for energy consumers, policy-makers and producers. This is largely due to the belief that, whereas the problems may seem major between now and the year 2020, even greater problems will emerge post-2020. Experience compels recognition that the lead-times involved in meeting even these longer-term challenges means there must be no delay in getting the appropriate measures under way.

BIBLIOGRAPHY

Adamantiades, A. G., 1991, *Radioactive Waste Management – A Background Study*, World Bank,1991.

American Association for the Advancement of Science, *Science*, vol. 259, 12 February, pp.905–941. Washington DC, USA, 1993.

Anderson, D., *Energy and the Environment,* The Wealth of Nations Foundation, 1991.

Anderson, D., *The Energy Industry and Global Warming: New Roles for International Aid,* Overseas Development Institute, London, 1992.

Anderson, E.W., 'The Middle East and Hydropolitics', *WEC Journal* (December), WEC, London, 1991.

Arbatov, A. A., et al., *Soviet Energy – An Insider's Account,* The Centre for Global Energy Studies, 1991.

Ayres, R. U., *Energy Inefficiency in the US Economy: A New Case for Conservation,* IIASA, 1989.

Ayres, R.U., 'The Energy Policy Debate: A Case of Conflicting Paradigms', *WEC Journal* (July), WEC, London, 1992.

Barbier, E.B., *Economics, Natural Resource Scarcity and Development: Conventional and Alternative Views*, Earthscan, London, 1989.

Barde, J-P, et al.,*Valuing the Environment: Six Case Studies,* Earthscan, London, 1991.

Barnes, D. F., *Population Growth, Wood Fuel and Resource Problems in Sub-Saharan Africa,* World Bank, 1990.

Barnes, P., Imran, M., *Energy Demand in Developing Countries. Prospects for the Future,* World Bank, 1990.

Barnes, P., *The OIES Review of Energy Costs,* Oxford Institute of Energy Studies, 1991.

Barthold, L., *Technology Survey Report on Electric Power Systems,* World Bank, 1989.

Bashmakov, I., *Energy and Europe: The Global Dimension,* USSR Academy of Sciences, 1990.

Besant-Jones, J. E., *Private Sector Participation in Power through BOOT Schemes,* World Bank, 1990.

Besant-Jones, J., *The Future Role of Hydro Power in Developing Countries,* World Bank, 1989.

Best, G., 'Energy, Environment and Sustainable Rural Development', *WEC Journal* (December), WEC, London, 1992.

Boardman, B., *Fuel Poverty,* Belhaven, London, 1991.

Boardman, B., *Paying for Energy Efficiency*, NSCA, Brighton, England, 1992.

Boden, T.A. et al., *Trends '91: A Compendium of Data on Global Change,* Oak Ridge National Laboratory, Tennessee, 1991.

Bolin, B. et al., *The Greenhouse Effect, Climate Change, and Ecosystems,* Wiley, New York, 1986.

Brown, L.R. et al., *State of the World: A Worldwatch Institute Report on Progress Toward a Sustainable Society,* Norton, New York, 1984 – 1992 (annual).

Brown L.R. et al., *Vital Signs 1992: The Trends That Are Shaping Our Future,* Norton, New York, 1992.

Butera, F., *Renewable Energy Sources in Developing Countries: Successes and Failures in Technology Transfer and Diffusion*, PFE Rome, 1989.

Cairncross, F., *Costing the Earth,* Random Century Ltd., London, 1991.

CEC, *Proposal for a Council Decision Concerning the Promotion of Energy Efficiency in the Community*, 1991.

CEC, 'Technological and Economical Development Outlook for Renewable Energy Sources for Electricity Generation', (in *Senior Expert Symposium on Electricity and the Environment*) IAEA, 1991.

CEC, *Energy in Europe: A View to the Future* (September), Brussels, 1992.

Chandran, T.R.S., 'Electricity and Environment, Policy Aspects in Developing Countries', (in *Senior Expert Symposium on Electricity and the Environment*), IAEA, 1991.

Christie, I. et al., *Energy Efficiency: The Policy Agenda for the 1990s*, Policy Studies Institute/Neighbourhood Energy Action, London, 1992.

Churchill, A.A., *Financing Energy Enterprises in the 1990s,* World Energy Council Pacific Asia Regional Energy Forum, Sydney, 1991.

Churchill, A.A., Saunders, J. R., *Financing of the Energy Sector in Developing Countries,* World Bank, 1989.

Churchill, A.A., *Technology Transfer and Training of Manpower in the Energy Sector,* Fourth Symposium on Pacific Energy Co-operation, Tokyo, 1990.

Churchill, A.A., *Private Power: The Regulator Implications,* World Bank/Singapore National Committee/World Energy Council ASEAN Energy Conference, 1992.

Cipolla, C.M., et al., *The Economic Decline of Empires,* Methuen, London, 1970.

Cipolla, C.M., et al., *The Economic History of World Population,* Penguin Books, Harmondsworth, 1978.

Clare, R. et al., *Tidal Power: Trends and Developments,* Institution of Civil Engineers/ Telford, London, 1992.

Clark, J.G., *The Political Economy of World Energy: A Twentieth Century Perspective,* Harvester/ Wheatsheaf, London, 1990.

Clark, W. C., *Usable Knowledge for Managing Global Climate Change,* The Stockholm Environment Institute, 1990.

Cline, W.R., *The Economics of Global Warming*, Institute for International Economics, Washington DC, 1992.

Cline, W.R., *Global Warming: The Economic Stakes*, Institute for International Economics, Washington DC, 1992.

Cline-Cole, R. A., et al., *Wood Fuel in Kano,* UN University Press, 1990.

Colombo, U., et al., *Energy for a New Century – the European Perspective*, Report of "Groupe des Sages", 1990.

Colombo, U., *Energy Resources and Population,* Pontifical Academy of Sciences Study Week on "Resources and Population", Rome, 1991.

Connally, P., *Energy Finance – the Global Outlook*, presentation at the Conference "Energy Issues in Nigeria: Today and Tomorrow" in Lagos, 1991.

Coote, B., *The Trade Trap – Poverty and the Global Commodity Markets*, Oxfam UK and Ireland, 1992.

Cordukes, P. A., *A Review of Regulation of the Power Sector in the Developing Countries,* World Bank, 1990.

Daly, H.E., *Steady-State Economics,* W.H.Freeman, San Francisco, 1977.

Derrick, A., 'Renewable Energy Technologies in Developing Countries', *WEC Journal* (December), WEC, London, 1991.

Dobozi, I., *Impact of Market Reform on Soviet Energy Consumption,* SNS Stockholm, 1990.

Dornbusch, R. et al., *Global Warming: Economic Policy Responses,* M.I.T. Press, Cambridge, Massachusetts, 1991.

Drollas, L. et al., *Oil: The Devil's Gold,* Duckworth, London, 1989.

Dutkiewicz, R.K.,'Energy Concerns and Prospects in Sub-Saharan Africa', *WEC Journal* (December), WEC, London, 1991.

Energy Journal, The, Special Issue on Global Warming, Volume 12, Number 1, 1991.

European Energy Charter, The, Closing Document of the Conference of the Hague, December 1991.

Everest, D., *The Greenhouse Effect. Issues for Policy Makers,* The Royal Institute of International Affairs and Policy Studies Institute, 1988.

Fells, I. et al., *UK Energy Policy Post-Privatisation,* Scottish Nuclear, Glasgow, 1991.

Fells, I. et al., *Moving Forward: UK Energy Policy Post-Privatisation,* Scottish Nuclear, Glasgow, 1992.

Final Summary Statement from The Conference on Sustainable Development, Science and Policy, 1990, NAVF, Oslo.

Fisher, D., *Options for Reducing Greenhouse Gas Emissions,* The Stockholm Environment Institute, 1990.

Fisher, D., *Paradise Deferred: Environmental Policymaking in Central and Eastern Europe,* Energy and Environment Programme, Royal Institute of International Affairs, London, 1992.

Fitzgerald, K. B., Barnes, D., McGranahan, G., *Interfuel Substitution and Changes in the Way Households Use Energy,* World Bank, 1990.

Flannery, B.P. et al., *Global Climate Change: A Petroleum Industry Perspective,* International Petroleum Industry Environmental Conservation Association (IPIECA), London, 1993.

Freeman, C., et al., *Long Waves in the World Economy,* Butterworth, London, 1983.

Frisch, J-R., Brendow, K., Saunders, R., *World Energy Horizons 2000 – 2020,* WEC, 1989.

Frisch, J-R., *Future Stresses for Energy Resources,* WEC, 1986.

Frisch, J-R., *Energy 2000-2020: World Prospects and Regional Stresses,* WEC, 1983.

Gaidar, Y., Article in the UK, *Financial Times*, January 1992.

Gata, S. Z., *The Impact of Policy and Institutional Infrastructure on the Management of Energy Enterprises in Developing Countries,* WEC Harare Forum, 1990.

Gattinger, M., Halbritter, J., Voigtländer P., *Emissionen und Umwelt,* Siemens, 1990.

Goldemberg, J. et al., *Energy for a Sustainable World*, Wiley, New Delhi, 1988.

Goldemberg, J., "Leap-frogging": A New Energy Policy for Developing Countries, *WEC Journal* (December), WEC, London, 1991.

Gouse, S.W. et al., Potential World Development Through 2100: The Impacts on Energy Demand, Resources and the Environment, *WEC Journal* (December), WEC, London, 1992.

Gray, J. E., Davis K., Harned J. (eds), *Energy Supply and Use in Developing Countries,* University Press of America, 1988.

Grubb, M., The *Greenhouse Effect: Negotiating Targets,* The Royal Institute of International Affairs, 1989.

Grubb, M., *Energy Policies and the Greenhouse Effect: Policy Appraisal (vol. I),* Royal Institute of International Affairs, London, 1990.

Grubb, M., *Energy Policies and the Greenhouse Effect: Country Studies and Technical Options (vol. II),* Royal Institute of International Affairs, London, 1991.

Grübler, A. et al., *Inter-Generational and Spatial Equity Issues of Carbon Accounts,* IIASA, Laxenburg, Austria, 1992.

Grübler, A., Nakicenovic, N. and Schäfer, A., *Summary of IPCC/EIS-II-ASA International Workshop on Energy-Related Greenhouse Gases Reduction and Removal, 1-2 October 1992, Status Report SR-93-1.* IIASA, Laxenburg, Austria, 1992.

Guertin, D.L. et al., *US Energy Imperatives for the 1990s: Leadership, Efficiency, Environmental Responsibility, and Sustained Economic Growth,* University Press of America, Maryland, 1992.

Haefele, W., *Energy Technologies for the First Decade of the Twenty-First Century,* UN-ECE, 1989.

Hanisch, T., *A Comprehensive Approach to Climate Change*, CICERO, 1991.

Harlow, I., 'Nuclear Power in the OECD: Is There Life After Dearth?' *WEC Journal* (July), WEC, London, 1992.

Helm, D. et al., *Economic Policy Towards the Environment,* Blackwell, Oxford, 1991.

IAEA, *Nuclear Power Reactors in the World,* 1991.

IEA, *Energy Conservation in IEA Countries,* IEA/OECD, 1987.

IEA, 'Energy Sources and Technologies for Electricity Generation', (in *Senior Expert Symposium on Electricity and the Environment*), IEA 1991.

IEA, *Greenhouse Gas Emissions – The Energy Dimension*, IEA/OECD, 1991.

IEA, *Energy Efficiency and the Environment,* IEA/OECD, 1991.

IEA, *Climate Change Policy Initiatives,* IEA/OECD, Paris. (Contains UN Framework Convention on Climate Change and Intergovernmental Negotiating Committee's Resolution thereon), 1992.

IIASA, *Technological Progress, Structural Change and Efficient Energy Use: Trends Worldwide,* Laxenburg, Austria [Internal Draft], 1989.

IIASA, *Science and Sustainability, Selected Papers on IIASA's 20th Anniversary,* Laxenburg, Austria , 1992.

IIASA, *Long-Term Strategies for Mitigating Global Warming: Towards New Earth*, Laxenburg, Austria [Internal Draft], 1992.

IIASA, *Proceedings of International Workshop on Costs, Impacts and Possible Benefits of CO_2 Mitigation*, 28-30 September, 1992, Laxenburg, Austria, forthcoming 1993.

IIASA, *Proceedings of IPCC/EIS-IIASA International Workshop on Energy-Related Greenhouse Gases Reduction and Removal*, 1-2 October, 1992, Laxenburg, Austria, forthcoming 1993.

Imamura, M.S. et al., *Photovoltaic System Technology: A European Handbook*, CEC/H.S. Stephens, Felmersham, England, 1992,

International Chamber of Commerce (ICC), *WICEM II Second World Industry Conference on Environmental Management – Conference Report and Background Papers,* ICC, 1991.

IPCC, *Climate Change, The IPCC Scientific Assessment,* Cambridge University Press, 1990.

IPCC, *Climate Change 1992: The Supplementary Report to the IPCC Scientific Assessment*, Cambridge University Press, 1992.

IPCC, *Climate Change, The IPCC Impacts Assessment*, WMO and UNEP, 1990.

IPCC, *Preliminary Guidelines for Assessing Impacts of Climate Change,* Environmental Change Unit, Oxford/ Centre for Global Environmental Research, Japan, 1992.

Jackson, T., *Efficiency Without Tears: 'No-Regrets' Energy Policy to Combat Climate Change,* Friends of the Earth, London, 1992.

Jäger, J., *Responding to Climate Change: Tools for Policy Development,* The Stockholm Environment Institute, 1990.

Jäger, J. et al., *Climate Change: Science, Impacts and Policy,* C.U.P., Cambridge, England, 1991.

Jenkin, F.P., *The Future Role of Energy in the (European) Community* in Proceedings of the Conference "New Developments in the International Energy Marketplace" in Amsterdam 1991.

Johansson, T., Bodlund, B., Williams, R.H., *Electricity. Efficient End Use and New Generation Technologies and Their Planning Implications,* Lund University Press & Chartwell-Bratt, 1989.

Johansson, T.B. et al., *Renewable Energy: Sources for Fuels and Electricity,* Island Press, Washington DC, 1993.

Kaya, Y., Nakicenovic, N., Nordhaus, W.D., Toth, F.L. (eds) *Costs, Impacts and Benefits of CO_2 Mitigation, Proceedings of a Workshop held on 28-30 September 1992.,* IIASA, Laxenburg, Austria, forthcoming 1993.

Kennedy, P.M., *The Rise and Fall of the Great Powers,* Random House, New York, 1988.

Kennedy, P.M., *Preparing for the Twenty-First Century*, Harper Collins, London, 1993.

Khatib, H. Al-, Energy in the Middle East and North African Region, *WEC Journal* (December), WEC, London, 1991.

Khatib, H. and Munasinghe, M., *Future of Electricity,* IEA International Conference on the New Electricity 21, Tokyo, 1992.

King, K., Kumar, M., Malik, U., *Environmental Considerations in Energy Development*, Asian Development Bank, 1991.

Kingston, M., *Co-operation Between the Public and Private Sector in the Provision of Finance for Power Projects,* SADCC, 1990.

Kitamura, R., *Life-Style and Travel Demand*, in "A Look Ahead: Year 2020", 1988.

Lewis, D. et al., Developing Countries: the Land of the Dammed?, *WEC Journal* (December), WEC, London, 1991.

McDonald, A., Haefele, W., *Energy in a Finite World*, IIASA, 1981.

McLachlan, M. and Itani, I., *International Comparisons: Interpreting the Energy/GDP Ratio,* Canadian Energy Research Institute, 1991.

Markandya, A. et al., *The Earthscan Reader in Environmental Economics,* Earthscan, London, 1992.

Maunder, W.J., *The Human Impact of Climate Uncertainty,* Routledge, London, 1989.

Mintzer, I.M. et al., *Confronting Climate Change: Risks, Implications and Responses,* C.U.P., Cambridge, England, 1992.

Moore, E.A. and Smith, G, *Capital Expenditures for Electric Power in the Developing Countries in the 1990s,* World Bank, 1990.

Moore, E., Crousillat, E., *Prospects for Gas-Fuelled Combined-Cycle Power Generation in the Developing Countries,* World Bank, 1991.

Moynet, G., *Electricity Generating Cost Evaluation Made in 1990 for Plant to be Commissioned in 2000,* UNIPEDE Congress, Copenhagen, 1991.

Mukai, J., 'Promotion of Electric Power Policies in Consideration of Japan's Environment' (in *Senior Expert Symposium on Electricity and the Environment*), IAEA,1991.

Munslow, B. et al., *The Fuelwood Trap: A Study of the SADCC Region,* Earthscan, London, 1988.

Nadezhdine, E., *Future Supply and Demand Scenarios of the USSR and Eastern Europe – Eastern Perspectives,* World Energy Council Forum, Budapest, 1991.

Nakicenovic, N. et al., *CO_2 Reduction and Removal: Measures for the Next Century,* IIASA, Laxenburg, Austria, 1992.

Nakicenovic, N., Grübler, A., Bodda, L. and Gilli, P-V, *Technological Progress, Structural Change and Efficient Energy Use: Trends Worldwide and in Austria.* Verbundgesellschaft, Vienna, 1990 (in German).

Nakicenovic, N., Grübler, A., Inaba, A.,et al, 'Long-term Strategies for Mitigating Global Warming', in *Energy - the International Journal, Issue May*, 1993.

National Academy of Sciences (US), et al., *Policy Implications of Greenhouse Warming: Mitigation, Adaptation and the Science Base,* National Academy Press, Washington DC, 1992.

NEA, 'Trends and Outlook for Nuclear Power Development Including Advanced Nuclear Reactors', (in *Senior Expert Symposium on Electricity and the Environment*), IAEA, 1991.

Nekrasov, A. S., *The Growing Role of Electricity in the Energy Spectrum*, World Energy Council, 1990.

Netherlands Ministry of Economic Affairs, *Memorandum on Energy Conservation: Strategy for Energy Conservation and Renewable Energy Resources*, SDU, The Hague, 1990.

Nitze, W.A., *The Greenhouse Effect: Formulating A Convention*, Royal Institute of International Affairs, London, 1990.

Nordhaus, W.D., 'Economic Growth and Climate: The Carbon Dioxide Problem', in *American Economic Review*, February, 1977.

Nordhaus, W.D., 'A Survey of the Costs of Reduction of Greenhouse Gases', *Energy Journal,* Fall issue, 1990.

Nordhaus, W. D., 'To Slow or Not to Slow: The Economics of the Greenhouse Effect', in *The Economic Journal* 101, July 1991.

Nordisk Ministerråd, *Critical Loads for Nitrogen and Sulphur,* Gotab, Stockholm, 1986.

Nordisk Ministerråd, *Acid Precipitation Literature Review,* Gotab, Stockholm, 1986.

O'Brien, B. J., *Postponing Greenhouse. Climate Change – Facts, Issues and Policies in 1990,* Frank Daniels, 1990.

OECD, *Environmental Policy Benefits: Monetary Valuation*, Paris, 1989.

OECD, *Managing Technological Change in Less-Advanced Developing Countries,* OECD, 1991.

OECD, *Estimation of Greenhouse Gas Emissions and Sinks, Final Report August 1991,* OECD, 1991.

OECD, *Climate Change: Evaluating the Socio-Economic Impacts,* OECD, 1991.

OECD, *Energy Taxation and Price Distortions in Fossil Fuel Markets: Some Implications for Climate Change Policy,* Economics Department Working Papers, No. 110, Paris, 1992.

OECD, *The Costs of Reducing CO_2 Emissions: Evidence from GREEN,* Economics Department Working Papers No. 115, Paris, 1992.

OECD, *The Costs of Reducing CO_2 Emissions: A Comparison of Carbon Tax Curves with GREEN,* Economics Department Working Papers No. 118, Paris, 1992.

OECD, *Costs of Reducing CO_2 Emissions: Evidence from Six Global Models,* Economics Department Working Papers No. 122, Paris, 1992.

OECD, *New Issues, New Results: The OECD's Second Survey of the Macroeconomic Costs of Reducing CO2 Emissions,* Paris, 1992.

OECD, G*lobal Effects of the European Carbon Tax,* Economics Department Working Papers No. 125, Paris, 1992.

OECD, *OECD Economic Studies No. 19: The Economic Costs of Reducing CO2 Emissions,* Paris, 1993.

OECD-NEA/IAEA, *Uranium – Resources, Production and Demand,* published biennially.

Office of Technology Assessment (USA), *Changing by Degrees: Steps to Reduce Greenhouse Gases,* Washington DC, 1991.

Office of Technology Assessment (USA), *Energy Technology Choices: Shaping Our Future,* Washington DC, 1991.

Office of Technology Assessment (USA), *Improving Automobile Fuel Economy: New Standards, New Approaches,* Washington DC, 1991.

Office of Technology Assessment (USA), *Building Energy Efficiency,* Washington DC, 1992.

Office of Technology Assessment (USA), *Fueling Development: Energy Technologies for Developing Countries,* Washington DC, 1992.

Olson, M., T*he Rise and Decline of Nations: Economic Growth, Stagflation, and Social Rigidities,* Yale University Press, New Haven, 1982.

Pachauri, R. K., *Major Energy Issues of the Developing World,* WEC Harare Forum, 1990.

Parry, M., *Climate Change and World Agriculture*, Earthscan, London, 1990.

Pearce, D., (ed.), *Blueprint 2*, Earthscan Publications Ltd, 1991.

Pearce, D., Markyanda, A., Barbier, E.B., *Blueprint for a Green Economy,* Earthscan Publications Ltd, 1989.

Pearce, D. et al., *The Social Cost of Fuel Cycles,* Centre for Social and Economic Research on the Global Environment/UK Department of Trade and Industry, London, 1992.

Pearce, D., *Economic Values and the Natural World*, Earthscan Publications Ltd., 1993.

Petrou, B. N., *Promoting Investment for Natural Gas Exploration and Production in Developing Countries,* World Bank, 1989.

Pezzey, J., *Impacts of Greenhouse Gas Control Strategies on UK Competitiveness,* HMSO, London, England, 1991.

Proceedings of the "Senior Expert Symposium on Electricity and the Environment" in Helsinki 1991, organised by CEC, SMEA, ECE, IAEA, IBDR, IEA, IIASA, NEA, UNEP, WHO and WMO, published by IAEA.

Proceedings of the Seminar "Energy Issues in Developing Countries" in Washington 1991, WEC Committee on Energy Issues in Developing Countries.

Proceedings of the Conference "Energy 2000" in London 1992, IBC.

Proceedings of the Conference "New Developments in the International Energy Marketplace" in Amsterdam 1991, IIR Limited International Division.

Proceedings of the "Pacific Asia Regional Energy Forum: Regional Energy Strategies for the Future" in Sydney 1991, WEC Australian Member Committee.

Proceedings of the "Regional Energy Forum for East and Southern African Countries" in Harare 1990, WEC.

Proceedings of the Conference "Energy Issues in Nigeria: Today and Tomorrow" in Lagos 1991, WEC Nigerian Member Committee.

Proceedings of the Conference "Coal in the Environment" in London 1991, World Coal Institute Conference and Exhibition, World Coal Institute.

Proceedings of the Conference "The Future of Asia-Pacific Economies" (FAPE IV) in New Delhi 1991, Indian Council for Research on International Economic Relations, New Delhi and Asian and Pacific Development Centre, Kuala Lumpur.

Radetzki, M., *Prospects for USSR Energy Exports After Perestroika,* SNS Stockholm, 1990.

Rana, K. N., 'Environment, Energy and Infrastructure', in *The Future of Asia-Pacific Economies,* 1991.

Rijsberman, F. R., Swart, R. J., *Targets and Indicators of Climatic Change,* The Stockholm Environment Institute, 1990.

Roberts, J. et al., *Privatising Electricity: The Politics of Power,* Belhaven, London, 1991.

Roland K. (ed)., *The Role of Petroleum in Sustainable Development,* PETRAD Publication No. 1, 1991.

Russell, J., *Environmental Issues in Eastern Europe: Setting An Agenda,* Royal Institute of International Affairs, London, 1990.

Russell, J., *Energy and Environmental Conflicts in East/Central Europe: The Case of Power Generation,* Royal Institute of International Affairs, London, 1991.

SADCC, *Power Co-operation in the West Region of SADCC,* 1991.

SADCC, *Future Electricity Strategy for the SADCC Region,* 1991.

Schäfer, A., et al., *Inventory of Greenhouse-gas Mitigation Measures: Examples from the IIASA Technology Data Bank,* IIASA [Internal Draft], Laxenburg, Austria, 1992.

Schipper, L. et al., *Energy Efficiency and Human Activity: Past Trends, Future Prospects,* C.U.P., Cambridge, England, 1992.

Schipper L. et al., *World Energy: Building A Sustainable Future,* Stockholm Environment Institute, Stockholm, 1992.

Schipper, L., Cooper, R. C., *Energy Use and Conservation in the USSR – Pattern, Prospects and Problems, Lawrence Berkeley Laboratory, 1990.*

Schipper, L., *Lifestyles and Energy,* Office of Technology Assessment, U.S. Congress, 1991.

Schmidheiny, S. et al., *Changing Course: A Global Business Perspective on Development and the Environment*, MIT, Cambridge, Massachusetts, 1992.

Schneider, H., Schulz, W., *Investment Requirements of the World Energy Industries,* WEC, 1987.

Schneider, S.H., *Global Warming: Are We Entering the Greenhouse Century?,* Lutterworth, Cambridge, England, 1990.

Scientific American, *Energy for Planet Earth*, Special Issue September 1990.

Seung Yoon Rhee, et al, *Energy Indicators of Developing Member Countries of ADB,* Asian Development Bank, 1989.

Silas, C.J. et al., *Energy Imperatives for the 1990s,* Atlantic Council, Washington DC, 1990.

Skinner, R.G. et al., 'Assessment of Policy Responses to Climate Change and Their Likely Effects on the Energy Sector', *WEC Journal* (December), WEC, London, 1992.

Smith, I.M. et al.,'Greenhouse Gas Emissions and the Role of Coal', *WEC Journal* (December), WEC, London, 1992.

Smyser, C., 'Competition, Cost-Effectiveness and Control in Global Environment Issues', *WEC Journal* (July), WEC, London, 1992.

Soussan, J., O'Keefe, P., Munslow, B., *Urban Fuelwood – Challenges and Dilemmas,* Butterworth-Heinemann Ltd, 1990.

Starr, C., 'Global Energy and Electricity Futures', *IEEE Power Engineering Review,* August 1991.

Stokes, G. et al., *Trends in Transport and the Countryside,* Countryside Commission, Manchester, England, 1992.

Strong, M., 'Prospects for a New Developing Countries' Agenda in the 21st Century', *WEC Journal* (December), WEC, London, 1991.

Summers R. and Heston. A., 'The Penn World Table (Mark 5): An Expanded Set of International Comparisons, 1950 – 1988', *The (US) Quarterly Journal of Economics,* May 1991.

Suzor, N. C., Bouvet, P.E., *Identifying the Basic Conditions for Economic Generation of Public Electricity from Surplus Bagasse in Sugar Mills,* World Bank, 1991.

Taylor L., Brown, I., Boyle, S., *Lesson from Japan – Separating Economic Growth from Energy Demand*, Association for Conservation of Energy, London, 1990.

Teja, R.S. and Bracewell-Milnes, B., *The Case for Earmarked Taxes – Government Spending and Public Choice,* The Institute of Economic Affairs, London, 1992.

Teplitz-Sembitzky, W., *Regulation, Deregulation or Reregulation – What Is Needed in the LDCs Power Sector?,* World Bank, 1990.

The World Commission on Environment and Development, *Our Common Future,* Oxford University Press, New York, 1987.

Thorpe, T.W., *A Review of Wave Energy, Vol I: Main Report,* ETSU/DTI, London, 1992.

Tietenberg, T., *Environmental and Natural Resource Economics,* Scott, Foresman, Glenview, Illinois, 1988 (2nd Ed.).

Tomitate, T., *Energy and Environmental Issues*, The Institute of Energy Economics, Japan. Japan-US Energy Policy Consultations, Hawaii. Global Climate Change: US-Japan Cooperative Leadership for Environmental Protection, 1991, Atlantic Council of the United States, Washington, 1991.

UK Dept. of Environment, *Climate Change: Our National Programme for CO_2 Emissions,* DoE, London, 1992.

UK Dept. of Trade & Industry, *Renewable Energy Advisory Group: Report to the President of the Board of Trade,* HMSO, London, 1992.

UK House of Commons Energy Committee, *Energy Policy Implications of the Greenhouse Effect,* HMSO, London, 1989.

UK House of Commons Energy Committee, *The Cost of Nuclear Power,* HMSO, London, 1990.

UK House of Commons Energy Committee, *The Fast Breeder Reactor,* HMSO, London, 1990.

UN Committee for Development Planning, *Elements of an International Development Strategy for the 1990s,* UN, New York, 1989.

UN Conference on Trade and Development, *Combating Global Warming: Study on a Global System of Tradeable Carbon Emission Entitlements,* UN, New York, 1992.

UN Department of Technical Co-Operation for Development, *Energy Sources for Electricity Supply Relevant to Developing Countries*, UN, 1986.

UN Economic Commission for Europe, *The State of Transboundary Air Pollution,* UN, 1989.

UN Economic Commission for Europe, *Optimum Use of Primary Energy Resources*, UN, 1990.

UN Economic Commission for Europe, *Interrelationship between Environmental and Energy Policies,* UN, 1990.

UN Economic Commission for Europe, *Energy Reforms in Central and Eastern Europe,* UN, 1991.

UN Economic Commission for Europe, *The Environment in Europe and North America: Annotated Statistics 1992,* UN, New York, 1992.

UN Environment Programme, *Saving Our Planet: Challenge and Hopes,* UNEP, Nairobi, 1992.

UN Economic Commission for Europe, 1991–1992, Energy Efficiency 2000 Project, continuously published proceedings/reports UN, 1990, Global Outlook 2000.

UN Economic Commission for Europe, *Energy Reforms in Central and Eastern Europe – The First Year,* UN, 1991.

UN Economic and Social Commission for Asia and the Pacific, *Energy Resources Development Problems in the Escap Region,* UN, 1985.

UNCTAD, *Joint Ventures as a Channel for the Transfer of Technology,* UN, 1988.

UNIPEDE Group of Experts EURPROG, *Programmes and Prospects for the Electricity Sector 1989 – 1995, 2000, 2005 and 2010.* Nineteenth Edition, 1991.

US Department of Energy, 'Trends in Research and Development of Advanced Fossil Fuel Technologies for Electric Power Generation', in *Senior Expert Symposium on Electricity and the Environment,* IAEA, 1991.

US Department of Energy, 'Policy Aspects of Electricity and the Environment, Integrating Environmental Concerns into Planning to Meet Electric Demand', in *Senior Expert Symposium on Electricity and the Environment,* IAEA, 1991.

USEA, *Global Climate Change – An Energy Industry Perspective,* The United States Energy Association, 1990.

USEA, *Getting Down to Business: A Strategy for Energy Efficiency in the United States,* USEA, Washington DC, 1992.

USSR Academy of Sciences, *Scenarios for Energy Development in the USSR,* Moscow International Energy Club, 1990.

Vedavalli, R., *Domestic Energy Pricing Policies,* World Bank, 1990.

Vouyoukas, E.L., *Carbon Taxes and CO_2 Emissions Targets: Results from the IEA Model,* OECD, Paris, 1992.

Walubengo, D., 'Biomass Availability, its Use and Consequences in Sub-Saharan Africa', *WEC Journal* (December), WEC, London, 1991.

Warrick, R.A., et al., *Climate and Sea Level Change Observations, Projections and Implications*, Cambridge University Press, Cambridge, England, 1993.

Wayne, R.P., (2nd Ed.), *Chemistry of Atmospheres,* Oxford University Press, Oxford, England, 1991.

WEC Study Committee, *An Assessment of Worldwide Energy-Related Atmospheric Pollution,* WEC, 1989.

WEC, *International Energy Data*, 1989.

WEC Study Committee, *Environmental Effects Arising from Electricity Supply and Utilisation and Resulting Costs to the Utility,* WEC, 1988.

WEC, *Survey of Energy Resources*, 1992.

Wigley, T.M.L. et al., Implications for Climate and Sea Level of Revised IPCC Emissions Scenarios, *Nature,* vol. 357, 28 May, 1992.

Wigley, T.M.L., *How Important are Carbon Cycle Model Uncertainties?,* CICERO Seminar, Oslo, Norway, 29 November-2 December, 1992.

William, F M., *US Energy Strategy: Prospects and Policies,* 1990.

Williams, J.R., *The Natural Gas Demand in Europe in a Long-Term Perspective,* The Sixth European Gas Conference, Oslo, 1991.

The World Bank, *Sub-Saharan Africa – From Crisis to Sustainable Development,* 1989.

The World Bank Industry and Energy Department, *Review of Electric Tariffs in Developing Countries During the 1980s,* World Bank, 1990.

The World Bank, *Poverty,* Oxford University Press, 1990.

The World Bank, *Energy Finance – the Global Outlook,* 1991.

The World Bank, *Development and the Environment,* Oxford University Press, 1992.

The World Bank, *Social Indicators of Development, 1991-92,* World Bank/Johns Hopkins University Press, Baltimore, 1992.

The World Bank, *World Energy Subsidies and Global Carbon Emissions,* Public Economics Division, Washington DC, USA, 1992.

The World Bank, *Energy Efficiency and Conservation in the Developing World: a World Bank Policy Paper,* Washington DC, USA, 1993.

World Resources Institute, *World Resources 1990-1991,* Oxford University Press, 1990.

World Resources Institute, *World Resources 1992-93: A Guide to the Global Environment,* Oxford University Press, Oxford 1992.

World Resources Institute (Dower, R.C. et al), *The Right Climate for Carbon Taxes: Creating Economic Incentives to Protect the Atmosphere,* W.R.I., Washington DC, 1992.

Wright, J. K., *The Global Impact of Nuclear,* University of Gent, 1989.

Wuebbles, D.J. et al., *Primer on Greenhouse Gases*, Lewis, Michigan State, 1991.

Yergin, D., *The Prize: The Epic Quest for Oil, Money and Power,* Simon & Schuster, New York, 1991.

APPENDIX A

THE REGIONS AND COUNTRIES IN THE REGIONS

NORTH AMERICA

Canada   USA

LATIN AMERICA and the CARIBBEAN

Argentina	Guatemala	Venezuela
Bahamas	Guyana	Islands:
Belize	Haiti	Antigua
Bermuda	Honduras	Barbados
Bolivia	Jamaica	Dominica
Brazil	Mexico	Grenada
Chile	Nicaragua	Guadeloupe
Colombia	Panama	Martinique
Costa Rica	Paraguay	Netherlands
Cuba	Peru	Antilles
Dominican Republic	Puerto Rico	Santa Lucia
Ecuador	Suriname	St Kitts
El Salvador	Trinidad / Tobago	St Vincent
French Guyana	Uruguay	Virgin Islands

WESTERN EUROPE

Austria	Greece	Portugal
Belgium	Iceland	Spain
Cyprus	Ireland	Sweden
Denmark	Italy	Switzerland
Finland	Luxembourg	Turkey
France	Malta	United Kingdom
Germany (united)	Netherlands	Yugoslavia
	Norway	

CENTRAL and EASTERN EUROPE/ COMMONWEALTH of INDEPENDENT STATES (of the former USSR)

CENTRAL and EASTERN EUROPE

Albania	Czech and Slovak	Hungary
Bulgaria	Federal Republic	Poland
	(CSFR)	Romania

COMMONWEALTH of INDEPENDENT STATES (of the FORMER USSR)

The Commonwealth of Independent States

Estonia	Georgia	Lithuania
	Latvia	

MIDDLE EAST and NORTH AFRICA

Algeria	Kuwait	Sudan
Bahrain	Lebanon	Syrian Arab Republic
Egypt	Libya	Tunisia
Iraq	Morocco	United Arab Emirates
Iran	Oman	Yemen Arab
Israel	Qatar	Republic
Jordan	Saudi Arabia	

SUB-SAHARAN AFRICA

Angola	Gambia	Reunion
Benin	Ghana	Rwanda
Botswana	Guinea	Sao Tome and
Burkina Faso	Guinea-Bissau	Principe
Burundi	Côte d'Ivoire	Senegal
Cameron	Kenya	Seychelles
Cape Verde	Lesotho	Sierra Leone
Central African	Liberia	Somalia
Republic	Madagascar	South Africa
Chad	Malawi	Swaziland
Comoros	Mali	Tanzania
Congo	Mauritania	Togo
Djibouti	Mauritius	Uganda
Equatorial Guinea	Mozambique	Zaire
Ethiopia	Namibia	Zambia
Gabon	Niger	Zimbabwe
	Nigeria	

PACIFIC

CENTRALLY PLANNED ASIA

Campuchea
China (Peoples
  Republic)

Hong Kong
Korea (Dem Rep)
Laos

Mongolia
Vietnam

PACIFIC COUNTRIES

Australia
Brunei
Fiji
Indonesia
Japan
Malaysia
Mayanmar
New Zealand
Papua New Guinea

Philippines
Republic Of Korea
Singapore
Taiwan, China
Thailand
Smaller Islands:
  American Samoa
  French Polynesia
  Gilbert – Kiribati

Guam
New Caledonia
New Hebrides
Pacific US Trust
Solomon
Tonga
Western Samoa
Vanuatu

SOUTH ASIA

Afghanistan
Bangladesh
Bhutan

India
Maldives
Nepal

Pakistan
Sri Lanka

APPENDIX B

REGIONAL GROUPS

NORTH AMERICA

Regional Co-ordinator
Dr John W Landis
USA

Assistant Regional Co-ordinator
Dr Arthur J O'Connor
Canada

W J Bowen	A M Ferrer	L G Stuntz
USA	USA	USA
G A L Capobianco	R W Fri	A Taylor
Canada	USA	Canada
M Cleland	J E Gray	J R Waldron
Canada	USA	USA
P Cockshutt	Abe Haspel	B K Worthington
Canada	USA	USA
	D McKellar-Gulardo	
	USA	

LATIN AMERICA and the CARIBBEAN

Regional Co-ordinator
Mr Juan Eibenschutz
Mexico

It was not possible to form a regional group. Representatives of the Regional Co-ordinator, led by Ing Gerardo Novarrete Bazan and Antonio Alonso Concheiro together with Sr Tatit-Holtz from OLADE, have visited each country in the region following initial analysis of the results of a questionnaire sent to 180 addresses.

WESTERN EUROPE

Regional Co-ordinator
Mr Pierre Desprairies
France

Joint Regional Co-ordinator
Mr Paul Alba
France

Special Adviser
Mr Jacques Hartmann
Independent Consultant Aquitaine

X B De La Tour France	M Jefferson UK	S de F B Paes Portugal
J J C Bruggink Netherlands	H Lee UK	R Querol Spain
B Cales France	R Leonato Spain	S Robinson UK
F Careme France	K Leydon EEC	A Saullo Italy
G Carta Italy	J M Martin France	M Saillard France
D Champlon France	F Moisan France	G Semrau Germany
J J Escudero Spain	B Nelson Sweden	H-C Sorensen Denmark
C Girard France		Olavi Vapaavuori Finland

CENTRAL and EASTERN EUROPE and the COMMONWEALTH of INDEPENDENT STATES (of the former USSR)

CENTRAL and EASTERN EUROPE

Regional Co-ordinator
Prof Dr Marek Jaczewski
Poland

T Jászay Hungary	J Suva CSFR	J Martinek CSFR
T Krastev Bulgaria	D Vaverka CSFR	G Liciu Romania

The COMMONWEALTH of INDEPENDENT STATES, GEORGIA and the BALTIC STATES

Regional Co-ordinator
Prof N K Pravednikov

Co-ordinator Adjunct
Prof Dmitri B Volfberg

CENTRAL EXPERTS

I I Kondratenko	M H Gaseev	V M Z'ikov
B A Davidov	B M Kozlov	A I Kuzovkin
I V Granin	S E Kazakov	N G Shamrayev
V I Potapov	O F Hudyakov	V L Likhachev

REPRESENTATIVES of the former USSR REPUBLICS

A N Kurashov Russian Federation	V M Kasymova Kirghizia	B V Unusov Tadzhikia
V F Stoliarov Ukraine	P Tamkivi Estonia	Y T Komendant Moldova
F I Molochko Belorussia	T M Akhmedov Uzbekistan	D T Arshakyan Armenia
R S Musina Turkmenia	D I Chomakhidze Georgia	V P Mishkinis Lithuania
T Mandaria Kazakhstan	K N Ramazanov Azerbaidzan	N A Zeltinsh Latvia

MIDDLE EAST and NORTH AFRICA

Regional Co-ordinator
Dr Hisham Khatib
Jordan

Rashad Abu Ras Jordan	Murfat Badawi Arab Fund for Economic and Social Development	Abdel Aziz Al'Turki OAPEC
Fawaz Karmi Jordan		Said Yassin Arab Thought Forum

SUB-SAHARAN AFRICA

EAST and SOUTHERN AFRICA

Regional Co-ordinator
Dr Z S Gata
Zimbabwe

P W Freeman
South Africa

J Madzongwe
Zimbabwe

C Y Wereko-Brobby
Ghana

D Walubengo
Kenya

J Chadzingwa
Zambia

M I Gielink
South Africa

S C Desai
Côte d'Ivoire

R K Dutkiewicz
South Africa

P Victus
Tanzania

J Bond
African Development
Bank

R M Harlen
Zimbabwe

P Robinson
Zimbabwe

K Akapelwa
Zambia

Haile Lul Tebicke
Ethiopia

WEST AFRICA

Regional Co-ordinator
Prof I H Umar

The regional group was drawn from Professor Umar's local associates.

PACIFIC

Joint Regional Co-ordinator
Dr R R Booth
Australia

Joint Regional Co-ordinator
Mr Jia Yunzhen
China

Takao Tomitate
Japan

R W Myers
New Zealand

V Krishnaswamy
Asian Development Bank

Shankar Sharma
Singapore

P J Graham
New Zealand

Budi Sudarsono
Thailand

Hoe Sung Lee
Korea

Bong Su Lee
Republic of Korea

M K H Tsang
Hong Kong

With assistance from the WEC Member Committees of the Pacific Region and other individuals.

SOUTH ASIA

Regional Co-ordinator
Mr S L Khosla
India

A Bhattacharyya
India

R K Pachauri
India

Bhim Subba
Bhutan

M I Beg
India

R K Sachdev
India

Hilal A Raza
Pakistan

J Gururaja
India

K N Majumdar
India

Aslam Iqbal
Pakistan

J N Maggo
India

S Maudgal
India

K D M C Bandara
Sri Lanka

Rita Nangia
India

G D Sootha
India

C B A Fernando
Sri Lanka

E A S Sarma
India

M U Boon Kyi
Myanmar

Nazrul Islam
Bangladesh

C K Sharma
Nepal

Ismail A Gadir
Maldives

APPENDIX C

GLOBAL AND REGIONAL STATISTICS

	1960	1970	1980	1990	2020*
North America	198.7	226.5	251.9	275.9	326.4
Latin America	218.1	285.7	362.7	448.1	716.3
Western Europe	371.5	407.2	433.5	454.1	489.2
Central and Eastern Europe	81.1	88.1	95.3	100.2	111.0
CIS	214.3	242.8	265.5	288.6	343.9
Middle East & North Africa	115.0	149.9	200.3	271.0	543.3
Sub-Saharan Africa	214.2	278.6	370.0	501.6	1 195.3
Pacific[1]	1 032.0	1 293.0	1 559.2	1 806.9	2 428.4
(includes CPA)[1]	(714.8)	(903.1)	(1 084.7)	(1 248.4)	(1 652.5)
South Asia	574.7	726.1	909.5	1 146.0	1 937.9
World	**3 019.6**	**3 697.9**	**4 447.9**	**5 292.4**	**8 091.7**

[1] Data for the Pacific Region include Centrally Planned Asia, which are also shown separately
* Projection by UN
Source: World Population Prospects 1990, E.91.XIII.4, UN/DIESA Population Studies No 120

Table C1a   Global and Regional Population, millions

	1960–1970	1970–1980	1980–1990	1990–2020*
North America	1.3	1.1	0.9	0.6
Latin America	2.7	2.4	2.1	1.6
Western Europe	0.9	0.6	0.5	0.2
Central and Eastern Europe	0.8	0.8	0.5	0.3
CIS	1.3	0.9	0.8	0.6
Middle East & North Africa	2.7	2.9	3.1	2.3
Sub-Saharan Africa	2.7	2.9	3.1	2.9
Pacific[1]	2.3	1.9	1.5	1.0
(includes CPA)[1]	(2.4)	(1.8)	(1.4)	(0.9)
South Asia	2.4	2.3	2.3	1.8
World	**2.0**	**1.9**	**1.8**	**1.4**

[1] Data for the Pacific Region include Centrally Planned Asia, which is also shown separately
* Projection by UN
Source: World Population Prospects 1990, E.91.XIII.4, UN/DIESA Population Studies No 120

Table C1b   Global and Regional Population Increase, % per Annum

	1960	1970	1980	1990	2020*
North America	1 983.7	2 905.2	3 844.5	5 120.3	10 430
Latin America	482.2	840.9	1 564.8	1 822.0	6 630
Western Europe	1 693.4	2 718.7	3 694.0	4 664.0	9 500
Central and Eastern Europe	197.7	295.3	428.1	431.2	970[1]
CIS	568.0	975.0	1 339.9	1 676.3	3 300[1]
Middle East and North Africa	191.6	378.1	711.6	834.0	3 070
Sub-Saharan Africa	180.2	310.9	461.4	522.0	2 250
Pacific[2]	845.7	1 668.2	2 840.9	4 912.8	16 110
(includes CPA)[2]	(261.0)	(402.2)	(691.4)	(1762.2)	(7 740)
South Asia	296.1	426.2	604.9	1 040.0	3 420
World	**6 438.5**	**10 518.4**	**15 490.0**	**21 022.6**	**55 700**

[1] GDP in Central and Eastern Europe and CIS is assumed to fall by 25% from 1990 to 1992. Economic growth thereafter is assumed to be 4.0 and 3.5% p.a. respectively.
[2] Data for the Pacific Region include Centrally Planned Asia, which is also shown separately
* Projection by WEC - Cases B, B₁ and C
Sources: Roy DJ, Consultant to WEC Commision;
Summers R. and Heston. A., 1991, The Penn World Table (Mark 5): An Expanded Set of International Comparisons, 1950 - 1988, The (US) Quarterly Journal of Economics May 1991

Table C2a Gross Domestic Product, by Volume, billionUS$ (at 1985 values)

	1960–1970	1970–1980	1980–1990	1990–2020*
North America	3.9	2.8	2.9	2.4
Latin America	5.7	6.4	1.5	4.4
Western Europe	4.8	3.1	2.4	2.4
Central and Eastern Europe	4.1	3.8	0.1	2.7[1]
CIS	5.6	3.2	2.3	2.3[1]
Middle East & North Africa	7.0	6.5	1.6	4.4
Sub-Saharan Africa	5.6	4.0	1.2	5.0
Pacific[2]	7.0	5.5	5.6	4.0
(includes CPA)[2]	(4.4)	(5.6)	(9.8)	(5.1)
South Asia	3.7	3.6	5.6	4.0
World	**5.0**	**3.9**	**3.1**	**3.3**

[1] GDP in Central and Eastern Europe and CIS is assumed to fall by 25% from 1990 to 1992. Economic growth thereafter is assumed to be 4.0 and 3.5% p.a. respectively.
[2] Data for the Pacific Region include Centrally Planned Asia, which is also shown separately
* Projection by WEC - Cases B, B₁ and C
Sources: Roy DJ, Consultant to WEC Commission:
Summers R and Heston A, 1991, The Penn World Table (Mark 5): An Expanded Set of International Comparisons, 1950 - 1988, The (US) Quarterly Journal of Economics May 1991

Table C2b Gross Domestic Product Growth Rates, % per Annum

	1960	1970	1980	1990	2020*
North America	9 983	12 826	15 262	18 559	31 955
Latin America	2 211	2 943	4 314	4 066	9 256
Western Europe	4 558	6 677	8 521	10 271	19 419
Central and Eastern Europe	2 438	3 352	4 492	4 303	8 739
CIS	2 650	4 016	5 047	5 808	9 596
Middle East & North Africa	1 666	2 522	3 553	3 077	5 651
Sub-Saharan Africa	841	1 116	1 247	1 041	1 882
Pacific[1]	819	1 290	1 822	2 719	6 634
(includes CPA)[1]	(365)	(445)	(637)	(1 412)	(4 684)
South Asia	515	587	665	908	1 765
World	**2 132**	**2 844**	**3 483**	**3 972**	**6 884**

[1] Data for the Pacific Region include Centrally Planned Asia, which is also shown separately
* Projection by WEC - Cases B, B₁ and C

Table C3a   Gross Domestic Product per Capita, US$ (at 1985 values)

	1960–1970	1970–1980	1980–1990	1990–2020*
North America	2.5	1.8	2.0	1.8
Latin America	2.9	3.9	–0.6	2.8
Western Europe	3.9	2.5	1.9	2.1
Central and Eastern Europe	3.2	3.0	–0.4	2.4
CIS	4.2	2.3	1.4	1.7
Middle East & North Africa	4.2	3.5	–1.4	2.0
Sub-Saharan Africa	2.9	1.1	–1.8	2.0
Pacific[1]	4.6	3.5	4.1	3.0
(includes CPA)[1]	(2.0)	(3.7)	(8.3)	(4.1)
South Asia	1.3	1.3	3.2	2.2
World	**2.9**	**2.0**	**1.3**	**1.8**

[1] Data for the Pacific Region include Centrally Planned Asia, which is also shown separately
* Projection by WEC - Cases B, B₁ and C

Table C3b   Gross Domestic Product per Capita Growth Rates,
% per Annum

	1960	1970	1980	1990	2020*
North America	1 143	1 762	1 991	2 157	2 337
Latin America	162	259	431	577	1 397
Western Europe	662	1 072	1 306	1 462	1 726
Central and Eastern Europe	135	229	336	292	319
CIS	441	732	1 085	1 447	1 529
Middle East & North Africa	35	70	162	317	864
Sub-Saharan Africa	92	142	208	266	690
Pacific[1]	510	806	1 258	1 843	3 482
(includes CPA)[1]	(321)	(374)	(621)	(950)	(2 009)
South Asia	126	193	268	446	1 015
World	**3 306**	**5 265**	**7 045**	**8 807**	**13 359**

[1] Data for the Pacific Region include Centrally Planned Asia, which is also shown separately
* Projection by WEC - Case B
Sources: UN Energy Statistics Yearbook, WEC

Table C4a   Primary Energy Requirement, Mtoe

	1960–1970	1970–1980	1980–1990	1990–2020*
North America	4.4	1.2	0.8	0.3
Latin America	4.8	5.2	3.0	3.0
Western Europe	4.9	2.0	1.1	0.6
Central and Eastern Europe	5.4	3.9	−1.4	0.3
CIS	5.2	4.0	2.9	0.2
Middle East & North Africa	7.2	8.8	6.9	3.4
Sub-Saharan Africa	4.4	3.9	2.5	3.2
Pacific[1]	4.7	4.6	3.9	2.1
(includes CPA)[1]	(1.5)	(5.2)	(4.3)	(2.5)
South Asia	4.4	3.3	5.2	2.5
World	**4.76**	**2.96**	**2.26**	**1.40**

[1] Data for the Pacific Region include Centrally Planned Asia, which is also shown separately
* Projection by WEC - Case B
Sources: UN Energy Statistics Yearbook, WEC

Table C4b   Primary Energy Requirement Growth Rates, % per Annum

	1960	1970	1980	1990	2020*
North America	5.75	7.78	7.90	7.82	7.16
Latin America	0.74	0.91	1.19	1.29	1.95
Western Europe	1.78	2.63	3.01	3.22	3.53
Central and Eastern Europe	1.66	2.60	3.53	2.91	2.87
CIS	2.06	3.01	4.09	5.01	4.45
Middle East & North Africa	0.30	0.47	0.81	1.17	1.59
Sub-Saharan Africa	0.43	0.51	0.56	0.53	0.58
Pacific[1]	0.49	0.62	0.81	1.02	1.43
(includes CPA)[1]	(0.45)	(0.41)	(0.57)	(0.76)	(1.22)
South Asia	0.22	0.27	0.29	0.39	0.52
World	1.09	1.42	1.58	1.66	1.65

[1] Data for the Pacific Region include Centrally Planned Asia, which is also shown separately
* Projection by WEC - Case B

Table C5a   Primary Energy per Capita, toe per Capita

	1960–1970	1970–1980	1980–1990	1990–2020
North America	3.1	0.2	−0.1	− 0.3
Latin America	2.0	2.7	0.8	1.4
Western Europe	4.0	1.4	0.7	0.3
Central and Eastern Europe	4.6	3.1	−1.9	< 0.1
CIS	3.9	3.1	2.1	− 0.4
Middle East & North Africa	4.4	5.6	3.8	1.0
Sub-Saharan Africa	1.7	1.0	−0.6	0.3
Pacific[1]	2.3	2.6	2.4	1.1
(includes CPA)[1]	(−0.8)	(3.3)	(2.9)	(1.6)
South Asia	1.9	1.0	2.8	1.0
World	2.7	1.1	0.5	< 0.1

[1] Data for the Pacific Region include Centrally Planned Asia, which is also shown separately
* Projection by WEC - Case B

Table C5b   Primary Energy per Capita Growth Rates, % per Annum

	1960	1970	1980	1990	2020*
North America	958.0	1 844.4	2 731.4	3 475.5	4 650
Latin America	72.0	160.5	385.0	598.1	2 350
Western Europe	611.7	1 238.6	1 892.1	2 468.4	3 900
Central and Eastern Europe	74.5	184.1	336.0	362.0	600
CIS	292.1	735.6	1 274.9	1 718.4	2 400
Middle East & North Africa	10.2	36.6	117.2	311.4	1 350
Sub-Saharan Africa	30.2	74.2	148.2	224.6	700
Pacific[1]	230.0	615.1	1 196.9	2 106.0	5 700
(includes CPA)[1]	(70.3)	(140.4)	(354.6)	(699.0)	(2 650)
South Asia	22.8	71.2	139.9	343.3	1 350
World	**2 301.5**	**4 960.3**	**8 221.6**	**11 607.7**	**23 000**

[1] Data for Pacific Region include Centrally Planned Asia, which are also shown separately
* Projection by WEC - Case B
Sources: UN Energy Statistics Yearbook; WEC

Table C6a Total Electricity Consumption (*not as Primary Energy*), TWh

	1960–1970	1970–1980	1980–1990	1990–2020*
North America	6.8	4.0	2.4	1.0
Latin America	8.3	9.1	4.5	4.7
Western Europe	7.3	4.3	2.7	1.5
Central and Eastern Europe	9.5	6.2	0.7	1.7
CIS	9.7	5.7	3.0	1.1
Middle East & North Africa	13.6	12.3	10.3	5.0
Sub-Saharan Africa	9.4	7.2	4.2	3.9
Pacific[1]	10.3	6.9	5.8	3.4
(includes CPA)[1]	(7.2)	(9.7)	(7.0)	(4.5)
South Asia	12.1	7.0	9.4	4.7
World	**8.0**	**5.2**	**3.5**	**2.3**

[1] Data for Pacific Region include Centrally Planned Asia, which are also shown separately
* Projection by WEC - Case B
Sources: UN Energy Statistics Yearbook; WEC

Table C6b Growth Rates for Electricity Consumption, % per Annum

	1960	1970	1980	1990	2020*
North America	4.82	8.14	10.84	12.60	14.20
Latin America	0.33	0.56	1.06	1.34	3.27
Western Europe	1.65	3.04	4.36	5.44	7.97
Central and Eastern Europe	0.92	2.09	3.53	3.61	5.35
CIS	1.36	3.03	4.80	5.95	7.03
Middle East & North Africa	0.09	0.24	0.59	1.15	2.47
Sub-Saharan Africa	0.14	0.27	0.40	0.45	0.58
Pacific[1]	0.22	0.48	0.77	1.17	2.36
(includes CPA)[1]	.(0.10)	.(0.16)	.(0.33)	.(0.56)	(1.61)
South Asia	0.04	0.10	0.15	0.30	0.70
World	**0.76**	**1.34**	**1.85**	**2.19**	**2.84**

[1]Data for the Pacific Region include Centrally Planned Asia which is also shown separately
* Projection by WEC - Case B
Sources UN Energy Statistics Yearbook; WEC

Table C7a   Electricity Consumption per Capita, MWh per Capita

	1960–1970	1970–1980	1980–1990	1990–2020*
North America	5.4	2.9	1.5	0.4
Latin America	5.5	6.6	2.3	3.0
Western Europe	6.3	3.7	2.2	1.3
Central and Eastern Europe	8.6	5.4	0.2	1.3
CIS	8.3	4.7	2.2	0.6
Middle East & North Africa	10.7	9.1	7.0	2.6
Sub-Saharan Africa	6.6	4.2	1.1	0.9
Pacific[1]	7.9	4.9	4.3	2.4
(includes CPA)[1]	(4.7)	(7.7)	(5.5)	(3.6)
South Asia	9.5	4.6	6.9	2.9
World	**5.8**	**3.3**	**1.7**	**0.9**

[1] Data for the Pacific Region include Centrally Planned Asia which is also shown separately
* Projection by WEC - Case B.
Sources UN Energy Statistics Yearbook; WEC

Table C7b   Growth Rates for Electricity Consumption per Capita, % per Annum

	Fossil fuels:			Nuclear Energy	Renewables:			Total
	Coal	Oil	Natural Gas		Hydro.	Traditional	"New"	
North America	508	809	497	145	127	38	34	2 158
Latin America	22	218	80	3	80	125	50	578
Western Europe	333	568	254	169	99	20	19	1 462
Central and Eastern Europe	156	49	64	11	5	4	4	293
CIS	365	378	569	47	50	26	11	1 446
Middle East and North Africa	7	167	117	0	5	21	1	318
Sub-Saharan Africa	68	38	4	1	9	141	6	267
Pacific [1]	734	486	108	64	69	351	31	1 843
(includes CPA) [1]	(575)	(100)	(14)	(0)	(30)	(218)	(13)	(949)
South Asia	126	60	25	1	20	204	10	446
World	2 319	2 773	1 718	441	464	930	166	8 811

[1] Data for the Pacific Region include Centrally Planned Asia (CPA), which are also shown separately.
Source: UN Energy Statistics Yearbook: WEC

Table C8   Fuel Mix in 1990, Mtoe

	Fossil fuels:			Nuclear Energy	Renewables:			Total
	Coal	Oil	Natural Gas		Hydro.	Traditional	"New"	
North America	400	793	601	188	162	46	147	2 337
Latin America	79	483	296	26	235	179	99	1 397
Western Europe	352	534	354	244	149	20	73	1 726
Central and Eastern Europe	98	67	105	27	6	5	11	319
CIS	236	355	744	69	58	31	36	1 529
Middle East and North Africa	17	368	412	0	18	38	11	864
Sub-Saharan Africa	141	165	29	6	31	299	19	690
Pacific [1]	1 423	797	342	203	191	414	112	3 482
(includes CPA) [1]	(1 154)	(273)	(126)	(40)	(105)	(257)	(54)	(2 009)
South Asia	289	207	94	30	70	291	34	1 015
World	3 035	3 769	2 977	793	920	1 323	542	13 359

[1] Data for the Pacific Region include Centrally Planned Asia (CPA), which are also shown separately. Projection by WEC - Case B

Table C9   Fuel Mix in 2020 for Case B, Mtoe

	Fossil fuels:			Nuclear Energy	Renewables:			Total
	Coal	Oil	Natural Gas		Hydro.	Traditional	"New"	
North America	−108	−16	+104	+43	+35	+8	+113	+179
Latin America	+57	+265	+216	+25	+155	+54	+49	+819
Western Europe	+19	−34	+100	+75	+50	0	+54	+264
Central and Eastern Europe	−58	+18	+41	+16	+1	+1	+7	+26
CIS	−129	−23	+175	+22	+8	+5	+25	+83
Middle East and North Africa	+10	+201	+295	0	+13	+17	+10	+546
Sub–Saharan Africa	+73	+127	+25	+5	+22	+158	+13	+423
Pacific [1]	+689	+311	+234	+139	+122	+63	+81	+1 639
(includes CPA) [1]	(+579)	(+173)	(+112)	(+40)	(+75)	(+39)	(+42)	(+1 060)
South Asia	+163	+147	+69	+29	+50	+87	+24	+569
World	+716	+996	+1 259	+352	+456	+393	+376	+4 548

[1] Data for the Pacific Region include Centrally Planned Asia (CPA), which are also shown separately.
Based on projection by WEC - Case B

Table C10   Change in Regional Fuel Mix 1990–2020, Mtoe

	Fossil fuels:			Nuclear Energy	Renewables:			Total
	Coal	Oil	Natural Gas		Hydro.	Traditional	"New"	
North America	−21	−2	+21	+30	+28	+21	+332	+8
Latin America	+259	+122	+270	+767	+194	+43	+98	+142
Western Europe	+6	−6	+39	+44	+51	0	+284	+18
Central and Eastern Europe	−37	+37	+64	+145	+20	+25	+175	+9
CIS	−35	−6	+31	+47	+16	+19	+227	+6
Middle East and North Africa	+143	+120	+252	n.a.	+260	+81	n.a.	+172
Sub–Saharan Africa	+107	+334	n.a.	n.a.	+244	+112	+217	+158
Pacific [1]	+94	+64	+217	n.a.	+177	+18	+261	+89
(includes CPA) [1]	(+101)	(+173)	(n.a.)	(n.a)	(+250)	(+18)	(+350)	(+112)
South Asia	+129	+245	+276	n.a.	+250	+43	+240	+128
World	**+31**	**+36**	**+73**	**+80**	**+98**	**+42**	**+227**	**+52**

[1] Data for the Pacific Region include Centrally Planned Asia (CPA), which are also shown separately.
n.a. Not appropriate to express the change as a percentage (zero or very low value in 1990)
Based on projection by WEC - Case B

Table C11 Change in Regional Fuel Mix 1990–2020, percent

	Fossil fuels:			Nuclear Energy	Renewables:			Total
	Coal	Oil	Natural Gas		Hydro.	Traditional	"New"	
North America	23	38	23	7	6	2	1	100
Latin America	4	38	14	0	14	22	8	100
Western Europe	23	39	17	12	7	1	1	100
Central and Eastern Europe	53	17	22	4	2	1	1	100
CIS	25	26	39	3	4	2	1	100
Middle East and North Africa	2	52	37	0	2	7	0	100
Sub–Saharan Africa	26	14	2	< 0.5	3	53	2	100
Pacific [1]	40	26	6	3	4	19	2	100
(includes CPA) [1]	(61)	(11)	(1)	(0)	(3)	(23)	(1)	(100)
South Asia	28	14	6	< 0.5	4	46	2	100
World	**26**	**31**	**20**	**5**	**5**	**11**	**2**	**100**

[1] Data for the Pacific Region include Centrally Planned Asia (CPA), which are also shown separately.

Table C12 Regional Fuel Shares 1990, percent

	Fossil fuels:			Nuclear Energy	Renewables:			Total
	Coal	Oil	Natural Gas		Hydro.	Traditional	"New"	
North America	17	34	26	8	7	2	6	100
Latin America	6	34	21	2	17	13	7	100
Western Europe	20	31	21	14	9	1	4	100
Central and Eastern Europe	31	21	33	8	2	2	3	100
CIS	15	23	49	5	4	2	2	100
Middle East and North Africa	2	43	48	0	2	4	1	100
Sub–Saharan Africa	20	24	4	1	5	43	3	100
Pacific [1]	41	23	10	6	5	12	3	100
(includes CPA) [1]	(57)	(14)	(6)	(2)	(5)	(13)	(3)	(100)
South Asia	29	20	9	3	7	29	3	100
World	**23**	**28**	**22**	**6**	**7**	**10**	**4**	**100**

[1] Data for the Pacific Region include Centrally Planned Asia (CPA), which are also shown separately.
Based on projection by WEC - Case B

Table C13   Regional Fuel Shares 2020 – Case B, percent

	1960	1970	1980	1990	2020*
North America	0.58	0.61	0.52	0.42	0.22
Latin America	0.34	0.31	0.28	0.32	0.21
Western Europe	0.39	0.39	0.35	0.31	0.18
Central and Eastern Europe	0.68	0.78	0.78	0.68	0.33
CIS	0.78	0.75	0.81	0.86	0.46
Middle East & North Africa	0.18	0.19	0.23	0.38	0.28
Sub-Saharan Africa	0.51	0.46	0.45	0.51	0.31
Pacific[1]	0.60	0.48	0.44	0.38	0.22
(includes CPA)[1]	(1.23)	(0.93)	(0.90)	(0.54)	(0.26)
South Asia	0.43	0.45	0.44	0.43	0.30
World	**0.51**	**0.50**	**0.45**	**0.42**	**0.24**

[1] Data for the Pacific Region include Centrally Planned Asia, which is also shown separately
* Projection by WEC - Case B

Table C14a Energy Intensity (Total Primary Energy in toe per 1000US$ of GDP at 1985 values),

	1960–1970	1970–1980	1980–1990	1990–2020*
North America	+0.51	-1.57	-2.04	-2.1
Latin America	-0.87	-1.11	+1.41	-1.3
Western Europe	+0.09	-1.09	-1.20	-1.8
Central and Eastern Europe	+1.28	+0.12	-1.46	-2.4
CIS	-0.34	+0.76	+0.64	-2.1
Middle East & North Africa	+0.13	+2.09	+5.26	-1.0
Sub-Saharan Africa	-1.11	-0.13	+1.23	-1.7
Pacific[1]	-2.19	-0.87	-1.64	-1.8
(includes CPA)[1]	(-2.76)	(-0.35)	(-4.98)	(-2.4)
South Asia	+0.62	-0.22	-0.33	-1.2
World	**-0.26**	**-0.95**	**-0.82**	**-1.8**

[1] Data for the Pacific Region include Centrally Planned Asia, which is also shown separately
* Projection by WEC - Case B

Table C14b Rates of Change in Energy Intensity, % per Annum

	Sulphur [2]			Nitrogen [2]			Carbon [3]		
	1990	2020	Change	1990	2020	Change	1990	2020	Change
	Mt	Mt	%	Mt	Mt	%	Gt	Gt	%
North America	12.1	5.8	−52	5.5	3.2	−42	1.55	1.49	−4
Latin America	3.2	7.1	+122	1.4	2.7	+93	0.26	0.68	+162
Western Europe	10.4	4.5	−57	3.7	2.3	−38	1.00	1.06	+6
Central and Eastern Europe	3.9	2.2	−44	1.0	0.7	−30	0.25	0.23	−8
CIS	12.4	7.4	−40	4.0	2.9	−28	1.08	1.03	−5
Middle East and North Africa	2.2	4.9	+123	1.0	2.0	+100	0.22	0.59	+168
Sub–Saharan Africa	1.9	4.4	+132	0.7	1.6	+129	0.11	0.31	+182
Pacific [1]	15.1	22.2	+47	5.7	9.1	+60	1.27	2.43	+91
(including CPA) [1]	6.9	14.4	+109	3.2	6.3	+97	0.72	1.56	+117
South Asia	3.4	7.5	+121	1.1	2.4	+118	0.20	0.55	+175
World	64.6	66.1	+2	24.0	27.0	+13	5.90	8.37	+42

[1] Data for the Pacific Region include Centrally Planned Asia (CPA), which are also shown separately.
[2] The emissions are calculated as millions of metric tonnes of elemental sulphur and nitrogen
[3] The emissions are calculated as 1000 millions of metric tonnes (Gtonnes) of elemental carbon
Based on projection by WEC – Case B

Table C15   Emissions of Sulphur, Nitrogen and Carbon

Case B - "Reference"

The Commission's Case B for 2020 is an update (by the original author Dr J-R Frisch and the PMU) of the Moderate Economic Growth Scenario in the Report "World Energy Horizons 2000-2020" presented at the WEC Montreal Congress 1989. That Report was prepared following wide consultation within the WEC. Recent developments in the Commonwealth of Independent States of the former USSR, as well as in the countries in Central and Eastern Europe, are incorporated into the projection. This results in a projection which indicates only a slight increase in energy demand (6%) from 1990 to 2020 in these regions, which is considerably lower than projected in the Montreal Report. Recent experience in many developing countries indicates a larger growth in energy use up to 1990 than was projected in the Montreal Report. Projections for the OECD area are virtually unchanged. In total these changes give a marginal net reduction of global energy demand by 2020 (a reduction from 13.5 Gtoe to 13.4 Gtoe) compared with the Report to the Montreal Congress.

For the different fuels there is a significant increase in the use of natural gas (3.0 Gtoe instead of 2.4 Gtoe) and of "new" renewable energy sources (0.5 Gtoe instead of 0.37 Gtoe based on the work of the WEC Committee on Renewable Energy Sources) and a reduction in the use of coal and nuclear (3.0 Gtoe instead of 4.05 Gtoe and 0.8 Gtoe instead of 1.1 Gtoe respectively) compared with the Montreal Report.

Three other cases have been developed. It must be emphasised that none of them can be described as "business as usual": they all assume some improvement on past rates of performance.

Case A - "High Growth"

Case A assumes a higher economic growth in developing countries, 1% p.a. higher than the Case B. The improvement in energy intensity is also somewhat lower than in Case B (1.6% p.a. instead of 1.9%). These changes would drive global energy demand up to about 17.2 Gtoe. On the supply side this would lead to increased use of all fuels (except "traditional" energy).

Case B$_1$ - "Modified Reference"

Case B$_1$ is a sub-case of Case B. This case assumes a weaker performance on improving energy intensity in the Central and Eastern Europe/CIS countries and a dramatically slower and delayed improvement within the developing countries.

Case C - "Ecologically Driven"

Case C assumes a greater improvement of energy intensity than Case B (2.4% p.a. instead of 1.9% p.a.) which curbs the global energy demand to 11.3 Gtoe by 2020. Further it assumes a larger contribution from "new" renewable energy sources (1.4 Gtoe instead of 0.6 Gtoe, based on the WEC Committee on Renewable Energy Resources) and a smaller contribution from all other sources, especially from coal.

Table C16   Description of the four WEC Cases

Case	A	B₁	B	C
Name	High Growth	Modified Reference	Reference	Ecologically Driven
World General Data				
Population (millions)	8 092	8 092	8 092	8 092
Economic Growth Rate (% per Annum)	3.8	3.3	3.3	3.3
GDP (trillion US$)*	64.7	55.7	55.7	55.7
GDP per Capita (US$)	8 001	6 884	6 884	6 884
World Primary Energy				
Total Energy Demand (Mtoe)	17 208	16 008	13 359	11 273
Energy Demand per Capita (toe/Capita)	2.13	1.98	1.65	1.39
Energy Intensity (toe/1000US$)	0.27	0.29	0.24	0.20
Primary Energy Mix (Mtoe)				
Coal	4 852	3 814	3 035	2 128
Oil	4 594	4 532	3 769	2 898
Natural Gas	3 648	3 561	2 977	2 486
Nuclear	982	981	793	693
Hydro	999	987	920	661
Traditional	1 323	1 323	1 323	1 060
New Renewables	810	810	542	1 347
Primary Energy Demand in the Regions (Mtoe)				
North America	2 444	2 338	2 337	1 829
Latin America	2 231	2 104	1 397	1 307
Western Europe	1 814	1 725	1 726	1 319
Central and Eastern Europe	360	360	319	265
CIS	1 674	2 039²	1 529	1 266
Middle East and North Africa	1 296	1 134	864	791
Sub-Saharan Africa	1 279	1 053	690	608
Pacific	4 258	3 795	3 482	2 988
(including CPA) ¹	(2 327)	(2 007)	(2 009)	(1 768)
South Asia	1 852	1 460	1 015	900
Emissions				
Sulphur (Mtonnes)	98.1	87.9	66.0	42.8
Nitrogen (Mtonnes)	37.9	33.5	26.9	20.9
Carbon (Gtonnes)	11.46	10.23	8.37	6.34

* trillion = million-milion (10^{12})
¹ Data for the Pacific Region include Centrally Planned Asia which is also shown separately
² Case B₁ assumes a reduced improvemnt in energy intensity in the CIS – see Table C16

Table C17   Basic Data for the four WEC Cases

	Fossil fuels:			Nuclear Energy	Renewables:			Total
	Coal	Oil	Natural Gas		Hydro.	Traditional	"New"	
North America	477	756	600	181	163	46	221	2 444
Latin America	441	715	434	49	265	179	148	2 231
Western Europe	369	540	379	249	148	20	109	1 814
Central and Eastern Europe	117	78	102	36	6	5	16	360
CIS	263	348	821	93	65	31	53	1 674
Middle East and North Africa	125	597	500	0	20	38	16	1 296
Sub–Saharan Africa	435	275	184	12	46	299	28	1 279
Pacific [1]	1 841	921	444	278	192	414	168	4 258
(includes CPA) [1]	(1 408)	(282)	(163)	(46)	(91)	(257)	(80)	(2 327)
South Asia	784	364	184	84	94	291	51	1 852
World	**4 852**	**4 594**	**3 648**	**982**	**999**	**1 323**	**810**	**17 208**

[1] Data for the Pacific Region include Centrally Planned Asia (CPA), which are also shown separately.
Based on projection by WEC - Case A

Table C18   Regional Fuel Mix 2020 Case A, Mtoe

	Fossil fuels:			Nuclear Energy	Renewables:			Total
	Coal	Oil	Natural Gas		Hydro.	Traditional	"New"	
North America	19	31	25	7	7	2	9	100
Latin America	20	32	19	2	12	8	7	100
Western Europe	20	30	21	14	8	1	6	100
Central and Eastern Europe	33	22	28	10	2	1	4	100
CIS	16	21	49	5	4	2	3	100
Middle East and North Africa	10	46	39	0	1	3	1	100
Sub–Saharan Africa	34	22	14	1	4	23	2	100
Pacific [1]	43	22	10	6	5	10	4	100
(includes CPA) [1]	(61)	(12)	(7)	(2)	(4)	(11)	(3)	(100)
South Asia	42	20	10	4	5	16	3	100
World	28	26	21	6	6	8	5	100

[1] Data for the Pacific Region include Centrally Planned Asia (CPA), which are also shown separately.
Based on projection by WEC - Case A

Table C19 Regional Fuel Shares 2020 Case A, percent

	Fossil fuels:			Nuclear Energy	Renewables:			Total
	Coal	Oil	Natural Gas		Hydro.	Traditional	"New"	
North America	381	737	599	190	164	46	221	2 338
Latin America	258	813	401	51	254	179	148	2 104
Western Europe	322	528	353	244	149	20	109	1 725
Central and Eastern Europe	108	71	118	36	6	5	16	360
CIS	371	382	1 010	122	70	31	53	2 039
Middle East and North Africa	53	524	485	0	18	38	16	1 134
Sub-Saharan Africa	274	359	45	8	40	299	28	1 053
Pacific [1]	1 503	861	386	263	200	414	168	3 795
(includes CPA) [1]	(1 141)	(260)	(125)	(40)	(104)	(257)	(80)	(2 007)
South Asia	544	257	164	67	86	291	51	1 460
World	3 814	4 532	3 561	981	987	1 323	810	16 008

[1] Data for the Pacific Region include Centrally Planned Asia (CPA), which are also shown separately.
Based on projection by WEC - Case B₁

Table C20   Regional Fuel Mix 2020 Case B₁, Mtoe

	Fossil fuels:			Nuclear Energy	Renewables:			Total
	Coal	Oil	Natural Gas		Hydro.	Traditional	"New"	
North America	16	32	26	8	7	2	9	100
Latin America	12	39	19	2	12	9	7	100
Western Europe	19	31	20	14	9	1	6	100
Central and Eastern Europe	30	20	33	10	2	1	4	100
CIS	18	19	49	6	3	2	3	100
Middle East and North Africa	5	46	43	0	2	3	1	100
Sub–Saharan Africa	26	34	4	1	4	28	3	100
Pacific [1]	40	23	10	7	5	11	4	100
(includes CPA) [1]	(57)	(13)	(6)	(2)	(5)	(13)	(4)	(100)
South Asia	37	18	11	5	6	20	3	100
World	**24**	**29**	**22**	**6**	**6**	**8**	**5**	**100**

[1] Data for the Pacific Region include Centrally Planned Asia (CPA), which are also shown separately.

Based on projection by WEC - Case B₁

Table C21 Regional Fuel Shares 2020 Case B₁, percent

	Fossil fuels:			Nuclear Energy	Renewables:			Total
	Coal	Oil	Natural Gas		Hydro.	Traditional	"New"	
North America	213	493	487	160	134	36	306	1 829
Latin America	117	378	245	25	148	144	250	1 307
Western Europe	147	375	313	224	114	15	131	1 319
Central and Eastern Europe	74	59	76	25	5	3	23	265
CIS	159	230	655	65	52	20	85	1 266
Middle East and North Africa	12	330	378	0	9	27	35	791
Sub–Saharan Africa	104	146	15	5	15	239	84	608
Pacific [1]	1 117	684	260	164	136	344	283	2 988
(includes CPA) [1]	(967)	(247)	(71)	(38)	(76)	(215)	(154)	(1 768)
South Asia	185	203	57	25	48	232	150	900
World	2 128	2 898	2 486	693	661	1 060	1 347	11 273

[1] Data for the Pacific Region include Centrally Planned Asia (CPA), which are also shown separately.
Based on projection by WEC - Case C

Table C22   Regional Fuel Mix 2020 Case C, Mtoe

	Fossil fuels:			Nuclear Energy	Renewables:			Total
	Coal	Oil	Natural Gas		Hydro.	Traditional	"New"	
North America	12	27	26	9	7	2	17	100
Latin America	9	29	19	2	11	11	19	100
Western Europe	11	28	24	17	9	1	10	100
Central and Eastern Europe	28	22	29	10	2	1	8	100
CIS	12	18	52	5	4	2	7	100
Middle East and North Africa	2	42	48	0	1	3	4	100
Sub–Saharan Africa	17	24	2	1	2	40	14	100
Pacific [1]	37	23	9	6	5	11	9	100
(includes CPA) [1]	(55)	(14)	(4)	(2)	(4)	(12)	(9)	(100)
South Asia	21	22	6	3	5	26	17	100
World	**19**	**26**	**22**	**6**	**6**	**9**	**12**	**100**

[1] Data for the Pacific Region include Centrally Planned Asia (CPA), which are also shown separately.
Based on projection by WEC - Case C

Table C23   Regional Fuel Shares 2020 Case C, percent

APPENDIX D

Extract from:
"CLIMATE CHANGE 1992:
The Supplementary Report to the
IPCC[1] Scientific Assessment"
Cambridge University Press, 1992, pp 5/6 and 19/20

Our Major Conclusions

Findings of scientific research since 1990 do not affect our fundamental understanding of the science of the greenhouse effect and either confirm or do not justify alteration of the major conclusions of the first IPCC Scientific Assessment, in particular the following:

- emissions resulting from human activities are substantially increasing the atmospheric concentrations of the greenhouse gases: carbon dioxide, methane, chlorofluorocarbons, and nitrous oxide;

- the evidence from the modelling studies, from observations and the sensitivity analyses indicate that the sensitivity of global mean surface temperature to doubling CO_2 is unlikely to lie outside the range 1.5 to 4.5°C;

---

[1] The Intergovernmental Panel on Climate Change (IPCC) Secretariat was set up in May 1988 by the World Meteorological Organisation and the United Nations Environment Programme to carry out a regular assessment of the climate change issue, providing the basis for development of realistic and effective internationally accepted strategies for addressing climate change.

- there are many uncertainties in our predictions particularly with regard to the timing, magnitude and regional patterns of climate change;

- global mean surface air temperature has increased by 0.3 to 0.6°C over the last 100 years;

- the size of this warming is broadly consistent with predictions of climate models, but it is also of the same magnitude as natural climate variability. Thus the observed increase could be largely due to this natural variability; alternatively this variability and other human factors could have offset a still larger human-induced greenhouse warming;

- the unequivocal detection of the enhanced greenhouse effect from observations is not likely for a decade or more.

There are also a number of significant new findings and conclusions which we summarize as follows:

Gases and Aerosols

- Depletion of ozone in the lower stratosphere in the middle and high latitudes results in a decrease in radiative forcing which is believed to be comparable in magnitude to the radiative forcing contribution of chloroflurocarbons (CFCs) (globally-averaged) over the last decade or so.

- The cooling effect of aerosols[1] resulting from sulphur emissions may have offset a significant part of the greenhouse warming in the Northern Hemisphere (NH) during the past several decades. Although this phenomenon was recognized in the 1990 report, some progress has been made in quantifying its effect.

- The Global Warming Potential (GWP) remains a useful concept but its practical utility for many gases depends on adequate quantification of the indirect effects as well as the direct. We now recognise that there is increased uncertainty in the calculation of GWPs, particularly in the indirect components and, whilst indirect GWPs are likely to be

---

[1] The scientific definition of "aerosol" is an airborne particle or collection of particles, but the word has become associated, erroneously, with the propellant used in "aerosol sprays". Throughout this report the term "aerosol" means airborne particle or particles.

significant for some gases, the numerical estimates in this Supplementary Report are limited to direct GWPs.

- Whilst the rates of increase in the atmospheric concentrations of many greenhouse gases have continued to grow or remain steady, those of methane and some halogen compounds have slowed.

- Some data indicate that global emissions of methane from rice paddies may amount to less than previously estimated.

Scenarios

- Steps have been taken towards a more comprehensive analysis of the dependence of future greenhouse gas emissions on socio-economic assumptions and projections. A set of updated scenarios has been developed for use in modelling studies which describe a wide range of possible future emissions in the absence of a coordinated policy response to climate change.

Modelling

- Climate models have continued to improve in respect of both their physical realism and their ability to simulate present climate on large scales, and new techniques are being developed for the simulation of regional climate.

- Transient (time-dependent) simulations with coupled ocean-atmosphere models (CGCMs), in which neither aerosols nor ozone changes have been included, suggest a rate of global warming that is consistent, within the range of uncertainties, with the 0.3°C per decade warming rate quoted by IPCC (1990) for Scenario A of greenhouse gas emissions.

- The large-scale geographical patterns of warming produced by the transient model runs with CGCMs are generally similar to the patterns produced by the earlier equilibrium models except that the transient simulations show reduced warming over the northern North Atlantic and the southern oceans near Antarctica.

- CGCMs are capable of reproducing some features of atmospheric variability on intra-decadal time-scales.

- Our understanding of some climate feedbacks and their incorporation in the models has improved. In particular, there has been some clarification of the role of upper tropospheric water vapour. The role of other processes, in particular cloud effects, remains unresolved.

Climate Observations

- The anomolously high global mean surface temperatures of the late 1980s have continued into 1990 and 1991 which are the warmest years on record.

- Average warming over parts of the Northern Hemisphere mid-latitude continents has been found to be largely characterized by increases in minimum (night-time) rather than maximum (day-time) temperatures.

- Radiosonde data indicate that the lower troposphere has warmed over recent decades. Since meaningful trends cannot be assessed over periods as short as a decade, the widely reported disagreements between decadal trends of air temperature from satellite and surface data cannot be confirmed because the trends are statistically indistinguishable.

- The volcanic eruption of Mount Pinatubo in 1991 is expected to lead to transitory stratospheric warming. With less certainty, because of other natural influences, surface and tropospheric cooling may occur during the next few years.

- Average warming over the Northern Hemisphere during the last four decades has not been uniform, with marked seasonal and geographic variations; this warming has been especially slow, or absent, over the extratropical north-west Atlantic.

- The consistency between observations of global temperature changes over the past century and model simulations of the warming due to greenhouse gases over the same period is improved if allowance is made for the increasing evidence of a cooling effect due to sulphate aerosols and stratospheric ozone depletion.

The above conclusions have implications for future projections of global warming and somewhat modify the estimated rate of warming of 0.3°C per decade for the greenhouse gas emissions Scenario A of the IPCC 1990 Report. If sulphur emissions continue to increase, this warming rate is likely to be reduced, significantly in the Northern Hemisphere, by an amount dependent on the future magnitude and regional distribution of the emissions. Because sulphate aerosols are very short-lived in the atmosphere, their effect on global warming rapidly adjusts to increases or decreases in emissions. It should also be noted that while partially offsetting the greenhouse warming, the sulphur emissions are also responsible for acid rain and other environmental effects. There is a further small net reduction likely in the rate of global warming during the next few decades due to decreases in stratospheric ozone, partially offset by increases in tropospheric ozone.

Research carried out since the 1990 IPCC Assessment has served to improve our appreciation of key uncertainties.

There is a continuing need for increased monitoring and research into climate processes and modelling. This must involve, in particular, strengthened international collaboration through the World Climate Research Programme (WCRP), the International Geosphere Biosphere Programme (IGBP) and the Global Climate Observing System (GCOS).

Key Uncertainties and Further Work Required

The prediction of future climate change is critically dependent on scenarios of future anthropogenic emissions of greenhouse gases and other climate forcing agents such as aerosols. These depend not only on factors which can be addressed by the natural sciences but also on factors such as population and economic growth and energy policy where there is much uncertainty and which are the concern of the social sciences. Natural and social scientists need to cooperate closely in the development of scenarios of future emissions.

Since the 1990 report there has been a greater appreciation of many of the uncertainties which affect our predictions of the timing, magnitude and regional patterns of climate change. These continue to be rooted in our inadequate understanding of:

- sources and sinks of greenhouse gases and aerosols and their atmospheric concentrations (including their indirect effects on global warming)

- clouds (particularly their feedback effect on greenhouse-gas-induced global warming, also the effect of aerosols on clouds and their radiative properties) and other elements of the atmospheric water budget, including the processes controlling upper level water vapour

- oceans, which through their thermal inertia and possible changes in circulation, influence the timing and pattern of climate change

- polar ice sheets (whose response to climate change also affects predictions of sea level rise)

- land surface processes and feedbacks, including hydrological and ecological processes which couple regional and global climates

Reduction of these uncertainties requires:

- the development of improved models which include adequate descriptions of all components of the climate system

- improvements in the systematic observation and understanding of climate-forcing variables on a global basis, including solar irradiance and aerosols

- development of comprehensive observations of the relevant variables describing all components of the climate system, involving as required new technologies and the establishment of data sets

- better understanding of climate-related processes, particularly those associated with clouds, oceans and the carbon cycle

- an improved understanding of social, technological and economic processes, especially in developing countries, that are necessary to develop more realistic scenarios of future emissions

- the development of national inventories of current emissions

- more detailed knowledge of climate changes which have taken place in the past

- sustained and increased support for climate research activities which cross national and disciplinary boundaries; particular action is still needed to facilitate the full involvement of developing countries

- improved international exchange of climate data.

Many of these requirements are being addressed by major international programmes, in particular by the World Climate Research Programme (WCRP), the International Geosphere Biosphere Programme (IGBP) and the Global Climate Observing System (GCOS). Adequate resources need to be provided both to the international organization of these programmes and to the national efforts supporting them if the new information necessary to reduce the uncertainties is to be forthcoming. Resources also need to be provided to support on a national or regional basis, and especially in developing countries, the analysis of data relating to a wide range of climate variables and the continued observation of important variables with adequate coverage and accuracy.

APPENDIX E

Possible Implications of the WEC Commission's Energy Cases for Atmospheric CO₂ Concentrations, Global-Mean Temperature and Sea-Level Rises

The UN Framework Convention on Climate Change[1] has called for the stabilisation of greenhouse gas concentrations in the atmosphere at a level which could prevent "dangerous anthropogenic interference" with the climate system (Article 2). The Convention does not define "dangerous anthropogenic interference" but does define "adverse effects of climate changes" as changes in the physical environment or biota resulting from climate change "which have significant deleterious effects on the composition, resilience or productivity of natural and managed ecosystems or on the operation of socio-economic systems or on human health and welfare" (Article 1:1).

"Climate change" is defined as change attributed directly or indirectly to human activity that alters the composition of the global atmosphere "and which is in addition to natural climate variability observed over comparable time periods" (Article 1:2).

The Convention notes that "there are many uncertainties in predictions of climate change, particularly with regard to the timing, magnitude and regional patterns thereof."

---

[1] By late March 1993, 161 countries plus the European Community had signed the Framework Convention and 17 had ratified it (out of the 50 required for the Convention to enter into force).

The Parties to the Convention have "the aim of returning individually or jointly to their 1990 levels these anthropogenic emissions of carbon dioxide and other greenhouse gases not controlled by the Montreal Protocol" (Article 4.2(b)). However, it is not the case that the Parties, developed countries or otherwise, are required absolutely to achieve this goal by the year 2000 (as sometimes claimed). The Convention calls upon developed countries to take policies and measures which "will demonstrate they are taking the lead in modifying longer-term trends in anthropogenic emissions consistent with the objective of the Convention" recognising that the return by the end of the present decade to earlier levels of anthropogenic emissions of carbon dioxide and other greenhouse gases not controlled by the Montreal Protocol would contribute to such modification" (Article 4.2(a)).

Developed countries are required by the Convention to provide "financial resources, including the transfer of technology, needed by the developing country. Parties to meet the agreed full incremental costs of implementing measures" that are covered by the key commitments (Article 4.3). However, "the extent to which developing country Parties will effectively implement their commitments under the Convention will depend on the effective implementation by developed country Parties of

Case	1990	A		B		C	
		2050	2100	2050	2100	2050	2100
Global Energy Demand (Gtoe)	8.8	27	42	23	33	15	20
Fossil Fuels (% of Primary Energy)	77	58	40	57	33	58	15
Nuclear (% of Primary Energy)	5	14	29	15	28	8	11
New Renewables (% of Primary Energy)	2	15	24	14	26	20	50
Annual CO_2 Emissions from Fossil Fuels (GtC)	5.94	14.87	16.59	12.18	11.72	7.25	2.45
Annual CO_2 Emissions from Fossil Fuels % Change on 1990		+150	+179	+105	+97	+22	−59
Atmospheric CO_2 Concentrations (ppmv)	355	536	708	494	617	449	469
Increase in Atmospheric CO_2 Concentrations – Change on 1990 (ppmv)		+181	+353	+139	+262	+94	+114

Table E.1   Illustrations of Possible Long-Term Impacts of Energy Use on Climate

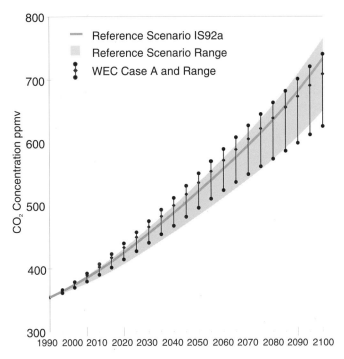

Figure E.1   Atmospheric CO_2 Concentrations

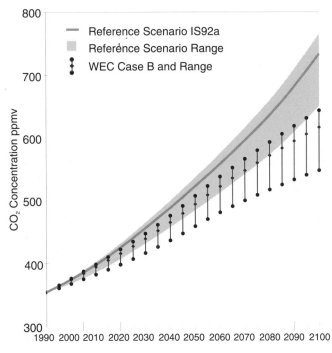

Figure E.2   Atmospheric CO_2 Concentrations

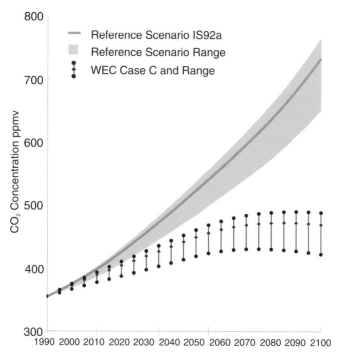

Figure E.3   Atmospheric CO_2 Concentrations

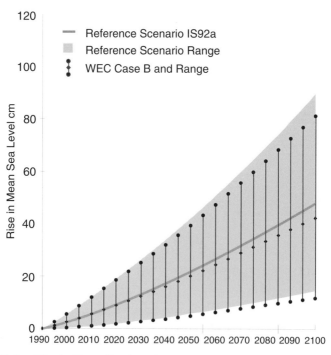

Figure E.4   Rise in Mean Sea Level

	IS92a	WEC Case			
		A	B₁	B	C
1990	355	355	355	355	355
2020	426	434	426	416	404
2050	523	536		494	449
2100	733	708		617	469
Note: The pre-industrial atmospheric concentration of CO_2 (1750–1800) is believed to have been 280 ppmv					

Table E.2 Atmospheric CO_2 Concentrations (parts per million by volume)

	IS92a	WEC Case			
		A	B₁	B	C
2020	0.52	0.56	0.53	0.49	0.44
2050	1.16	1.22		1.02	0.82
2100	2.46	2.42		2.05	1.37

Table E.3 Rise in Global-Mean Temperature (°C) on 1990 Levels

	IS92a	WEC Case			
		A	B₁	B	C
2020	9.3	9.6	9.4	9.0	8.5
2050	21.9	22.9		20.2	17.6
2100	48.0	48.2		42.4	32.6

Table E.4 Rise in Mean Sea Level (cm) on 1990 Levels

their commitments under the Convention related to financial resources and transfer of technology and will take fully into account that economic and social development and poverty eradication are the first and overriding priorities of the developing country Parties" (Article 4.7).

In Chapter 5 of this report it was pointed out that this Commission's High Growth Case (Case A) lies close to the IPCC's IS92a Scenario (their "mid-estimate" scenario in terms of Fig. A 3.1, "Climate Change 1992", p.81 – their two lower scenarios being based on an extremely low 6.4 billion world population projection for the year 2100).

For illustrative purposes, Cases A, B (Reference) and C (Ecologically Driven Case) have been extended to 2100 and their implications for atmospheric concentrations of CO_2, change in global-mean temperature, and change in global-mean sea level by the years 2050 and 2100 have

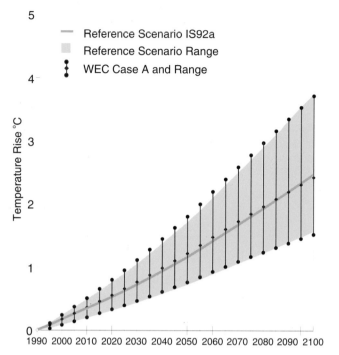

Figure E.5 Rise in Global Mean Temperature

been calculated by the internationally respected Climatic Research Unit of the University of East Anglia, Norwich, England (Tables E.1–4).

This work was undertaken by Professor T.M.L. Wigley[1] and Dr. M. Hulme of the Climatic Research Unit who supplied future estimates of atmospheric CO_2 concentrations, global-mean temperature change, and global-mean sea-level change based upon the Commission's energy Cases. The estimates were generated using the MAGICC climate model.

The estimates for Cases A, B and C are provided in the charts where "WEC Case x and Range" refers to the WEC Case examined. "Reference Scenario IS92a" and the shaded range around it refers to the IPCC's Scenario IS92a for purposes of comparison. [Professor Wigley contributed jointly with P.T. Barnett Chapter 8 of IPCC: "Climate Change: The IPCC Scientific Assessment", 1990, and was a lead author of Chapter 2 of "Climate Change 1992: IPCC Scientific Assessment", 1992.]

The IPCC's IS92a figures are compared with the Commission's Cases in Tables E.2, E.3 and E.4. (Case B_1 was not continued beyond 2020.)

It is stressed that these Cases and the estimates based upon them are for illustrative purposes only. They illustrate that if the hypothesis about enhanced global warming and potential climate change is broadly correct

---

[1] Professor Wigley is now at the University of Boulder, Colorado, USA.

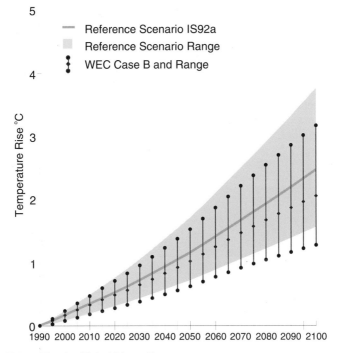

Figure E.6   Rise in Global Mean Temperature

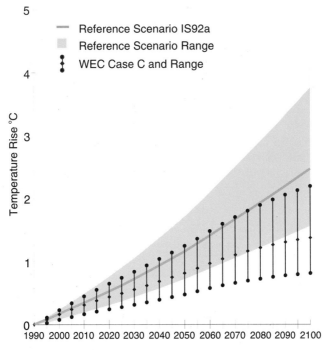

Figure E.7   Rise in Global Mean Temperature

then, using a highly respected research unit and climate model, the consequences are likely to be as set down here.

Readers are left to draw their own conclusions as to the severity of the challenge the world may face, and the extent of abatement and adaptation measures that may be demanded.

INDEX

Assessment (1992) 146, 297–302; *see also* GCOS; IGBP; WCRP
Iraq 92
iron and steel 117
irrigation 119
Italy 229

Japan 41, 48, 113, 159, 184; diversification away from oil 55; environmental standards 66; Institute of Energy Economics 220; reducing growth rate 221; steel production 117
Johansson, T B 93
joint ventures 99, 178

Karachi 138
Kazakhstan 105, 195, 196
Khatib, H 56n
Kirgizstan 196
Korea, Republic of 41, 68, 92, 117, 125; energy consumption per capita 69
Kozloduy 200
Kuala Lumpur 138

land-use planning/changes 124, 142
Latin America 41, 74, 138, 173–8, 263, 267; equity capital inflows 32
Latvia 196
lead 63, 138
"leap-frogging" process 49, 70, 135
leguminous crops 142
less developed countries 159, 217
life expectancy 39, 45, 46
life-styles 173–5, 205, 213
lighting 48, 122–3
limestone 230
Lithuania 196
local pollution 137–9; abatement of 235, 236; ameliorating 230–1; associated with fossil fuel use 150; complaints 147; controlling 221; current level of concern 135; reduction of 161, 179–81; significant, in some cities 70
London 138
Los Angeles 138
lower quality fuels 213
LPG (liquefied petroleum gas) 52, 121, 124

Malaysia 70, 71, 217
Manila 138
manufacturing industry 56, 115–19, 196–7
marginal costs 58, 59, 130–1
markets 59, 190, 219–20, 228; access to 162, 178, 185; capital 43, 101; distortions 130; effective energy supply through 164; energy 33–4, 208–9, 236; free, encouraging 222; infrastructure 199; international 185, 210, 215; oil 215; open and competitive 184; regional co-operation in 208–9; role of

governments in 160; *see also* economies in transition
measles 138
mechanisation 119
mega-cities 74
mergers 61
methane 42, 140, 297, 298–9; concentrations in the atmosphere 137; emitted by fossil fuel provision and use 137; global emissions 66; human emissions 141; major source of production 142; natural emissions from wetlands 141
methanol 52, 170
Mexico 70, 78 demographic data 46
Mexico City 71, 74, 138
Mexico, Gulf of 177
Meyers, S 84
Middle East 41, 57, 98, 105, 201–4, 264; percentage of probable world oil resources 97, 201; regional coordinator 269; risk of oil price shocks from growing dependency on 183
Mikhailov, V N 200
Moldavia 196
monopolies 61, 99, 168
Montreal Protocol (1986) 304; London Amendments (1990) 143
motor vehicles: efficiency 52, 53, 54, 182; energy services provided by 112; improvements in design 53; non-commercial 171; ownership 52, 54; potential for domination of motor car in developing countries 54; public 138; reducing emissions 53; shared occupancy of private cars 124; volatile organic compounds from 149
motor driven systems 126–7
Munasinghe, M 56n

natural emissions 140, 141
natural gas 81, 97, 119, 170, 189, 236; availability 157, 226, 243; compressed 124; demand for 88; efficiency of power plants 48; importing 227; increases in 55; more people competing for 152; net exporter of 193; production 198; role expected to increase 182; supplies 108, 152, 157; world price of 85; *see also* reserves
natural resources 70, 214
New Delhi 138
"new" renewables 42, 93–6, 149, 151, 183; accelerating the development of 81, 82, 154; availability 237; expansion 106, 108; future role 60; opportunities for 213; percentage demand 50; priority to provision of 103; *see also* biomass (modern); geothermal; hydro; oceans; solar; wind
New Zealand 159